the
weight
of
air

a story of the lies
about addiction
and the truth
about recovery

david poses

SANDRA JONAS
PUBLISHING

Sandra Jonas Publishing House
PO Box 20892
Boulder, CO 80308
sandrajonaspublishing.com

Printed in the United States of America
26 25 24 23 22 21   1 2 3 4 5 6 7 8

Book and cover design by Sandra Jonas

Publisher's Cataloging-in-Publication Data

Names: Poses, David, author.
Title: The Weight of Air: A Story of the Lies about Addiction and the Truth about
     Recovery / David Poses.
Description: Boulder, CO : Sandra Jonas Publishing, 2021. |
Identifiers: LCCN 2021933178 | ISBN 9781954861992 (hardcover) |
     ISBN 9781954861978 (paperback) | ISBN 9781954861923 (ebook)
Subjects: LCSH: Poses, David. | Depressed persons—Biography. | Recovering
     addicts—Biography. | LCGFT: Autobiographies. | BISAC: BIOGRAPHY &
     AUTOBIOGRAPHY / Social Activists.
Classification: LCC HV5805 .P6747 | DDC 362.293092 — dc23
LC record available at http://lccn.loc.gov/2021933178

This is for you

contents

author's note   *vii*

part one: 1995   *1*

part two: 1996   *73*

part three: 1999   *129*

part four: 2000   *183*

epilogue   *235*

acknowledgments   *239*

playlist   *241*

about the author   *243*

CONTENTS

author's note

I recreated the scenes and dialogue in this book from memory and journal entries. Some of the names and details were changed by request. I'm not a doctor, and the information presented should not be used for diagnosis or treatment or as a substitute for professional care. Please accept my apologies for the stigmatizing language. I don't condone the use of such offensive words and phrases, but it would have been dishonest to exclude them.

part one

1995

one

Rob was right. My plan is a fucking disaster.

It made perfect sense yesterday. I'd kick here at Mom's house while she was in Florida. No distractions. No one around. Rob would have my car so I couldn't leave. This would be different, not like the other times I tried. And in just a few days, the whole mess would be behind me.

But that was before the last hit of heroin raced out of every pore, before the puking, before my legs started twitching—before all the bones in my body felt like they were disintegrating.

And I know it'll only get worse.

Rob warned me. "When you're shooting this much dope," he said between urgent puffs on a crack pipe, "you don't just decide to quit. I'll take you to the methadone clinic. Or you can do a slow taper. Or get on buprenorphine."

No, I told him. I needed to do it my way.

Now all I want is relief.

The volume on the stereo is cranked. Johnny Rotten screams about blood and bile and bodies. I wipe vomit off my face with one of Mom's soft fancy towels and stumble out of the bathroom and down the hall, past dozens of photographs in uniform frameless frames. Most are of me and my brother, Daniel. Our mother is in some. Our father is in none. I stop at a picture taken at a beach when I was eleven and Daniel was eight. He's smiling maniacally. I look blank, my lips pressed into a thin line.

Before he left, Rob put six blue Klonopin on the kitchen counter. "When you can't stand it another second, take *one*," he said.

I toss all six into my mouth and swallow. One comes up in a puddle of yellow and brown phlegm. It stays down when I chase it with ginger ale.

I wait. Nothing happens. How long before I feel something?

Outside, snow is falling. Seconds take hours to pass. Doubled over, one arm wrapped around my stomach, I call the apartment Rob and I have shared since December. The phone rings and rings and rings. I try his beeper. "We're sorry. This number is no longer in service."

I slide down to the floor and light a cigarette. Squinting and swatting at tendrils of smoke, I remember the empty bags Rob threw in the trash after we shot up. On a heap of paper towels and coffee grinds, I spot two glassine envelopes with archaic Hotstepper stamps—the closest you'll get to quality assurance on a ten-dollar bag of heroin.

Grabbing a steak knife, I split the bags and use the dull edge to scrape the creases. With the flat end of a syringe, I mix the powder and water in a spoon, and then I suck the concoction into the chamber. No lighter. No cooking. No cotton. My stomach clenches with anticipation.

I tighten a belt around my upper arm and hold it in my teeth and make a fist. When the vein pops, I stab it with the needle and release the medicine into my bloodstream. Tension disappears from my body in less than a second. My insides begin to warm. My legs stop twitching. I can breathe again—for the moment.

The countdown to withdrawal resets. I'll try again when this wears off. I can do this. For fuck's sakes, if I can't get through the day without a tiny speck of powder, I don't deserve to live. Next month, I'll be nineteen or I'll be nothing.

I turn off the stereo and collapse on the couch. On TV, a kid hits a baseball over a fence in a Little League game, and his proud father charges onto the field. Cut to the inside of a McDonald's, where he tousles his son's hair and they enjoy a celebratory Happy Meal together.

I close my eyes.

Is this a dream? My father never randomly shows up here. I hear him say Mom's name. He speaks with the authority of a switchblade.

"Robin, wake up and smell the coffee," his voice booms from the kitchen. "Your son's a dope fiend."

I'm lying on my stomach on the couch. Everything hurts. When I sit up, I start to cough uncontrollably. It's dark outside. The clock on the VCR says 6:05—a.m. or p.m.?

A guy I've never seen before lumbers into the living room. His doughy paunch jiggles behind a New York Mets jersey. Number sixteen. "Bob," he calls over his shoulder, "the dope fiend is up."

My father pokes his head into the room, the cordless phone cradled in his neck, and gives me a long, narrow-eyed once-over. His hair is more salt and less pepper than it was a year ago, the last time we saw and spoke to each other.

"Bob, waddaya want me to do?"

"I don't know, Howie. Maybe sit on him so he doesn't do something stupid again? He's too whacked out to know we're trying to help him."

Howie grabs my arm and the back of my head and forces me to the floor. "This is tough love, brother," he says.

The carpet scrapes against my cheek like sandpaper. I squirm and wriggle under his weight, and he shifts forward, planting his giant ass into the base of my spine. I laugh nervously.

"Something funny, dope fiend?"

"Your breath smells like Doritos and coffee."

"And you look like a friggin' clown with that orange hair."

"I think I'm gonna puke."

"You're out of your gourd if you think I'm falling for that again."

I cough up bile, and my nose starts to bleed. Howie yanks me to my feet and points to the floor. "I'm sure your mom wants to come home to this friggin' mess."

A trail of blood stretches from the kitchen to the front door, where a broken glass jar sits next to a pile of loose change.

"How much dope did you think you'd score with that?"

What happened last night?

Dad joins us, squeezing the bridge of his nose as if he has a headache.

"I take it the ex-wife wasn't too thrilled?"

"She can't help it," Dad says. "It's hard not to sound crazy when you're crazy."

I'm not a violent person, but I want to punch him in the face.

My self-proclaimed saviors carry me out of the house in a T-shirt and boxers and load me into the back of Dad's BMW like a cheap rug. He squeals out of the driveway. The Pointer Sisters' "Neutron Dance" comes on the stereo, and he pumps up the volume. Bobbing his head, he sings along with made-up lyrics involving rutabagas and watermelons.

Splayed across the back seat, I curl into the fetal position and watch the streetlights blur by. "Where are we going?" I manage to yell above the music.

"Don't worry about it, dope fiend."

It's still dark outside when we careen into the emergency entrance at United Hospital in Port Chester. The clock on the dash says 7:45. It must be p.m.

A nurse hustles me into a small triage area and closes the curtain. She opens a sealed package of surgical scissors, cuts off my clothes without explanation, and helps me into a gown—the kind that leaves little to the imagination in the rear.

Howie slips in. "Your old man'll catch up once he's dotted the *i*'s and crossed the *t*'s."

"Are you allergic to any medications?" the nurse asks.

"Yeah," Howie says. "Dope."

The nurse stabs my thigh with a shot of Clonidine and drops the needle into a red biohazard container. She grabs a wheelchair and pats the seat.

"His legs ain't broke," Howie says.

"Sorry," the nurse says, unapologetically. "Hospital policy."

She wheels me down a wide yellow corridor lined with posters of iconic Westchester County locations. I've gotten high at most of them over the past three years. The beach at Rye Playland. Saxon Woods Park in Mamaroneck. Downtown Tarrytown, facing the Hudson River. I used to stop at an abandoned warehouse before school and shoot up in my car.

I got decent grades. I was the top-seeded player on my high school tennis team. And I was on heroin.

Struggling to keep up, Howie gasps about kicking in a friggin' jail cell around twenty hard motherfuckers. "This is a picnic," he says, "kicking in a friggin' hospital."

My last visit to a hospital was two years ago, when Mom's cancer came back. I remember her first battle better. Dad took Daniel and me to see her after surgery. I thought it was going to fix her, but she looked frail, and her voice was groggy and barely audible.

When we left her room, I asked Dad if Mom was going to die. He finally answered in the elevator. "Probably," he said, as if it were an overcast day and I'd asked if it might rain. I put on a brave face as we walked to the car in silence. Nobody was in the pay booth at the parking lot, and Dad started to drive around the gate. But then he realized he couldn't do it without scratching his new Jaguar and let loose a string of f-bombs.

At the end of the corridor, a burly security guard uses his body as a shield while punching numbers into a keypad. A wide door opens in stop-start motion. The nurse pushes me into a room cut in half by a giant turquoise shower curtain.

Two TVs are mounted to the wall, one opposite each bed. My roommate moans as he watches *The Price Is Right* on mute.

The nurse hangs bags of clear liquids on a pole and attaches a narrow tube that ends in a wide needle. After swabbing the inside of my elbow with rubbing alcohol, she sticks in the IV with a sympathetic smile.

"Get comfy," she says. "You'll be here a few days unless other plans were—"

Dad arrives out of breath. "Yep," he says, hunched over, his hands on his thighs. He glances at Howie. "Joey's on it."

Who the fuck is Joey?

I stare up at the foamy white tiles in the ceiling covered with Rorschach-pattern water stains. One resembles the outline of Florida, minus the panhandle. Another could be a unicorn. I ask if anyone sees the unicorn in the ceiling. Silence.

My mom would see the unicorn if she were here. She'd find other things too. One of her biggest complaints about my father over the years, apart from his lack of a conscience, is his inability to see the face in the man in the moon.

"Get some rest, sweet boy," Dad says, laying the back of his hand on my forehead. "This would have been much worse if you hadn't called."

two

I t's 5 a.m. Bunny rabbits scamper across the TV screen, going "bok bok b'kok" like chickens and pooping chocolate eggs. An announcer with an aristocratic British accent says, "Easter is coming. Load up on Cadbury Crème Eggs."

I could really use some chocolate right now to coat the acid in my gut and distract me from the sledgehammer pounding every inch of my body. I hit the button on the wall next to my bed. A nurse with kind eyes appears. I swing my legs over the edge of the bed and tell her I want to go home.

"Uh, hold on a sec," she says, backing into the hall. I watch her shadow's arms flail and somebody else's shadow run to her. They whisper.

A doctor in a crisp white lab coat enters and lectures me about the high rate of relapse among "junkies" who fail to complete a medically supervised detox and drug treatment and blah blah blah. I yank out the IV and take a few steps.

The doctor raises his hands. "Whoa there, chief."

The nurse gets between us. In a singsong voice, she says, "The kitchen is clo-sed but I might know some-one who can pull some strings and get you some Jell-O . . ."

I stumble into the hallway and look for the exit.

The doctor follows, running his hand along the rail on the wall, his wedding ring clanging against the steel as he asks if I understand the consequences of my decision. I nod. In the lobby, he asks the receptionist for an AMA form. He thwaps it against the wall and clicks a pen.

"AMA stands for 'against medical advice,'" he says.

I sign without reading and go outside into the freezing cold, my bare ass exposed.

Shivering by the entrance, I remember the first time I bucked medical advice. In the seventh grade, after my orthodontist broke repeated promises to remove my braces next time, I took matters into my own hands—literally. It was a bitch to pry those fuckers off with my fingers, without a mirror, in fifth-period study hall. Not completely thorough, I made enough progress for Mom to notice. The next morning, as Dr. Berman lectured me about the permanent damage I'd caused to my enamel, he removed the remaining metal from my teeth.

The sun cracks its yolk on the horizon. I go back inside and call my father—collect—from a pay phone.

No blood in the foyer or on the carpet. No broken glass or loose change. I still don't remember what happened and don't want to ask. I muster a halfhearted thank-you.

"The people you really need to thank are Howie and Joey," Dad says. "You wouldn't be going to Hazelden if Joey hadn't made a few calls on your behalf."

He launches into a monologue about Joey's "miraculous recovery from dope fienddom" twenty years ago. With enough context, I realize Hazelden is a rehab and Joey is my aunt Jo, a hotshot lawyer who works for Sunbeam, the company that makes blenders and all kinds of other things.

The front door opens. I hear Mom crying, and my heart sinks. Of course she came home early. Her face looks unfamiliar and old and puffy, no makeup, giant purple bags under her eyes, and her short brown hair, always styled to perfection, is a staticky bird's nest.

I can taste her tears as she grips me in a tight hug. She lets go and hesitates before taking a seat on the couch, two cushions from Dad. I drop to the floor and sit across from my parents, hugging my knees, wishing I could disappear, trying to remember the last time they were together in the same room.

Choked up, Mom leans forward. "Why?"

Dad clasps his hands behind his head and closes his eyes.

I take a deep breath, swallow hard, and choose my words carefully, but not necessarily honestly. "Rob had some heroin. I asked to try it."

"*When*, David?"

"I don't know. Maybe six months ago."

Mom buries her head in her hands and sobs.

Dad gets up and roars. "You never held the boys accountable for anything, Robin. You've got Daniel at that boarding school because he got kicked out of every school around here, and David's in the city every night at Limelight and . . . How did you *not* know he was stoned out of his mind on drugs?"

My skin tightens, as if it's stuck to my bones. I want to say, "She didn't know I was stoned out of my mind because I wasn't. Heroin makes me feel normal." Instead I ask, "Do I have to go to rehab? This whole thing happened because I decided to quit—"

"Son, you and your mother are going to do what you're going to do—because that's what you've always done."

"That's *not* fair," Mom says.

"Robin, you want to bury your son? He'll be dead in a week if he doesn't go."

Mom starts to cry again. I agree to go to rehab.

"Please," she says, "promise me you'll never do . . . I can't even say it . . . that *shit* . . . again."

I promise. And I want so badly to mean it.

three

I t's almost noon when the plane descends from a clear blue sky into Minneapolis. The wheels touch down and the passengers applaud as if the pilot did us a huge favor by not crashing.

In the terminal, Creedence Clearwater Revival's "Heard It Through the Grapevine" crackles out of an overhead speaker. I flip through my CD case—eighteen discs from a collection of three thousand. Did I bring the right music to get through the next month?

Mom didn't say where someone from Hazelden would meet me, only that someone would. Headphones on, I follow signs to baggage claim, listening to Neil Young. *Live Rust.* On the escalator, I stay to the right as harried travelers scamper by. A woman with a giant purse crashes into me and apologizes. I feel proud, smiling and waving like no big deal. Then I feel stupid.

At the carousel, an older man holds a sign with my name on it. His swollen nose teems with dark veins. I wait for "I Am a Child" to end and then I approach.

"I'm David."

"Hey, Dave. I'm Pete."

I hate being called Dave.

My yellow duffel is the first thing out of the chute. I nab it and follow Pete on a twenty-minute trek to a blue van at the farthest reaches of the cold parking lot. He drives painfully slowly, his plump tongue poking through thin, cracked lips unless he's reading street signs aloud.

The radio is off. I'm riding shotgun. My eyes are heavy, but they refuse to close. I never went to sleep on heroin—I passed out. It's been almost a week since my last hit. My mind is racing, but I can't complete a thought, and my body still feels like it's being pulled apart by horses.

"Burger King. Dillard's. Blockbuster Video. Ramada Hotel."

On a wide strip-mall-lined boulevard, Pete hits the windshield with minty green washer fluid and fashions his hand into a visor as the wiper blades battle a splotch of bird shit.

"Better 'n sunglasses," he says. "'Cause your hand ain't getting lost or stoled."

I force a chuckle. Pete grins.

At the next intersection, he leans toward me and says, "Just so you know, I got the disease too."

What the fuck is he talking about?

"Yes siree Boberooney. My head came awful close to the blades a time or two."

Though I assume he's speaking metaphorically, I picture Pete's short gray hair in dangerously close proximity to whirring helicopter blades and an industrial fan.

"Looking for answers at the bottom of a bottle—till God took me in his arms."

Got it. He calls addiction a *disease*—which makes no sense.

We turn onto a narrow, windy road of split-levels and short driveways with minivans. Two lefts later, we approach a dozen absurdly tall speed bumps and an open gate next to a shed. Pete rolls down the window and nods to two security guards, who raise sandwiches wrapped in tin foil to toast our arrival.

A massive, modern pastel yellow structure appears. Wide columns support an overhang at the front entrance. I remember fifth grade and Mr. Tacelly's lesson on the three types of classic Greek columns: Doric, Ionic, and the other one. *What is it?*

Nancy, the director of counseling, greets me with a bear hug in the reception area. She's short and overweight with red spiky hair. In a thick Midwestern accent, she says, "Thank God you're here."

I resist the temptation to say, "Praise the Lord."

Nancy says my counselor, Ron, will be "out in a jiffy."

Approximately two jiffies later, a guy in a dark suit appears. "Nancy," he says, "can I borrow you?"

"Okay, Lester . . . but only if you give me back."

Lester and Nancy laugh their way to an office. I drop down on a flowered love seat and prop my feet on a coffee table between stacks of Hazelden's magazine, *Together*.

A mini fridge buzzes. *What's the third type of Greek column?*

A set of double doors open, and a girl with rectangular glasses and purple streaks in her long brown hair saunters in. After a quick nod in my direction, she dive bombs the love seat across from me, straightens her plaid Catholic-school skirt, and grabs an issue of *Together*.

"They should call it *This Is My Sucky, Fucking, Fucked-Up Life Now*," she says, flipping through the pages. "What the hell? Someone already did the crossword puzzle—in pen. Duh, dumbass. A five-letter game that starts with 'O' isn't 'Oprah.'"

"'Ouija.'"

"Damn, new guy. You're good."

The receptionist snaps, "Victoria."

"Big Brother doesn't like outgoings talking to incomings," Victoria whispers. "What're you in for?" she asks.

"Heroin."

"Well, well, well. Heroin. Very chic. How long were you on it?"

"About three years. What were you in for?"

"Weed, booze, coke, meth. You name it. Shrooms. Acid. You trip out?"

"I got scared away from hallucinogens in fifth grade."

"You dropped acid in *fifth grade*?"

"A cop came to my school for a drug prevention assembly. He said a kid from our high school took acid, thought he was an orange, and peeled off his skin."

"I'm sorry, but that is complete BS. Acid's the bomb. Of all the things I'm gonna miss, acid's right up there with coke, shrooms, weed—you smoke cheeba?"

"A few times."

"Drinking?"

"I got drunk once. I hate being intoxicated."

"You hate—dude, heroin's the most hard-core drug there is."

"It has a bad rap. Alcohol and pot fuck you up *way* more."

"Well, I never tried it. Nobody did heroin where I grew up. Where you from?"

"New York."

"City?"

"Just outside. Westchester County. Rye."

"No way! I'm from Greenwich."

The receptionist says "Victoria" again and shoots a stink eye while poking a straw into a can of Diet Dr. Pepper.

Victoria scurries around a half wall covered with framed awards and commendations for Hazelden's work on addiction recovery and flops onto an overstuffed upholstered chair with a lilac batik pattern. She crosses and uncrosses her legs a few times, then scribbles on a magazine page and tears it out and balls it up.

"Incoming!" she shouts, hurling the note into a nearby fichus plant. I retrieve and unravel it—her name and phone number.

"All right, Victoria," the receptionist says, "Pete's here."

On her way out, Victoria says, "Give me a call when you get home. We'll go to an AA meeting. Or something."

I sit back and imagine myself a month from now, driving around Greenwich's backcountry with her. Then it hits me. *Corinthian.*

four

Ron's gold track pants make a swishing sound as he walks toward me, his right hand outstretched. Tall and skinny with the impeccable posture my mother would love, he's probably in his late twenties. He yawns and apologizes for yawning while leading me through a maze of hallways to a small room with a twin bed, a chair with initials carved into the seat, a tall dresser—and no door.

"Call it a way station," he says, gesturing from the threshold like he's revealing a prize on a game show. "As long as there's no contraband in your bag and no red flags go up in your intake evaluation, you'll be in general population tomorrow morning." He follows me into the room and stands at the foot of the bed with his arms folded. I hug my bag and stare at the shiplap wall.

"Okay, so here's the deal," he says. "Every morning we're up at six, except Sundays when you can sleep in. That means *seven*. Group therapy every day, and AA and NA meetings. Physical fitness, meditation, recreation, lectures on sober living—the whole nine. Unless you have a doctor's note, everything's mandatory, so don't think about trying to ditch. Capisce?"

Does he want me to say "Sir, yes, sir"? I nod and drop my bag on the bed, trying not to laugh at his dorky impression of a drill sergeant.

"This will be your life for the next twenty-eight days. Once you've been here a week, you get phone privileges. Forty-five minutes a day. Abuse those privileges and sayonara the phone."

"I promised my mom I'd call when I—"

"Holy smokes, Dave. Has it been a week already? I could have sworn you just got here." He grins. "No, all kidding aside. Mom knows you're here. I just talked to her. Part of my daily routine is a check in with your folks."

"My parents are divorced."

"Yep."

"Will you talk to both of them every day?"

"Mom and Dad have as much to learn about recovery as you do. And fortunately for you and them, Hazelden does a terrific job of educating parents about enabling and tough love, everything they need to know to help you avoid old patterns when you're back home in six months or—"

"Six *months*?" He can't be serious. But it doesn't matter. Mom won't make me stay. She's never forced me to do anything. Seven days until phone privileges. Home in eight, max. This place is for serious drug addicts and hardened criminals.

"Dave. Coming here for a month is a great start, but that's all it is. A *start*. Recovery's a lifelong process. You'll want to go to aftercare when you leave here—a halfway house—we've got options all over the country. Some folks don't go home for eighteen months. Some never do. All depends on how bad your disease is. Questions?"

"Why do you call addiction a disease?"

Ron narrows his eyes. "You being facetious?"

"No."

"We call addiction a disease, Dave, because that's what it is."

"Er, when I think of disease, I think of cancer. My mom didn't choose to have it. It could've killed her."

"Bingo. We're saying the same thing, yeah?"

I smile. "I love the idea of you telling my parents that a disease made me stick needles in my arms, but they know it's my fault."

"Sorry, Dave, but that's baloney. *Buh-loney*. You have a disease. First step in AA is admitting we're powerless over the disease."

"But if I decided to start and I decided to stop—"

Ron winces and exhales hard. "Dave. You might have decided you *wanted* to stop, but you're here because your higher power saw you at rock bottom and said, 'Hey, look. There's Dave down there. Let me see if I can't give him a hand.'"

A security guard appears in the doorway, a tall, heavy-breathing dude with a greasy blond mullet. "Keith," he says, giving me a curt nod. He blows into a surgical glove and stuffs his sausage fingers inside, then opens the zipper on my bag.

While Keith commences the perfunctory "welcome to rehab" inspection, Ron picks up a big blue hardcover from the dresser and opens to "The Twelve Steps of Alcoholics Anonymous." He reads aloud and follows the words with his finger.

"Number one: We admitted we were powerless over alcohol—that our lives had become unmanageable. Number two: Came to believe that a Power greater than ourselves could restore us to sanity. Number three: Made a decision to turn our will and our lives over to the care of God as we understood him . . ."

Ron drones on about making a moral inventory, admitting our wrongs, asking God to remove our character defects, and making amends to everyone we've harmed.

He finally reaches number twelve. "Having had a spiritual awakening as the result of these steps, we tried to carry this message to alcoholics and to practice these principles in all our affairs." He snaps the book shut with one hand and gives it to me. "What do you think?"

"Seems awfully religious." When I talk to Mom, I won't need to make anything up. After a couple of conversations with Ron, she'll know this place is completely fucking bonkers.

"Not religious, Dave. *Universal.* The only way to keep this disease from being terminal is to put your life and will in God's hands and you work the steps."

"So, if God is keeping me clean, is it his fault if I relapse?"

Ron stands there, gaping at me in teapot stance, the back of his hands on his hips.

"Aha," Keith cries. "Contraband." He removes a can of Right Guard deodorant spray and gives it to Ron.

They probably assume it's one of those decoy cans my nana hides jewelry in, or maybe Hazelden has an environmental policy prohibiting aerosol deodorant?

Ron shakes the can in my face. "Should I get your folks on the horn? Have them book you on the next flight home?"

"Why?"

"Let me guess. It never occurred to you to monkey with the nozzle and get high off the fumes?"

"What?"

We lock eyes for a beat. He's not running me out of here—I'll leave on my own terms.

"All right, Dave. You get the benefit of the doubt, but give me one more reason and so help me God . . ."

Keith resumes the search and rattles off other banned household items: whipped cream, certain kinds of air conditioner cartridges, Purell. "Hand sanitizer's the most popular alcoholic beverage in the US prison system," he says.

"Hmm," I say. "I remember something in the news a while back about a politician's wife drinking nail polish remover. Kitty Dukakis?"

"Whoa, Nelly!" Keith says, elbow-deep in my bag. He slowly tweezes my Discman and CD case out with his fingers.

Ron snickers. "Dave, Dave, Dave, Dave. If I call your folks, what're the chances they say you knew we don't allow music to be brought in?"

"We can't have music?"

"That's not what I said. Clock radios are allowed, but you wouldn't know that because, obviously, you didn't bother reading the list."

"List?"

"Golly, Dave. Most folks bring clock radios because most folks read the list, which clearly states that you can listen to any station you can tune on the dial, but you cannot—I repeat—cannot bring Walkmans, Discmans, record players, LPs, CDs, tapes."

"Why?"

"Because it's a trigger, Dave. Music is a trigger."

"It'll be easier to live without dope than without music."

"Sorry. Them's the rules."

five

The window is narrow and rectangular, the kind you crank open, except the crank is gone. Ice on the screen partially obscures the view of a snow-covered field with random footprints and a wall of pine trees. I exhale onto the glass, draw a smiley face in the condensation, and watch it evaporate.

"Knock, knock," Pete says, rapping where the door should be. He slides a brown plastic cafeteria tray onto the dresser and leaves without another word. Three slimy slices of turkey, with some sort of gelatinous goo on the ends, on white bread, a small packet of mustard, and two slightly larger packets of ketchup. No sides. I don't eat anything.

As the sun sets, I lie down on the small bed. Headlights sweep across the ceiling and remind me of the nights when my father tucked me in at my mom's house. After he left my room, I'd stare at the ceiling until his headlights appeared. Then I'd run to the window and watch him do "tricks"—his term for veering off our long driveway onto the lawn and peeling doughnuts and figure eights. I'd brag about the show to my friends. "This is why it's great to have divorced parents!" Two years ago, when Mom sold the house, there were still patches of lawn where grass didn't grow.

No one I know has been to rehab. Is it all prayer and religious mumbo jumbo? Maybe some of it. The therapy is probably more like the weekly sessions Mom started taking me to when I was five. After the divorce. Fuck. What if she makes me stay here after all?

I overheard her tell one of my psychiatrists that I was "devoid of feelings." She was wrong. I *felt* everything. She used to ask—constantly—"Why are you so sad?" or "Don't you want to be happy?"

I didn't want to be sad, but I didn't know why I was sad or how *not* to be sad or how to talk about it. I was broken. I *felt* broken. My body ached. My stomach hurt. I couldn't sleep. Nothing was pleasurable. Every morning, I woke up knowing I'd failed before my feet hit the ground. At night, I'd lie in bed and wish for a terminal disease.

Mom would pull my shoulders back and say, "Body language speaks volumes about how you feel about yourself." And she'd say something similar when I failed to make eye contact during a conversation or didn't ooze with confidence.

"Someday, David, I hope it'll be important enough for you to decide to be happy."

Though I kept my shittiest feelings inside—even in therapy—three different shrinks diagnosed me with clinical depression by the age of sixteen. Their scientific explanations called for chemical solutions. But Prozac made me more depressed. Zoloft made it impossible for me to sleep (not terrible) or get an erection (not acceptable). Paxil made me sweaty and confused.

I knew what I needed. I'd known since the drug prevention assembly in fifth grade. The cop said cocaine made you angry, pot made you stupid, and if you drank alcohol, you weren't allowed to drive.

"Heroin is the worst drug," he said, and then lowered his voice to an ominous whisper. "It's a painkiller so powerful, it makes you not feel anything."

That sounded perfect to me. The last thing I needed was anger or an impediment to fulfilling my lifelong dream of driving into a tree at top speed. The idea of heroin gave me hope.

From the beginning of high school, all other substances were readily available and liberally consumed by my friends, who used weed and booze like an essential garnish for activities. Peer pressure was rampant with hallucinogens and cocaine. I experimented and hated the effects. Reality wasn't the problem. I was.

But I had no access to heroin. It might as well have been plutonium in my slice of suburbia.

· · ·

The bright hall light shines into my dark room, and a peculiar wet dog and corn chip smell fills the air. It's eerily quiet and I'm restless. I get up and pace the small room.

Rob doesn't know where I am. I couldn't call him or go by the apartment before I left. Will I ever see him again? Probably not.

When we first met during the summer between my freshman and sophomore year, Rob looked nothing like the junkie stereotype in his pleated khakis and polo shirt, his short hair neatly combed and parted to the side. He was seven years older than me, close with my friend Andrew's older brother and supposedly with Michael Alig, leader of the Club Kids. I'd seen them on talk shows. The self-proclaimed freaks and outcasts struck a chord.

The night Rob took me to Michael's Disco 2000 party at Limelight, we skipped to the front of a line that stretched down the block and around the corner and got in without having to pay or show ID. Rob introduced me to Michael, and I started hanging out with both of them and going to the clubs at least once a week. It was easy to lose myself in the dark rooms and loud techno music.

Soon after I told Michael I could attract rich, thirsty suburban kids to Limelight, USA, and Tunnel, he hired me as a promoter. It didn't matter that I wasn't old enough to enter a nightclub.

The Club Kids drank and used cocaine, ecstasy, and Special K, but they shunned heroin. When I found out Rob used heroin and asked for a hit, he said, "I wouldn't wish this on my worst enemy." He resisted for months, but I persisted.

He finally caved at the end of an all-nighter at Save the Robot, an after-hours club. I was sixteen, in the passenger seat of his grandmother's Chevy Celebrity, choking back tears as I told him about my struggle with depression.

"Please," I said. "This has been going on since I was a kid, but lately, I think about suicide all the time."

My heart raced as Rob shook an infinitesimal amount of rough beige powder onto the back of a magazine. I snorted it with a rolled-up five-dollar bill. As the bitter mix of heroin and coagulated snot dripped down the back of my throat, my body started to relax, and years of bottled-up shame, sadness, anger, and fear melted into warmth and safety. I wasn't high—I was *even*. I could breathe—for the first time.

The next morning, all I could think about was getting more.

. . .

I'm still pacing when Dr. Burton comes in and turns on the overhead light. He could pass for an English professor at a small liberal arts college: longish, unkempt gray hair, blue shirt buttoned to the top, collar buttons undone, one side jutting up. I sit on the edge of the bed, and he eases into the chair next to me and moans about his back.

"Sciatica. Not fun." He licks the tip of his index finger and flips to a blank page in a legal pad. "Do you prefer Dave or David?"

"David. Thanks for ask—"

"All right, Da-vid. Anyone in your family with a history of addiction?"

"My aunt Jo was a heroin addict in the '70s. Other than her, no one."

We breeze through my limited experience with pot and alcohol and my lack of experience with hallucinogens.

"Cocaine?"

"I snorted it a few times—smoked it more. Crack counts as coke, right?"

"How do you figure?"

"On a molecular level, powder is the hydrochloride salt form of coke, and crack has the added base that lets you smoke it, but it's just baking soda."

"How often did you smoke crack?"

"Thursday mornings, mostly. I had a job as a nightclub promoter. Wednesday's at Limelight ended at dawn on Thursday. I didn't want to fall asleep driving to school."

Dr. Burton nods and jots something down. He must know I don't belong here, right? Pen poised over the page, he asks about heroin.

"I started at sixteen, after every antidepressant known to man failed."

"We call that self-medicating."

"Exactly. Depression is pain. Heroin is a pain*killer*."

"How much did you use?"

"Two bags a day. Maybe three or four. Five."

"Shoot? Snort? Smoke?"

"I snorted at first and started shooting after a year or so."

"One day you said, 'Here's an idea'?"

"I was the kid who hated going to the doctor because of the finger prick."

"And yet . . ."

"I was in withdrawal. My nose was too stuffy and runny to snort. My friend Rob put the needle in. I had to close my eyes."

"So you got over your fear of needles?"

"Rob told me to make a fist and count backward from ten. By nine, I knew I'd never snort again."

"Ever share a needle?"

"No."

"Not even with Rob?"

"Never. We were militant about hygiene, and clean needles weren't a problem. There were plenty around. My brother had a prescription for—"

"Ah, you stole needles from your brother. Ever been arrested?"

"Never."

"Five bags a day isn't cheap. How'd you pay for it?"

"My job at the clubs."

"Isn't that something—a teenage nightclub mogul-entrepreneur, non-degenerate addict who had everything under control."

"I did."

"So why are you here?"

"I guess I got sick of being a junkie."

"You just said enough and quit?"

"I'd been thinking about it for a while. Then Rob and I were coming home from the Bronx in the middle of the night and a kid threw a brick at my car as we drove under a bridge. We pulled over. The kid was on the bridge laughing, and the top of the driver's side door frame was bent like an elbow. It could have easily gone through the windshield, and we would've died."

"In recovery, that's known as an epiphany, a sign from God. That how it felt?"

"I've always thought of God as Santa Claus for grown-ups."

"Uh-huh. And did you stop after the accident?"

I shake my head.

"You couldn't."

"I needed a plan. A few months after the accident—last week—when my mom went to Florida, I gave Rob all my money and my car so I'd have no way out, and . . ."

"Withdrawing from heroin is a serious medical condition."

"I'd kicked before. Rob said it'd be much worse this time—he tried to convince me to get on methadone or do a slow taper."

"Why not take his advice? There are safer, less excruciating ways to withdraw."

I choke up a little and stare at the wall. Finally I say, "I thought I deserved to suffer."

six

"Seven o'clock, Dave. You're late for a powwow with Nancy."

I sit up and rub my eyes, nowhere near well rested after yet another night of being jolted out of nightmares I can't remember but can tell are brutal.

Ron claps his hands. "C'mon. Shake your tail feathers."

I slide out of bed fully clothed and reach for my sneakers. He bounds into the hall and I follow, holding my toothbrush between my teeth and hopping on my right foot so I can wedge the back of my left sneaker over my ankle. We zig and zag down a series of brightly lit narrow corridors papered in an ugly floral pattern.

"What's the powwow about?" I mumble through the toothbrush.

"Intake eval. Dr. Burton's diagnosis."

When we arrive at Nancy's office, the door is open and she's at her desk, talking on the phone.

"Where's the bathroom?"

"You'll brush your teeth later."

"I have to pee too."

"This'll only be a few minutes."

Nancy hangs up and waves us in. Ron perches on the edge of the desk and futzes with a Green Bay Packer's mug. I drop my toothbrush into my shirt pocket and crumble into a chair.

Opening a folder, Nancy says, "Let's get down to brass tacks." She glances at a short, typed paragraph. "Cross-addicted. Textbook."

"That means you're not loyal to *a* drug," Ron adds. "You'll do *anything* to get high."

My mouth is dry and tastes like an ashtray, and my bladder is about to explode. I plant my hands on my thighs and push—hard, burning, sweaty palm-on-denim friction. "No! I've never taken a hallucinogen. I got drunk once. I hate alcohol."

Nancy and Ron exchange a look, two guards reacting to a prisoner proclaiming his innocence. "Now, Dave," she says. "You might hate alcohol now, but with this disease, you don't get to decide not to become an alcoholic. You're powerless."

"There wasn't a gun to my head. I made a conscious choice to—"

"The disease chooses," Nancy says. "The disease *is* the gun."

Sunlight hits the gems in her crucifix necklace, spraying a kaleidoscope of color on the wall. Diamonds or zirconia? Did she buy it for herself? She's not wearing a wedding ring. Do drug counselors make decent money? What kind of training do you need? I'd be a good counselor. I should start a rehab that doesn't march you up twelve steps and force God down your throat.

Ron hops off the desk and snaps his fingers in my face. "Earth to Dave. Do you copy? What. Religion. Were. You. Raised?"

"Jewish."

"So Hebrew school? Bar mitzvah? Whole nine?"

"Yeah, but where I grew up, Judaism was more of a cultural thing. Less synagogue, more country club."

"You told Dr. Burton you don't believe in God. That true?"

"Between the robes and beards and followers and trying to curry favor through good behavior—no, I don't believe in God."

"Dave."

"Maybe I'm biased. God didn't do anything to help my mom when she had cancer, but he helps junkies, drunks, and crackheads?"

"Dave, for this to work, you need to start by admitting you're powerless. Put your life and will in God's hands and you'll see."

"But if I'm powerless, how can I put my life and will in anyone's hands?"

"Dave."

"Okay, so there's a loophole. Somehow, I manage to put my life and will in God's hands. Aren't I still powerless?"

"Dave."

"What if God is a morning person, with bad taste in music and a yen for backgammon? What if he calls me Dave?"

Nancy chuffs air and runs a hand through her hair.

I cross my legs. Maybe that'll stop me from pissing myself. "There's no question I was addicted to heroin but—"

"*Are* addicted," Nancy says. "Once an addict, always an addict—even if you're not actively using."

"Heroin isn't the problem."

"Exactly," Ron says. "Just like Purell isn't the problem for the guys knocking it back in jail. When you're an addict and you're desperate enough for a high, you'll abuse anything that can be abused."

"Do you get what he's saying?" Nancy tilts her head.

"I get why drinking soap is abuse, but heroin is a painkiller. I ran out all the time. If I never even thought to drink a beer, why would I start chugging Purell?"

"*Denial*," Ron says. "It's not just a river in Egypt."

Nancy looks at Ron. "I think he knows the truth and he's scared. He's been squirming and wriggling since you two got here."

"I'm trying not to pee all over your chair."

Nancy rises to her feet and inhales deeply through her nose and lets it out slowly. "Why don't we let you get settled and we'll pick it up later. Sound good?"

Ron takes me through general population, and my stomach twists into knots as my world is compressed into an eternity on two and a half floors. We pass the kitchen, dining hall, and gymnasium and enter the small library, which has no shortage of Bible bibles and bibles for Alcoholics Anonymous and Narcotics Anonymous.

In a hall of offices and classrooms, some of the doors have placards next to them with names and titles etched in white on phony wood. On one, the letters are unevenly spaced in "therapist." It looks like "the rapist."

The bedrooms are downstairs, off long corridors with dark brown carpet that reaches halfway up the walls, below sconces with low-wattage light bulbs. All the rooms have doors.

Mine is a perfect square. Hunter green walls. A white popcorn stucco ceiling. Cheap plaid flannel curtains. Four twin beds made with military corners and covered with navy blue blankets, the hard kind of wool you don't want near your body. Adjacent to every bed is a short, wide dresser with three drawers and a clock radio on all but mine.

"Obviously, your roomies read the list," Ron says.

A framed print from an Audubon book hangs on a wall. On another, a faded, sad-looking still-life watercolor of a fruit bowl.

The bathroom has a toilet, sink, and shower. No tub. The blurry vanity mirror appears to be unbreakable, depriving you of the option of shattering it and slitting your wrists.

"All righty then. Get yourself situated and I'll see you in group in a bit."

After Ron leaves, I count to twenty, grab my jacket, and take off for the smoking area.

A frozen drizzle falls on half a dozen diseased young adults in the small outdoor space, walled-in with wooden slats you can't see over. On a bench, a white kid with dreadlocks and bad acne draws disproportionately large penises on pictures of men in a Dillard's catalog. Two girls huddle and suck down Marlboro Lights.

The tall one says, "I told her—I was all, 'Rachel, if you're gonna live in denial, then move back in with your frickin' ex-frickin' boyfriend and go back to using.'"

A pale, skinny guy wearing a Chicago Blackhawks hat pulled low chuckles in the corner.

The tall girl says, "I'm sorry, Steve, but Rachel's a fucking cunt." She coughs up a wad of greenish-yellowish phlegm and spits it on the ground. "You think I'm wrong?"

"I'd agree," Steve says, "except Rachel lacks the warmth and depth of a vagina."

"Yeah, well, that cunt's made no frickin' progress. Especially with the fourth step."

The short girl turns to me. "That's when you're supposed to do a fearless moral inventory of yourself."

The tall girl goes inside. The short girl follows. Pausing at the door, she says, "Sorry to disappoint you, new guy, if you were expecting a parade when you got here."

seven

In one of the classrooms, eight of us, including Ron and both Rachel bashers, sit on folding metal chairs in a circle. Overhead, a couple of the fluorescent lights flicker on and off. We begin by reciting the Serenity Prayer:

> *God, grant me the serenity to accept the things I cannot change,*
> *The courage to change the things I can,*
> *And the wisdom to know the difference.*

Ron tells me that when the group welcomes a new member, everyone tells their story. Alex goes first. Identifying as "addict, alcoholic, eight days sober," he brags about getting high on angel dust and blowing up gas stations and claims to hold the record for highest blood alcohol content in Breathalyzer tests in seven Wisconsin towns. He beams with pride.

"I started getting fucked up at eleven," he says. "Drinking, smoking weed, huffing glue and gas, whatever I could get my hands on to escape the hell of my homelife."

I can't relate to this guy. As he tells how his father broke his wrist with a baseball bat, I remember fighting with Daniel over baseball cards and our father throwing them at a wall, dinging the corners of several Mark McGwire rookies.

Then there's Vanessa, the tall, phlegm-spitting Rachel basher, who says she's an addict and alcoholic, twenty days sober. She covers her face with her hands and recalls an uncle who physically abused her. Voice break-ing, she says, "My parents threw me out when I told them. They were all, 'You're destroying the family.'" She started smoking meth and sold her body to pay for it.

She talks about a warehouse roof where she used to have sex for meth money. I can't relate. All I can think of is when I was nine, I went over to a friend's house and climbed on his roof. His mom told my mom, who, for some reason, told my father, who took away my TV privileges. After he tucked me in and left, Mom invited me to watch TV in her master suite—an enormous bedroom with a bathroom, dressing room with mir-rored walls and four walk-in closets and a step-up study bigger than most of my friends' bedrooms.

Venessa says, "The worst hour of my life was on that roof. Four guys in a row. One pulled my hair so hard, I thought my scalp was coming off. When it was over, the last guy went 'You're a fucking whore. I hate you' and spat in my face."

While Mom and I watched Bruce Willis and Cybill Shepherd tackle a mystery and exchange clever witticisms on *Moonlighting*, I sat in her lap, breathing her perfume as she stroked my hair. When the show was over, I fake yawned, stumbled to my room, and slid under the covers. Seconds later, Mom came in, and I pretended to be asleep. She knelt beside me, kissed my forehead, and said "I love you." I made a slight snoring sound. Mom said, "One of these days, I hope you'll say 'I love you' to *me*."

Claire, the shorter Rachel basher, is an addict and alcoholic, twenty-two days sober. Talking with her hands, she says "the disease" made her steal to pay for the hundred grand worth of meth she banged into her jugular. "I woke up in an emergency room to a bunch of doctors going, 'Um, hon, you had enough meth in your system to kill a freakin' rhino.' I thought that was cool."

Until she hit rock bottom. She closes her eyes, and when they open, she whispers about a massive overdose in the parking lot of an outpatient rehab. "That's when you know you're powerless—when you're getting high in rehab."

No story is complete without at least one trip to the nebulous, figura-tive place known as "rock bottom," where God rescues addicts. For Jared, fourteen days sober, it was the back of a police car, following an arrest for possession with intent to sell a large volume of liquid LSD. For Phil, five days sober, it was a bakery—he drove drunk through the front window on a Sunday morning. Pulling strands of wool from his mukluks, he thanks God for the intervention specialist his parents hired. "I didn't know I was out of control until then."

"You're up, Dave," Ron says. Before I say a word, he says, "Dave's struggling with our belief that addiction is a disease and only God has the power to restore us to our sanity." He asks me if I'm a lost cause or willing to be open-minded.

"I'm open," I lie.

"Well, good," he says. "Who accepts the challenge?"

Everyone raises a hand.

At dinner, I sit by myself at a round table with ten chairs and poke at a pile of overcooked spaghetti and bland meatballs. Steve joins me. A twenty-one-year-old from some Chicago suburb, he's another stereotype-defying heroin addict—in blucher shoes with knotted lace ends and a white Oxford under a Northwestern sweatshirt. This is his second stint at Hazelden in as many years.

He removes his Chicago Blackhawks hat and explains the social order while double-fisting jelly sandwiches. "If this was high school, you'd have jocks at one table and nerds at another. In rehab, cliques are based on drug preference, and status comes from 'clean time.' You'd think it was a contest, the way people count and compare days."

"How long have you been clean?"

"Dunno. I haven't been keeping track."

After dinner, we file into the lecture room. I sit with Steve in the last row, talking music. It's nice to meet someone who shares my opinion of Prince's guitar prowess.

"I've been playing for ten years," he says. "If I'm alive in another ten, I still won't be able to play the solo at the end of "Let's Go Crazy." You play anything?"

"The stereo. I tried to learn guitar."

"You should learn. Chicks dig a guy who can express himself musically."

"I make mix tapes. The right songs with the right lyrics and a decorated cover."

Steve sings Prince's "Kiss" in a whispered falsetto. I laugh. Vanessa turns around in her seat and glares at me.

"You think it's funny now 'cause you don't get it," she says. "When you do, trust me—you won't be laughing."

eight

On the seventh day, they bestow phone privileges on me, and I make the first call to my mother.

"I think this is a mistake. Between the religion and the people and—"

"If you're not careful . . ." The seriousness in her voice makes my heart sink.

"What, I might accidentally become an alcoholic, chug a thing of hand sanitizer?"

"These people know what they're doing."

"It's a business. They'd lose money if they said I didn't need this, or the program wasn't a fit for my philosophical sensibilities."

"David, I think you need to listen to them."

"And give my life to Jesus? And admit I had as much choice about doing heroin as you had about cancer."

"I got cancer, David. You have an addiction. There's a difference."

"Not according to them."

Ron is outside the circle, leaning on the back of an unoccupied chair. "Why do we ask God to restore our sanity in the second step?"

"Because drugs fried our brains," Claire says.

"Drugs don't help," Ron says. "But it's the addiction that seriously impairs our cognitive thinking. That's why our lives become unmanageable."

He stops moving and hovers in front of me. "Dave, does that sound like powerlessness to you?"

"Not exactly."

Alex cracks a slight smile and chuckles, and Ron steps left, blocking my view of him. "I beg your pardon?"

"Seriously impaired doesn't mean impossible."

Vanessa says "Fuck you, Dave," and starts bawling. Gobs of mascara streak down her cheeks.

Ron grabs a box of Kleenex from the windowsill and hands them to her. She dabs the corner of her eyes and catches her breath. Crossing my arms, I slide down in the chair and stare at a missing chunk of linoleum on the other side of the circle.

"I thought it was me when I kept going back to that roof and those guys," Vanessa says. "Now that I know it was the disease, ain't nobody telling me it's my freakin' fault."

"You were powerless," Ron says. "That disease was trying to kill you."

"But I didn't know that until I hit bottom."

"Can't recover until you hit bottom," Ron says. "No one can."

"Maybe Dave hasn't hit bottom," Vanessa says. A balled-up tissue lands on my lap. I swat it away and feel everyone's eyes boring holes into my head.

"Dave's hit bottom," Ron says. "But his mom tells me he's never been honest with himself, and like the Big Book says, 'Those who do not recover are people who cannot or will not completely give themselves to this simple program, usually men and women who are constitutionally incapable of being honest with themselves.'" He crouches in front of me. "Make sense?"

"No. Are you saying that remission from a disease can only be achieved by putting your life and will in God's hands and not lying to yourself?"

"You're really in denial, Dave."

Before dinner, Ron summons me for another powwow with Nancy.

"Darn it, Dave," she says, hammering her fist on her desk. "I'm just plain miffed."

I fake a cough to hide a laugh.

"It's not a joke," Ron says. "Unless you want to end up dead in a ditch, you must start taking responsibility for your actions and *let go and let God.*"

"Why does God get the credit if I'm *not* dead in a ditch, but anything bad is my fault?"

"This isn't about credit and blame," Nancy says.

"But if I'm powerless, how can I also be responsible?"

Nancy twiddles a pencil between her index and middle fingers. "You might think I'm some old fuddy-duddy, but twenty-two years ago, I was a junkie, living with my boyfriend. One day, in the dead of winter, when we were both sick and had no money and owed every dealer in town, Jim said he was going for a walk. Two hours later, he came back with five bags of dope. I didn't ask how he got it—didn't matter. We were saved." She stabs the pencil into her Green Bay Packers mug.

"The next morning, four cops showed up and arrested him. Turned out, he'd cold-cocked an old lady and snatched her purse. We're talking about a guy who'd scoop up a spider with a newspaper and let it out the window instead of killing it, and there he was, in handcuffs, charged with assault and battery. Obviously, this was before I became a counselor, but even then, I got it. Jim was powerless. You tell me: Was he responsible for what he did?"

"Of course he was."

"And he was powerless."

"Well . . ."

Nancy scrunches her face. "He just up and walloped that poor old lady? Addiction had nothing to do with it?"

"Can't wait to hear this," Ron says, rubbing his hands.

"It's an equation." I look at Ron and then at Nancy. "I don't know what goes on in anyone else's head, but if it was me and it came down to mugging somebody or going into withdrawal, I'd go into withdrawal."

"So everybody's selfish and you're not," Ron says. "Everybody's—"

Nancy cuts him off. "Have you ever been in Jim's position?"

"No."

Ron says, "Keep living in denial and you will. I guarantee it."

"I don't want to be a junkie. I'd have no use for heroin if I wasn't depressed."

In a flabbergasted calm, Nancy says, "Heroin is pure evil, Dave. It has no medicinal value. None." She gets up and empties a bottle of water into a leafy, dark green potted plant. "You used because you're an addict. Once you admit that, you'll see that you never had a choice."

nine

Every day, a fresh batch of kids arrive and experience near-instantaneous religious awakenings. Ten days in, I still don't see how this is going to help me.

In group, "addict mentality" is the topic du jour. Ron says, "We rationalize and justify because the truth is too painful. It's easier to tell yourself that you're getting high because your girlfriend left than it is to tell yourself that you're getting high because you have a disease."

Everyone nods in unison, a roomful of unblinking eyes.

"Dave, I take it you disagree?"

"I think it's easier to say I'm getting high because I have a disease than it is to say I don't know how to deal with the hole in my heart, so I'm spackling it over with dope."

"What were you spackling over?"

"I don't know."

"You don't know."

I pan around the circle. Everyone is looking at me, their faces washed in a sick green from the lighting. Tears form in my eyes. I bring my knees to my chest and put my feet on the seat. "It's a fucking hole. Holes are fucking empty."

Ron flashes an approving smirk.

"Nice to see you taking this shit seriously for a change," Vanessa says.

Staring at the floor, I wipe my eyes and say, "If it's shit, why would I take it seriously?" I wait for a laugh that doesn't come. A chair squeals. I look up. Vanessa approaches with a frown. I tell her I'm sorry. "When I get scared or nervous, I sometimes have a tendency to get what you might call mouthy."

Vanessa waves at me to get up. I think she's going to punch me but she hugs me instead. The contact feels good. She smells good. I can't stop crying, and my tears land in her oversprayed hair. I squirm away. She stays in my face—almost like a ritualistic dance—until I sit back down.

After group, Ron says, "Kudos, Dave. You really dug in today. It will get easier."

"It would be easier if I had music. My birthday's coming up. How about an exception to the no-music rule to celebrate the occasion? A few songs on my Discman?"

"Dave."

"How about one song?"

"How about we'll see? You keep opening up and maybe. How's that?"

Before lecture, Nancy goes up to the podium and says a lot of new people are arriving tonight. She reminds us for the hundredth time that physical contact with the opposite sex is prohibited—other than quasi-preapproved hugs in certain circumstances.

"Recovery is an extremely vulnerable time," she says. "You might meet someone and think you have something in common, but more likely, you're both desperate to soothe your wounds. That's why we have the rule and why we strongly encourage you to avoid getting romantically involved long after you leave here."

Every morning, a female aide unlocks a closet and wheels a double-decker cart to the area by the ladies' room. The cart overflows with makeup, perfume, deodorant—you name it. The girls locate what they need and line up to use them under supervision.

Save for the mornings when I happen to bump into Steve in the hall and we stop to yell moo at the girls being herded into the beautification room, my routine usually involves an uninterrupted walk to the smoking area. Today, I pause by the cart and try not to get caught staring at a new girl: mussed dark brown shoulder-length hair, plaid flannel shirt at least two sizes too big, short jean shorts with neon pink tights—that certain je ne sais quoi, even first thing in the morning.

Joking to Vanessa, the new girl says, "I had to come to rehab to learn you can get drunk off perfume."

I mosey over and introduce myself and relay my recent education in other common household products that will get you high.

"No fuckin' shit," Chessa says, reaching for a bottle of Calvin Klein Obsession. "When they told me, I was all, 'Hello? I paid a lot of money for this shit. You think I'm gonna drink it?'" She leans in close, grabs my arm, and lowers her voice. "I didn't literally pay a lot of money for it. I stole it, but you get the point."

Rocking on the heels of green low-top Chuck Taylors, Chessa looks at my thick slippers. "Your little piggies must be awfully toasty in those bad boys."

I slide off a slipper and show the underside of the tongue. "'Made from genuine leather. Lined with imitation shearling.' Yep, my feet feel like they're crammed up a rabbit's ass."

"Except no rabbit's ass is lined with imitation shearling. I'm pretty sure no rabbit's ass is lined with genuine shearling, either."

During a special afternoon lecture about I don't know what, Chessa and I sit next to each other, scribbling notes back and forth on a blank page in my AA book. "This is so boring. I'd rather be sitting in traffic. Tell me your darkest secrets." At the end, Chessa writes "You're so cool" and draws an arrow pointing toward me.

At dinner, Chessa enters the dining hall, waving my AA Book. "I must've taken it by mistake." She hands it to me, and for a fleeting, erotic moment, our hands touch. Index finger touching her lips, she glances at the book, which seems to have a slight bulge. Did she specifically take the book to write a note and put it inside? My blood races. I bus my tray, run to my room, and fan the pages. A scrap of paper falls out—a heart around the lyrics to the chorus of the Divinyls song "I Touch Myself." Chessa signed it in cursive.

It's as though all the music I listened to before that night came from crappy headphones plugged into a great stereo. The headphones weren't on my head, but I could hear music if the volume was cranked. Then Chessa yanked the headphones out of the jack. Now I can hear. The treble snaps. My entire body vibrates from the bass.

Ron steps into the smoking area. "Nothing like the rich, smoky taste of a skinny white flaming turd," he says. Everyone laughs like it's required. He curls his finger at me. I follow him inside to the coffee station.

"Nancy and I decided to make an exception to the music rule for your birthday."

"Thank—"

He held up his hand. "Bup, bup, bup. Hold on, Dave. Ground rules. You get one song. *One.* And you need to tell us what it is first, so think long and hard. Do not pick a trigger."

"Easy. 'So What' by Miles Davis."

Ron repeats the title and asks me to write down the words. I tell him it's an instrumental. "Instrumental? Why that song?"

"It's the longest track on the CDs I brought. I haven't listened to my music in two weeks, and I figure if I'm trying to stop overthinking the shit out of everything, what could be more apropos."

Before breakfast on March 11, Ron unlocks the contraband closet and retrieves my Discman and CD case. "Happy Birthday," he says, standing uncomfortably close while I slide *Kind of Blue* from its sleeve.

Today is also the halfway point of my time here. Two weeks down, two to go.

As the music begins, I close my eyes and I'm in Rob's grandmother's Chevy Celebrity. I can see the sagging baby blue velvety fabric on the underside of the roof and cigarette butts in the ashtray, smoked to the filter. A phantom taste of dope teases the tip of my tongue, a hint of crack in the air. There's such a thing as *enough* heroin. You take a hit and don't immediately jones for more. Crack must be smoked until it's gone. Then you need more.

Crack changed Rob. I don't miss his crack-related lies, when he'd leave the apartment with $200, come back with two bags of dope and an impossible story, and then spend an hour in the bathroom. But I miss him.

When the song ends, I take off the headphones and give the Discman to Ron. He asks if I'm okay, as if he thinks I'm not.

"Yeah. I was just thinking. What's your history with drugs or alcohol?"

"Dave, the honest-to-God worst thing I ever did is smoke a cigarette. And I'll tell ya, I didn't even smoke the whole thing because my lungs were on fire after a couple of puffs. I don't know how you guys smoke all those cigarettes out there, day in, day out."

Ron locks the closet and admits to having an occasional beer. I don't respond.

"You don't think I'm cool anymore because I never got high?"

"I didn't think you were cool to begin with." I laugh. "No, seriously, all this time, we've been talking about addiction and you've never experienced—"

"Dave, the training we go through, is *pretty* intense. Trust me. I understand what you guys are going through better than you do."

ten

S teve, Chessa, Phil, and newcomers MJ and Doug greet their mothers and fathers. I'm the only one whose parents refuse to visit on the same weekend.

My father throws his arms around me. "Boy oh boy, are you a sight for sore eyes, my sonny boy." He says my aunt Jo sends her love and so do Donna and the kids—as if I have anything remotely approximating a relationship with his third wife and their infant offspring.

The counselors swoop in and take the parents for a group session. At five o'clock, we reconvene in the lobby, and Pete whisks us to a hibachi restaurant. Filing into the van, Chessa slips a folded note into my hand: "Impeccably timed tryst in the bathroom?"

At a table for two in the cavernous, mostly empty restaurant, Dad flips through a small, spiral-bound notebook. His handwriting—loopy and huge—could be mistaken for that of a serial killer. "Not easy, is it?" he says.

"Nope."

"Yep. Had a feeling."

"Yep."

"Well, I got a news bulletin for you. You're a dope fiend. Every day, for the rest of your life—even if you never do dope again—you'll be a dope fiend. Not a pleasant thought, is it?"

"No."

"Your dick's on a windowsill. You never know if the window's gonna slam shut."

I drop my gaze and futz with the tablecloth, pulling at a loose thread.

"Son, I didn't come here to blow smoke up your ass. So if it may please the court, allow me to explain a few things to you. Number one: I've seen this movie before. Two: If you want to croak, there isn't anything anyone can do. If you don't want to croak, you've got plenty of help. Howie shot dope for twenty-five years. My friend Cornell has drunk enough booze to fill a hundred Olympic-sized swimming pools. If that's not enough, then guess what—I've done more drugs and drunk more booze than you, everyone you know, and everyone they know, and everyone they know combined, times a hundred."

My body freezes. I scan my memory for clues. An occasional six-pack of beer in the fridge. A bottle of Remy Martin in the cabinet. I never saw him drink.

"Yoo-hoo, Dave. Look at me."

I slowly oblige.

"Son, I'm a fucking monster."

Dad points a chopstick at a skinny waiter standing next to me. How long has he been there? I order a teriyaki steak, rare. The self-proclaimed monster proclaims himself, also, a vegetarian.

"Seeing as I'm no longer eating critters, does the chef have some broccoli?"

The waiter nods.

"Then here's what let's do. You tell him to take that broccoli and steam it with a little garlic and olive oil and whomp it together in a bowl."

The waiter shuffles off.

"People talk about bingeing for a couple of days, a week. Mine went on for years. My drug of choice was "whaddaya got." And if anything stood between me and it—let's just say I never lost. Only tried heroin once, thought, *Meh. This is making me tired. What's the point?* I did everything else, boy. The night you were conceived, I was tripping on acid. That might explain a few things, don't you think?" He throws little daggers with his eyes.

I say nothing.

"Eight years ago today—your eleventh birthday—I said enough and dragged myself to the twelve-thirty AA meeting in Rye. If you'd bothered to talk to me . . . See, all these years, you haven't had a clue that I know what the fuck time it is."

Looking around the room, I see straight lips and lifeless eyes on everyone from Hazelden. MJ's elbows are propped on the table, his chin on his fist. Steve is staring into space. I finally spot Chessa leaning against the wall by the bathrooms.

"Uh, I need to go to the bathroom."

"By all means. There's plenty more when you get back."

Chessa slowly backs down the alcove toward the ladies' room. I follow. Our lips are about to connect when her mom yells from across the restaurant. "Chessa, your food is here!"

I jump over the threshold. My heart is racing.

"Did they see us?"

"Not a chance, dude," she says, squeezing my arm. "How's it going?"

I grunt.

"That bad?"

"Worse. You?"

"It would have been better if you'd gotten here a minute ago. I would've fucked your brains out and given you a big hug. In that order."

Dinner is on the table when I return. With a mouthful of food, the sober vegetarian monster brings up the cherry tree outside my childhood home. "That was part of why your mother loved that house," he says. "Remember what happened to it?"

I remember the long pruning shears he used on the tree. I remember Mom asking him to stop when the tree was full, lush, and alive. And I remember her begging him to stop as it was slowly reduced to a stump.

"Dave, do you remember what happened to that tree?"

"It died?"

"Know why?"

I think, *Yes, you fucking asshole. You killed it.* I open my mouth and a confused no comes out.

"It died because your mother refused to let me do what needed to be done so it could live. That's always been the problem. She knows everything, and I'm as smart as a five-pound bag of potatoes. I wasn't about to go to war with her over a tree, but if she thinks she knows a better way to save your life and she wants to duke this one out, she'll find out what I'm made of."

The waiter comes with the bill and Dad takes out his wallet—a big gold paperclip from Tiffany—a gift from Mom before they were married. He separates a crisp hundred-dollar bill from a fat wad and lays it on the table.

"When you leave here at the end of the month, you'll bunk with me and get a job. Doesn't matter what. If somebody with a pile of dead horses wants to pay you to dig ditches, you do it. Your mommy and your grandfather didn't do you any favors, making your life so easy that you never had to go out and fend for yourself. You'll re-enroll in college somewhere local. And go to at least two AA or NA meetings a day, every day, and work the steps. When you get to the eighth and you've got a list of people you harmed and you're ready to make amends, I'm more than willing to accept your apology for the ways you've harmed me."

Dad takes a sip of water and crunches an ice cube as if to punctuate the point. My hands turn to fists under the table.

"Do you know how I spent my fortieth birthday?"

"We went to a Mets game."

"After I dropped you and Daniel off, I went back to my house and sat on the couch with a loaded pistol in my mouth. Know why I didn't pull the trigger?"

"Uh . . ."

"You and Dan. Without me, how would you two grow up to be men?"

The van is silent on the ride from dinner to the Marriott. After the parents file out and we get back on the road, Pete twists the volume knob on the radio. A commercial for a discount mattress store plays.

Rain splatters on the windows as we coast down a suburban street.

"I've been doing this a long time," Pete says, glancing into the rearview mirror. "Don't recall a dinner where anybody's folks left with smiles on their faces."

The van has three rows of benches. Doug and MJ in the middle, then Phil and Steve. Chessa and I are in the back. Alone. She leans forward and asks Pete to take the long way home.

"Scenic route it is. Nice night for a drive."

The mattress commercial ends, and "Lightning Crashes" by Live begins. I wasn't crazy about this song or the band before. Right now, it's perfect.

Chessa's fingers inch their way up my thigh. I take her cold, sweaty hand and give it a light squeeze.

Sometimes it's hard to separate fact from my father's hyperbolic bullshit. At four in the morning, I'm still awake, thinking he was telling the truth at dinner.

After the divorce, he moved to a small house in Port Chester, fifteen minutes and another world away. The men in his neighborhood wore gold chains with Italian horns. They nursed bottles of Michelob Light and looked quizzically at rusted, tireless cars on cinder blocks on their front lawns, scratching their heads with dirt-caked fingernails. In their presence, my lower-upper-class Jewish father transformed into a caricature, affecting a nonspecific accent as he told stories of growing up in a studio apartment in the Bronx. It was fiction—he was raised in a large, single-family home in an upscale suburban New Rochelle neighborhood.

More than once, I heard Dad insinuate that he was the subject of multiple FBI investigations. Why would the feds be interested in a guy who owned a large paint manufacturing company? He always carried a gun to work—a revolver in a vest holster—and kept a rifle or two in the closet and a handgun in his briefcase, wide open, on his desk. I never touched any of them.

When I finally summoned the courage to ask him why he packed such heat, he said, "Let me put it to you this way: if the other guy has a gun and you don't, guess who's gonna get shot?"

I clench my eyes shut and try to force myself to sleep. Will my body ever learn to shut down without dope? Will my brain ever shut up? I hit the back of my head against the wall next to my bed. Not too hard. It doesn't hurt but it's not pleasant. I do it again. Harder. Again. Harder. Again. Harder. My roommate in the bed next to me sits up. An outside floodlight illuminates his face. I see concern in his eyes.

"Uh, Dave, are you head-butting the wall?"

"My bed at home is bigger and, um, it's in the middle of the room and . . ."

A little before six, I get up and go to the smoking area. Fresh snow covers every surface. Steve is on the bench, blowing perfect smoke rings, poking his finger through the holes. He says his parents gave him a choice: go to a halfway house or get cut off when his time here is up.

"Nancy's pimping this place in West Palm Beach," he says. "And she wants me to go on Prozac." He takes off his Blackhawks hat, runs a hand through his close-cropped hair, and kicks snow from the treads of brand-new Nikes his mom shipped last week via Federal Express overnight priority.

"Did you give her the 'antidepressant double standard' speech?"

"She went fucking ballistic." Steve raises his voice an octave and imitates Nancy. "'Steven, please tell me you understand the difference between drugs and medicine.' I go, 'Sure, Nancy. Prozac's a bunch of chemicals, and dope's all natural. But it's illegal because back in the day, some white dudes in San Fran complained about white women sleeping with the Chinese guys who owned the opium dens. And coke's illegal because in the 1920s, they thought Black men on blow were impervious to bullets.'"

"The War on Drugs has to be unconstitutional, right?" I say. "All that stuff in the Declaration of Independence about life, liberty, and the pursuit of happiness."

"Think you'll stay clean after this?"

"I don't know. I hate all the hiding and lying and risks and everything but I can't imagine going the rest of my life without dope. You?"

"Are you kidding? First chance I get, I'm scoring."

During breakfast, the parents show up and stand in the back of the dining room, whispering. I imagine them at the Marriott earlier this morning: crowded around a small table, Styrofoam plates with cold scrambled eggs and turkey sausage, comparing notes about their fubar kids. My father undoubtedly dominated the conversation.

Nancy comes to my table. "When you're through, swing by my office for a powwow with your dad."

I wait for her to leave with the parents before getting up. To buy more time, I run downstairs to pick up a notebook in my room and bump into Chessa in the hallway. She lifts her shirt for half a second—small, beautiful breasts, hard nipples, a ring in the left.

Dad is in midsentence when I walk into Nancy's office. She motions for me to sit in the chair next to him, facing her desk. "Somebody had to be the grown-up for Dave and Daniel. No rules, no accountability, no responsibilities." Wiping invisible tears, he turns to me. "It's unforgivable, what your mother did to you."

Nancy says, "Bob, how many times have you been married?"

"Three."

"And how many kids?"

"Four."

"So two with Robin and—"

"Yes, but Dave and Daniel have always been my top priority. All their lives, I've never missed a school play or a Little League game."

That statement would be accurate if by "never" he meant "usually."

Nancy thumbs through a stack of pamphlets. "While you're here, we ought to talk about aftercare. We have a national network of facilities that specialize in helping people in Dave's position."

Dad reaches over and nudges me in the shoulder. "I tried to klaboodle a soccer ball over your head, but I clocked you in the bizonga by mistake. You were just a little nipper, maybe three, at Harvey and Alice's house. Blood starts pouring down your face and you just went down like kapow! Your mother's running around, screaming like a lunatic. 'What'd you do? What'd you do? Oh my God, you killed him!' I knew you were fine."

"Our facility in West Palm is probably the best option," Nancy says, passing a brochure to him. "Before I do any legwork, are there any financial considerations?"

"I just want my sonny boy back, so here's what let's do. You pick the place and send me the bill. What's the point of money if you don't use it at a time like this?"

"I was hoping you'd call," Mom says. "How's it going with your father?"

"He said he was a monster drug addict. Did you know?"

"Oh, David, I'm so sorry."

"You knew."

"I knew he did drugs. I didn't know he was a *monster* drug addict. I never knew where he was or what he did or . . . I remember one day when you were a baby, we came home from shopping and he was snorting coke in the kitchen."

"Did you say anything?"

"No, because I couldn't stand being lied to. He wasn't a good husband or father, and I knew it. Even after all this time, I hate him with a passion."

I fixate on that phrase as Mom goes on a tirade. My parents once were in love. Now they're in hate. At least they have that in common.

"What kind of piece of shit says he'll pay for his kid's college and then doesn't, and you find out when you show up on the first day and he says he can't afford it, and meanwhile, he's driving around in a goddamn Ferrari?"

"You've told me that you knew you were going to leave when I was a baby, so why'd you wait until I was four?"

"I stayed because I wanted you to have a brother or sister. My worst fear was that if something happened to me, you'd only have *him*."

eleven

Phil shows up to group in tears. His mom's insurance provider refuses to cover more time as an inpatient. He has to move back in with his parents and drive here from St. Paul every day.

I tell him, "Think of it as commuting. Your job is to get sober."

"Fuck you, Dave. You don't take anything seriously."

"Perfect segue for today's topic," Ron says, patting Phil's shoulder. "Rage is normal and natural, but you need a healthy release." He asks what makes us enraged and how we deal with it.

A new girl says her parents make her angry, and she takes it out on a dog-shaped pillow. A new guy hates himself more than anything and punches walls. Alex is enraged by everything and shoots semiautomatic firearms at cans (and possibly squirrels—I can't tell if he's kidding).

"Dave? Batter up."

"I don't really experience rage. When I was younger, I saw the way my mom reacted to my father and brother's random acts of destruction and I decided not to—"

"Let me stop you right there, Dave. Rage is a feeling. We can work with our higher power on how we *deal* with our feelings, but we don't get to decide *how* we feel. You see what I'm getting at, right? Let's try again. Dave. Batter. Up."

"I smashed a lot of Matchbox cars when I was eight or nine."

"Could you give us something a little more recent?"

"I broke a pair of glasses at an open house my mom took me to, when she first started talking about selling the house I grew up in. I might've been eleven. It was at a new condo development. The place was empty except for a stack of fliers about the unit and a pair of glasses on a windowsill in the kitchen. My mom and I were with this realtor lady. She got all buddy-buddy with Mom the second we got there—took her by the arm and showed us around, talking about square footage and closet space and Jacuzzis. Upstairs, in one of the kids' bedrooms, she got in my face and said, 'Someone would be a very lucky boy to live here, don't you think?' When she and Mom went to the master suite, I said I wanted to go back downstairs and check it out again. She was like, 'Why, certainly.'"

"Did you know you were going to break the glasses beforehand?"

"Oh yeah. It was premeditated. I went straight to the kitchen and grabbed them. I folded the temples back and forth the way you break a paper clip. Once they snapped off, I popped out the lenses and stomped on them."

"Get caught?"

"Nope."

"What'd you do with the broken pieces?"

"At first, I put everything in my pockets. Then I put them back on the windowsill."

"So you wanted to get caught."

"No, I didn't want to—I stopped because I was worried about getting caught."

"Then why'd you put the glasses back?"

"I don't know."

"Did you want to move to the condo?"

"I didn't want to move anywhere."

"Did you tell your mom that?"

"No."

At dinner, Steve says he chose the halfway house in West Palm Beach. We're alone at the table, staring down piles of beef stroganoff on plastic plates. I try to cheer him up by pointing to the Heimlich maneuver poster on the wall by the kitchen, an illustrated instructional guide.

"If the words were in a language you didn't understand and somebody told you it was about fully clothed anal sex, you'd believe it."

Steve slurps a limp noodle. "Sorry. I'm a little cranky."

"That's a *feeling*. Ron just told me feelings can't be controlled."

"You're just learning that now?"

I affect an exaggerated infomercial announcer's voice. "Addiction? Feelings? Some people call them hard to manage. At Hazelden, we call them diseases. Although you're completely fucking powerless, our imaginary friend, God, has the serenity you need to change the things you can't accept and accept the things you can't change."

"Sounds like Ron got you all kinds of riled up today in group."

I recap the session. Steve cringes. "I loved my Matchbox cars. You smashed yours?"

"I pretended they belonged to people I hated and dropped rocks on them."

"Four-wheel voodoo dolls. How long did that go on?"

"One day, I demolished this blue station wagon—same color as my neighbors' car, the Kennedys. Married parents living in the same house. I couldn't stand them. The next morning, my mom told my brother and me that Marney, the mother, dropped off Sarah—my age—at dance class and then she, the baby, and Peter—my brother's age—were in an accident. Peter and Marney were killed. It was awful. My brother was crying. He said, 'Peter was my best friend. I'll miss him.' I never smashed another car."

Nancy enters the room, her eyes narrowing as she approaches me. She says we need to talk after lecture and then gets behind the podium and introduces tonight's topic: the Thirteenth Step—an unofficial term for newcomers who are preyed upon, sexually, by program veterans.

Lauren, the speaker, identifies as an addict-alcoholic—cross-addicted. Twirling her curly hair nonstop, she tells her story: divorced parents, physical and psychological abuse, running away, turning to drugs. Between minor bouts of nervous laughter, she recalls multiple arrests for theft, solicitation, possession, and a rock-bottom epiphany that led her to an outpatient rehab.

"I started working the steps, going to meetings. There was this guy—fifty maybe. He invited me to supper and asked to be my sponsor. A little flirtatious, but I said okay and went to his place and . . . that's when it happened.

I thought recovery was about staying clean, but I realized after six months went by and I was still going to his place, that I hadn't begun to work on myself. If a man wasn't showing me affection, it was like I didn't exist."

When Lauren finishes, the room fills with applause. MJ cuts through the stampede. He whispers, "I saw you and Chessa in the van last night." Between the low volume and his Southern accent, I can't tell if he's congratulating or accusing. Before he says another word, Nancy is in our faces.

"Hope I'm not interrupting anything," she says.

Following her down the hall, I start planning a rebuttal to the accusations I expect her to make. In her office, she leaves the overhead lights off and turns on a desk lamp, apologizing for the darkness and saying something about the poisonous crud in fluorescent bulbs.

She sits but I stay standing, figuring I'd be in a stronger position to argue my case.

"With divorce," she says, "sometimes it's amicable, and sometimes it's a shit show. Nine times out of ten, we can cut through the malarkey and get folks on the same page for the sake of the kid, but there's always *one* mom and dad who can't see eye to eye. That's your folks. Now that I've met your dad in person, I get it. He's really something. Do you have any memories of peace between him and Mom? A conversation that didn't end up with them yelling at each other? An activity you did as a family?"

"We almost went to the Hard Rock Café for lunch on my twelfth birthday—all of us."

"Almost doesn't count. Ever have a meal with both your parents?"

I share my earliest memory: three years old, sitting at the kitchen table with Mom on one side holding Daniel, Dad across from them. He's not wearing a shirt. I can see the gold ankh symbol on a chain around his neck and his oatmeal. There was a corkboard on the wall behind him, covered in articles Mom had clipped from newspapers and magazines. I remember the words she wrote on masking tape around the border: "Caring is the art of sharing. Sharing is the art of giving. Giving is the art of loving."

"Is that it for peace? That one breakfast?"

"Yeah."

"Do you know the biggest sign of trauma?"

"Uh—the presence of some sort of trauma?"

"The biggest sign of trauma is not recognizing you've been through it. Or minimizing or denying it. Or joking about it."

Nancy pushes a box of tissues across the desk. "I think you know you need this," she says. "I think you've been running from the issues for so long that you're afraid to stop. That possible?"

"I don't think my issues even qualify as issues. It's not like I was raped or beaten. I never had to steal or sell myself."

"You keep minimizing, but you've spent your whole life on the battle-field, Dave. Your folks have been too caught up in trying to kill each other to see the scared little boy in the crossfire, riddled with bullets. That won't change if you clam up next weekend around Mom like you crammed up around Dad. You're safe here. It's okay to let your feelings out."

A lump the size of a baseball forms in my throat. Nancy rises to her feet and wraps her arms around me. I start to cry and melt into her.

twelve

'm eating a bowl of Cheerios when the dining room doors open with a crash and MJ bounds in, a shit-eating grin on his round tan face, wearing the kind of robe-and-pajama combo you see only on old people or black-and-white TV shows. He crouches next to me.

"We have the same problem," he whispers. "Laura and I are looking for a way to be alone. Any ideas?"

"Pray?"

MJ smiles and clasps his hands together.

The lights flash on and off. Standing by the door, Nancy announces the reopening of a path around the building. "Now that the snow's melting, you can take walks outside."

MJ winks at me. I turn around and Chessa runs her tongue along her lips.

"Ground rules," Nancy says. "You can go alone or in groups, but to make sure there's no funny business, boys go one way around the loop and girls go the other. There's a one-hour time limit. If I can get from beginning to end in fifty-eight minutes, so can you."

Before lunch, MJ and I conduct a reconnaissance mission on the gravel path through the woods. My lungs are searing, and my legs are rubber after five minutes of running. MJ isn't faring much better. Squeezing his sides, he hatches a scheme to pretend we're gay so the counselors will make us take walks with girls. I don't see it working.

Chessa agrees. "But where there's a will, there's a way," she says. "And my *way* is so fucking wet for your *will* right now."

At the start of our walk, MJ clicks a button on his fancy diving watch. We go at a consistent pace. Thirty minutes in, we make a small rock pile on the left side of the path. Then Chessa and Laura time how long it takes for them to reach the pile. We refer to the rendezvous location as the "G-spot."

On Thursday night in a dark corridor on the second floor, MJ, Laura, Chessa, and I whisper giddily about a dry run after breakfast, followed by the real deal later in the afternoon. I feel like I'm in a prison escape movie.

But I wake to thunderclaps and torrential downpours. The path is closed until further notice. Might as well be forever. My mom will be here tomorrow morning, and on Monday, I'm going home.

Clear skies on Saturday morning. The path is open, but I'm at the main entrance when Pete pulls up with Mom in the van. She gets out and starts to cry before dropping her bags. Then she holds her heart like it'll explode if she lets go and hugs and kisses me until we get to the lobby, where Nancy is waiting with a box of tissues. Mom takes one and blots her eyes.

"Your son's been doing fabulous work lately," Nancy says. "Really opening up."

"My father used to say I was worrying about the wrong kid when I told him how concerned I was about David's emotional sensitivity. I always knew where I stood with Daniel, but he has so much of his father's anger and impulsivity in him."

"Uh-huh," Nancy says. "Dave said he and his brother are very different."

"Night and day. That's why when Bob called last month and said 'Your son's a dope fiend,' I thought for sure he was talking about Daniel."

Nancy says, "Tell you what, Dave. Ron and I could use some time alone with Mom, so we'll find you after lunch."

Within minutes, MJ and I are sprinting down the path. Last fall's leaves flail in the wind. Twigs snap between our feet. Clouds tick across the sky. I can see my breath.

MJ slides on the wet gravel, falls on his ass, and then trots with a limp, panting. He elbows me, long before the G-Spot. There are three silhouettes in the distance.

"Not them."

"Laura told Vanessa."

"Why?"

"I don't know, dude. Why does anyone do anything?"

Chessa rushes me. She slides her cold hand up the front of my shirt and pushes me against a tree, moistening her lips with her tongue. She grabs the loops on my jeans and we kiss urgently, hard at first. Then everything slows and I run my hand under her jacket and tease the small of her back. Her skin is soft and smooth and familiar.

Our bodies pinned together, I can feel Chessa's heart beating, her lungs expanding and contracting. I time my breath to hers. For a short, blissful moment, I can breathe.

"Your son is a good kid with a bright future," Nancy says, looking at Mom and then at me. "Dave, you've shown everybody such love and warmth and compassion."

Where's she going with this bullshit?

"But," she continues, "you have to learn to be as good to yourself as you are to others."

"I've been saying that for years," Mom says. "You're too smart and handsome and funny and clever not to feel better about your—"

There's a knock at the door. An assistant asks Nancy and Ron to come into the hall. Seconds later, Nancy returns and tells me to join them.

"Anything you want to tell us, Dave?"

"About . . . ?"

"Chessa."

I make an impulsive decision to say I'm gay. I instantly regret it.

Nancy closes her eyes. Ron shakes his head.

"Fine. I'm in love with her. I can't help it."

"Oh, give me a break," Ron says. "Yes, you can."

"Love's a feeling. Last week, you said we can't control our feelings."

Nancy and Ron file back into her office, and I follow.

"I'm sorry, Robin," Nancy says. "Some new things have come to light." She lays out the situation, and Mom's eyes fill with tears. "You really had us fooled, Dave," Nancy says. "Ron and I were just telling Mom how far you've come, but evidently—"

Ron wags his finger at me. "Evidently, nothing's changed since day one. You're still in addict mentality mode, still in denial, still haven't reached out to your higher power."

"I can't force myself to believe in God."

"Nobody's forcing you to believe in God," Mom says. "Your higher power could be a sneaker for all anybody cares. You just need something to believe in."

"I have something—myself."

"Dave." Ron lets out a loud sigh. "You can't be your own higher power."

"Why?"

"Because."

"Because why?"

"Because you just can't. A higher power is something greater than ourselves."

"If I can't do this without God, that's not exactly a vote of confidence in me."

"It's not you, Dave. *Nobody* can do it alone."

"So atheists are fucked?"

I look at Mom, and for a moment, I think she understands. Then Nancy says, "This is what I meant about the jokes," and Mom's face goes cold.

"Robin," Nancy says, "this is where tough love comes into play." She looks me in the eye. "Dave, we're asking you to leave."

"What if I don't want to go?"

Mom drops her head in her hands, and Nancy flashes me a smirky frown. "You have fifteen minutes to pack, and then you have two choices: I can get you a bed tonight at our halfway house in West Palm—you can be on a plane in an hour—or if you don't like that, we'll drop you off at the airport and you're on your own. If you choose to run—I don't care how strong or smart or funny you are—with God as my witness, you'll never outrun this disease."

thirteen

The terminal at Detroit International Airport is a quarter-mile corridor of mint green cinder-block walls. My connecting flight doesn't leave for another hour, so I take a seat at one of the bars. The bartender dries beer mugs with a rag like a scene in a Western movie. He nods at the tap. "Got Bud on draft. Bud Light, Miller, Michelob . . ."

I love the idea of alcohol—swishing a martini with big green olives stabbed with a small plastic sword, marinating in a generous pour, or any drink in a glass with an interesting shape and a garnish or just an umbrella—but I hate drinking. For a moment, I consider ordering something my grandfather occasionally gets at a restaurant—a perfect Rob Roy or a Manhattan—but I wouldn't take as much as a sip.

So I order a Coke instead. The bartender drags a glass through a trough of ice and fills it with soda.

When my parents got married, my grandparents gave them a fully stocked bar. What should have been a family room was literally a bar—a long, high slab of mahogany with a shiny brass rail for your feet, a dozen spinning bar stools, and a triple-tiered shelf lined with bottles. So many shapes and sizes and colors. I opened a few and smelled the contents but never tried anything.

If the bartender had said "We have morphine on intravenous drip, Percocet and Dilaudid pills, and transdermal fentanyl patches," I'd be high right now. I don't know how else to feel okay in my own skin. And I don't see God or AA changing that or helping me accept or forget it.

. . .

Mike picks me up at the West Palm Beach airport in a beige Oldsmobile Alero with a maroon passenger door—a shade lighter than his crispy skin. The floor is littered with fast-food wrappers and dirty Dunkin' Donuts cups.

Hot recycled air pumps from the vents as we cruise down a wide boulevard lined with strip malls teeming with pawn shops and liquor stores and places to wire money. This isn't Palm Beach. Mike fishes a partially smoked cigarette from the ashtray and lights it and talks about his latest relapse.

"Almost a year clean before I started sucking on that glass dick again. Weekend of my thirty-fifth birthday, I swing by my dealer for a bag of rocks, and I go home and pop one in a stem. Soon as I start sucking and the flame gets brighter, I see all these faces. My sister and ex-wife. My daughter. Parents. Everyone. My friggin' boss is there. They're all looking at me, going, 'Mike. What the F?' And I'm all, 'Fuck me.' That was January. I did two weeks of outpatient and then moved into the halfway house."

The long ash on Mike's cigarette falls on his dirty yellow tank top. He jiggles and wipes it away, leaving black smudges. "Ah, shit." He groans. "My fucking luck."

We coast into a handicapped spot in a sea of cracked pavement in front of a boxy, two-story structure with stucco siding and a white wrought-iron fence. No sign in front. Could be anything.

On a grimy white coral path, small lizards scamper to avoid being trampled. Mike opens the door. It's hotter inside than out. A straight-lipped receptionist fans herself with a pamphlet. "Tim," she yells, "Mike's back with the new guy."

Short and stout, maybe forty years old, Tim struts into the lobby and introduces himself as "the sheriff around these here parts." His belt looks kind of Western: black leather with white stitching and turquoise stones, a country club crest in place of a badge on his baggy blue polo shirt. We go to his small, dark office, where a noisy air conditioner sits in the window below a piece of cardboard.

Tim feels inside my bag but doesn't look. He pulls out my CD case and flips through. "You should get some Journey albums," he says. Cupping his hand over his ear, he belts out the beginning of "Don't Stop Believin'" and transitions to inverted whistling—that sound when you suck air in—as he shuffles my paperwork. He takes a folder from a file cabinet, empties the contents into the trash, turns it inside out, and writes my name on it.

"We do two things here. Heal and deal. Daily group therapy, AA/NA meetings, fitness program, and a chore wheel that rotates every morning. Unless you get a real, job-type job in the community, you participate in chores every day. It is possible to get an outside job. JJ cleans the locker room at a gym, and Vin works part time at Blockbuster Video. Play your cards right, and that's what you have to look forward to."

As the name suggests, the two dozen male residents are halfway (that is, somewhere) between rock bottom and functional. This could be a *Saturday Night Live* spoof of MTV's *The Real World*. Instead of attractive twenty-somethings lounging on sleek furniture, broken-down thirty- and forty-year old men lay on mismatched sofas with cigarette burns in the main lounge. They stare at the TV as if *Wheel of Fortune* holds the answer to all their problems.

Small fans push stale smoke in every direction of the open space, separated from the kitchen by a partial wall. The ceiling is high and arched. The white floor tiles are grimy and cracked and scuffed.

"Everybody, this is Dave. Dave, this is everybody."

Nobody says a word or looks at me.

"The guys have been lethargic since the AC conked out last week," Tim says. He sweeps a pamphlet off a bookshelf and waves it across his rear end.

One of the guys groans. "Jesus fucking Christ, Tim."

"Blame the chimichangas," Tim says. He shows me to the kitchen, whispers an apology for his noxious gas, and opens a commercial-grade refrigerator to a mess of store-brand condiments and plastic-wrapped packages of ground beef and chicken thighs. Everything has someone's name on it. Even a rotting banana. Brad.

My room is a triple at the end of the first floor. Tim says the bars on the windows are "to keep the bad element out, not to keep you in." He advises me to get a pair of flip flops unless "you want a wicked case of athlete's foot from the shower."

One of my roommates is lying on his bed, his lips moving as he reads a tattered Archie comic book. "He's been here since December," Tim says.

"And he'll probably be here after you're gone. You're still planning on sticking around until the end of August, right?"

"End of August?"

"Long as you have insurance or private pay and your account doesn't go into arrears, you can stay for two years. After a while, you get to be pretty big fish in this little pond."

The pay phone is in the basement. I call Chessa's halfway house and leave a message. I imagine a cheery Victorian mansion with a wackadoodle paint job, and Chessa amid a gaggle of eighteen-year-old girls in bras and panties, cavorting around a lush garden (never mind that it's twenty degrees in Duluth). Of all the locations in Hazelden's network, are any two farther apart than Chessa's and mine?

Steve hugs me when I find him in the smoking area—a small rock garden in the courtyard with a splintered picnic table and a sand-filled metal bucket for butts. He describes our housemates as "holier-than-thou evangelists."

"Everything's a cautionary tale with these assholes, or they're giving you shit for not having an attitude of gratitude. They're all, 'You think your life's hard? Try being a forty-year-old convicted felon, looking for a job. Try having three kids with three different baby mamas and a family court judge breathing down your neck for child support.'"

From the patio, a guy in a floral Hawaiian shirt yells, "You faggots coming to AA, or are you too busy sucking each other's dicks?"

"That's Dennis," Steve says. "Used to be a big-time contractor in New York. Now he's your average recovering crackhead with an attitude of gratitude."

Tim leads in-house AA meetings in the main living room. After we recite the Serenity Prayer, he asks, "Who has something to say?"

Robbie, thirty-two years old, describes a scene in his double-wide trailer outside Jacksonville. "Dun't get worse than being led out your place in handcuffs, nekkid, your kids holding onto your legs, crying, 'Daddy, don't go, don't go.'"

At the other end of the couch, Dennis digs his fingers into a tennis ball. Next to him is a shirtless guy picking a scab on his stomach. Mike pumps the straw up and down in his Slurpee cup, making it squeal against the plastic lid. Robbie tells him to stop and then backtracks to the incident that led to his arrest—a home invasion gone wrong.

Then it's Dennis's turn. A vein bulges in his forehead as he talks about setting up trust funds for his daughters when they were born and liquidating them years later to pay for crack. Glancing at the tennis ball in his hand, he compares his obsessive-compulsive disorder to OCS (obsessive crack smoking). "Powerless over both," he says. "Same thing." In the middle of an anecdote about the restraining order his wife filed against him, he side-arms his tennis ball at the shirtless scab-picker after he let out a loud yawn.

"Richie, am I boring you? You fucking faggot."

"Faggot? I'll faggot you, you faggot-ass faggot."

fourteen

Every weekday afternoon, Tim sends a small delegation to an outside AA meeting. He dispatches me on Friday with Dennis, Mike, and Robbie.

In the car, Dennis says this part of Florida is known as "recovery corridor," owing to the high concentration of treatment centers. Competition is fierce in detox, rehab, and halfway houses, he says. A place in nearby Jupiter was caught offering hundred-dollar Visa gift cards to addicts for checking in.

The AA meeting is in a church basement. Forty or fifty men and women of all ages and races, some in suits and others in shorts and tank tops. A younger guy apologizes for the coffee delay while dispensing Styrofoam cups by a table that appears to be caving from the weight of two large, gurgling carafes. On a clear plastic tray covered with stained doilies, there's a scattered smattering of crackers and corn chips and an upturned, hollowed-out green bell pepper filled with dip.

When the coffee is ready, plastic shots of cream and individual packets of every conceivable natural and artificial sweetener quickly disappear from a wicker basket. As the group stirs adulterants into coffee, a muscular older guy gets behind the podium and introduces himself. Alcoholic, twenty-two years sober. He thanks everyone for coming and makes a few announcements.

Another guy describes getting laid off yesterday and asking God for strength to get home without stopping at a bar or liquor store on the way. The room erupts in applause and "one day at a time" chants.

Dennis says, "It's hard enough to drive by a bar when life's peachy. When it's not, *fuggeddaboudit*. Every day we hear guys who thought they could have just one beer."

"That's how all my relapses started," Mike says.

"That's how *every* relapse starts. There's always a reason. Dog died. Wife left. Patriots lost. It's fuckin' Wednesday."

Grilled chicken and rice for dinner. I sit with Mike and Dennis and two guys whose names I don't know. Dennis asks me, "Do you really want to be here, or are you going through the motions just to shut Mom and Dad up?"

It takes a moment for me answer. "I don't know."

Dennis's hands connect slowly in two loud claps. "Now, there's an honest answer. Unlike your friend, Dickwad, over there." He nods toward Steve in the kitchen.

Later, after everyone gathers in the main lounge to watch *Law and Order*, Steve and I sign ourselves out and walk to a convenience store. Toto's "Rosanna" crackles out of a boom box behind the counter, and I admit it's one of my guilty pleasure songs.

"Me too," Steve says. "And it's actually very complicated. Key changes from G-major to F-major and back, with a half-time shuffle drum pattern. Five parts. On paper, they shouldn't work together, but they do."

By the main entrance, the ground beneath a row of banyan trees is littered with butts. We're sitting on the curved concrete benches when a security guy makes his rounds.

"It's 9:55. Five minutes to curfew."

Once the guard is out of earshot, Steve brings up the Juniper rehab center Dennis mentioned earlier. "Apparently, some local detox centers are so hard up they'll *give* you dope so you'll piss dirty and they can admit you." Rubbing his hands together, he asks if I want to investigate.

I don't immediately say yes, but it doesn't take long.

. . .

At first, I worry Chessa isn't getting my messages. Five days in, I worry she is getting them. I decide to call one more time and leave a message. Seconds after I hang up, the phone rings.

"Hello?"

"David?"

"Nana?"

"David?"

"Nana?"

"David, your mother told me you were in West Palm Beach."

"Uh-huh."

"At a place for drug addicts?"

Disappointing my grandparents feels far more severe than disappointing my parents. Especially my grandfather. That is the conversation I've been dreading.

"You know you shouldn't do drugs, right?"

"I know."

"Then what are you doing there?"

"I don't really know."

"We missed you last month when your mother and Daniel came down."

"I know. I wish I could've been there."

Steve skips downstairs and dances toward me. He mouths, *Hang up*.

"David?"

"Nana?"

"We want to see you. Take you to lunch. Do you need clothes? What are you doing tomorrow?"

"Hanging out with you."

When I get off the phone, Steve reaches into his pocket and pulls out a scrap of paper. "Supposedly, this guy's shit's crazy pure. And he'll meet anywhere, as long as we buy at least a bundle. Let's call him. Got a quarter?"

"Now?"

"Oh, dude. Hesitation means no."

"No, it's just . . . I don't want to tie up the phone. I just left a message for Chessa."

"If your girlfriend's anywhere like *this*, nobody's telling her when you call."

I go outside and take laps around the parking lot. I think about my mother. She used to say, "Life is about the choices we make and living with the consequences. If you want the car to go, put gas in the tank."

All afternoon, I roast in the sun, pacing, smoking, debating. Is mental gymnastics the key to sobriety? Overthink relapsing until you tire yourself out?

Before dinner, I find Steve alone in his room, lying on the floor.

"I can't do it. I can't risk getting kicked out after my mom just flew to Minnefuckingsota to watch me get kicked out of Hazelden."

Steve sits up, looking relieved. "Yeah, I threw the number away." He compares our situation to the prospect of getting a blow job from an ugly girl. "You know it'll feel good, but you know you'll regret it later."

"This proves we're not powerless. We should call Nancy and let her know."

He laughs.

The next morning, I wake to screaming. Sounds like Richie. I jump out of bed and race to the kitchen. Dennis is ramming his back against the wall, digging his fingernails into his tennis ball.

Tim stumbles into the building, his eyes open wide as if he's trying to adjust contact lenses without touching them. Mike and JJ whisk him through the main living area into the other wing. I ask what's going on. Dennis gives me a blank look and winds up and wings the tennis ball at the TV. Then he punches a hole in the wall.

Maybe Richie had a heart attack. But seconds later, Richie appears with a towel around his waist. He nods.

"Richie went to take a shower," Dennis says. "He found Steve on the floor." He lays his hands on my shoulders. "He's dead, David. Motherfucker OD'd."

I don't know what to do or think. I return to my room and grab my Discman and just stand there, trying not to hear the yelling and movement and sirens and walkie-talkies. Everything hurts, like I'm stuck in a bumper car while an entire carnival bashes me on all sides.

Once it's quiet, I go outside and sit on the curb. No idea how long I've been here when Nana's blue Sebring pulls up. The top is down. My grandfather, Herbie, is driving. My cousins call him Poppa, but I started using his first name when I was six.

I hop into the back seat behind Nana. Wind blasts my face as she bombards me with restaurant options.

"Bimini Boatyard's always good. Or that new Italian place on the Intercoastal."

My head is stuffy and throbbing. I make a random selection and ask if we can stop at a drugstore. "I think I'm coming down with something."

Nana cocks her head to the side. "You don't look sick."

"Leave him alone," Herbie says, glancing at me in the rearview mirror.

We pull into the next strip mall, and Nana and I go inside CVS, where I grab a bottle of DayQuil and NyQuil off a shelf. Nana snatches them and reads the labels aloud, stumbling over the ingredients nobody knows how to pronounce. She asks the pharmacist to recommend a cold medicine without alcohol. I tell her I don't have a problem with alcohol and the Quils are my go-to-remedies. Nana won't budge.

At lunch, three guys in suits in the booth next to us yell about guacamole.

"Did I tell you or did I tell you? Best guac anywhere."

"Sorry, but I went to a place in Phoenix last year that had killer fucking guac."

The suits lick their fingertips and sweep up small shards of corn chips and graze them through the remaining guacamole in a volcanic rock bowl.

"David," Nana says. "Are you going to eat?"

"Can I stay with you for a few days?"

"Why?" she asks, suspiciously.

"Of course," Herbie says.

Nana asks if something is wrong with the place in West Palm Beach. I tell her it's run by an evangelical Christian cult and I don't need Jesus to stay clean. When I say "I'm never doing drugs again," I know it's a fact.

fifteen

A tennis ball tied to a string dangles from the ceiling in the garage. The car stops when the ball touches the windshield. Herbie's side of the garage is a paint studio. He's a Fauvist, in love with Vlaminck. His Pontiac is in the driveway.

Tim doesn't push when I call and tell him I'm not coming back. I give him my mother's address to ship my things. All I have are the clothes I'm wearing and my Discman and whatever CD happens to be in it. I flop on the bed in the guest bedroom and stick my face in a pillow, breathing in the familiarity—Herbie's paintings on the walls, a stack of old photo albums I pore through during every visit, needlepoint pillows made by Nana. One is bright pink with "Phuque the Snow" in yellow.

Since I was a little kid, when the whole family converged at their house in Florida, I spent most of the time with Herbie. During the day, while everyone else was in the pool, he and I were in the garage. At night, while Mom, Daniel, and Nana watched TV with my aunt and uncle and cousins, Herbie and I sat outside. He'd point to stars and make up stories about life on Khakistan, where everyone wears tan pants. If a plane was in the sky, he'd say it was a UFO ferrying cigarettes and vodka and paintbrushes to distant galaxies. He loved to tell stories and encouraged me to find the story in everything.

We've been writing letters back and forth for years. When I was younger, he'd stick a twenty- or fifty-dollar bill in the envelope. As I got older, he started enclosing checks for a lot more, with spending suggestions: "This should be enough to sail around the world with an improper girl and 109 cases of cheddar cheese (ask the girl to provide suitable crackers)."

The smell of turpentine is strong in the garage, even with the window open. I sit on the hood of the golf cart, watching Herbie paint a frothy ocean of fat blue and white brushstrokes around a pencil sketch of a fisherman in a dingy. Samuel Barber's "Adagio for Strings" plays on a paint-stained tape deck, wedged between art books and tubes of oil paint on a metal shelf. Rows of canvases lean against the wall, waiting for a turn in the rotation inside.

Herbie lays his paintbrush on the lip of the easel and takes a step back. He says Ralph, his twin brother, got addicted to morphine in the 1950s, after a bad car crash.

"He went through hell to clean himself up," he says. "But he made it. You will too. I know you'll turn this into something good, maybe write a book about it."

"Maybe . . ."

"Why not? You're a fantastic writer. You always said that's what you wanted to be when you grew up."

A little before five, Nana gives a stern look when Herbie reaches for a bottle of Smirnoff in the living room. She says, "Cocktail hour starts at five." He glances at his watch periodically and at the bar—an ornately carved armoire he built when they lived in Yonkers. He had a woodshop, paint studio, and a darkroom.

At exactly five o'clock, Nana enters with a tray of cheese and crackers. She nods at the bar. "Okay already, Herbert. Jesus." He pours a drink and gestures to a shelf of CDs—all classical titles. He asks what I want to listen to. I almost pick his favorite: Mahler's Eighth Symphony. Instead, I choose Mozart's *Magic Flute.*

Facing each other, on cushy leather swivel chairs, we reminisce about the hot summer night when I was eight years old and we saw *Amadeus.* The theater manager warned us that the movie was nearly three hours long and the air conditioner was broken. Herbie said it was an important movie, so we sweated through it.

Swirling a glass of vodka and ice, Nana says, "We never did drugs."

"Bullshit. We smoked marijuana in Mexico in 1949."

"Bah—it didn't do anything."

"You laughed yourself silly and ate two giant bowls of candy in five minutes."

Nana says something about the pot roast and disappears into the kitchen. Herbie finishes his drink, pours another, and waves me to follow him down the hall to the guest bedroom, which doubles as his office. He flips on the light—there's an illustration of a man holding open an overcoat on the switch cover. A rectangular cutout makes the switch look like a penis.

He pulls a folder from his desk. Inside are drawings I made when I was much younger and the autobiography I wrote in second grade, *Full on Bread*.

"Always thought it was a great title," he says.

"Anytime we went to a restaurant, Mom used to tell me not to fill up on bread. But I never listened, and she never stopped me."

"You missed a lot of main courses."

Nana picks up bagels and lox before I'm awake. She makes me breakfast, and they take me shopping for shirts and pants and socks and underwear. And a Chicago Blackhawks hat—same as Steve's. Later, I go for a walk by myself and listen to *Nebraska*—the only Springsteen album I own. Once I'm out of sight of the house, I light a cigarette and fall into "Reason to Believe."

When the song ends, I drop the Camel and stomp it out. As a flurry of bright orange cinders rise from under my foot, I think Steve died so I would live. I think, *I'm going to write a book about this experience and dedicate it to him.*

The ashes turn black and scatter in a dense, sticky breeze. How could I be so arrogant? There is no omnipotent being, no master plan. I'm alive because of luck. It's that simple.

Back at the house, Nana says we're leaving for dinner at six. I ask Herbie for a razor and shaving cream.

"Check under the sink. On my side of the bathroom."

I find what I need amid a wall of prescription medications, one on top of another. I turn on the shower, undress, and lock the door, then open the cabinet again. Most of the labels are faded and facing inward. I'm relieved not to see anything interesting, but I continue to look. On the top of a big bottle, "PAIN" is scrawled in marker. I can make out the pharmacy's name and address and the contents: Darvocet. I shake the brown plastic bottle and run my finger over the peeling label.

Take one now to get it over with and deal with the guilt, or be distracted until I take one and deal with the guilt. I unscrew the cap and shake one of at least thirty oval red pills. One won't kill me. I get in the shower, tip my head back, and wash it down with hot water.

Coming out of the bathroom, I hear Frank Sinatra, a different, upbeat version of "Fly Me to the Moon." My grandparents are on the patio, sipping Smirnoff on the rocks. I ask Herbie who to call about a plane ticket home.

"You're leaving already?" he says.

"I probably shouldn't stay too long. A couple days?"

Nana says, "It'll be cheaper if we book a ticket a week in advance."

Control isn't the issue. Access is. No one would notice if the Darvocet vanished. I could take them all. I don't. Just one a day.

On the morning of my flight, Herbie and I leave through the garage and get into his car. The canvas with the fisherman and dingy is now covered in paint. He drives me to the airport—just the two of us.

"This is a blip," he says, idling at the curb on the departures level. "You have your whole life ahead of you. Whatever you do, I'll always be there to cheer you on."

We get out of the car and he holds me tightly and we say goodbye. I can't be proud of myself for leaving forty Darvocet. There's too much guilt over the seven. I want this feeling to go away and never come back.

I know what I have to do.

part two

1996

sixteen

A girl with short brown hair and big brown eyes comes into my dorm room singing to the Pixies' "Hey" on the stereo. Christine. An unfiltered Lucky Strike in her left hand, a worn copy of Henry Miller's *Air Conditioned Nightmare* in her right. She ogles my book collection, alphabetized by author on a tall, wide shelf.

"You a writer?" she asks.

I smile. Christine smiles back. "Thought so," she says, reaching for Burroughs's *Junkie*, facedown and open on my dresser. As she flips through the dog-eared pages, I try not to stare at the sliver of teal bra visible through a missed button on her white Oxford shirt.

"Think there were really farms like the place he went to to get clean?"

"If there were, they weren't like the rehab I went to."

Christine's eyes widen. "You went to . . . What'd you . . . Wait. You don't have to tell me if—"

"It's cool. I *was* a heroin addict. I've been clean for a year and a half."

"Isn't heroin like the hardest drug to quit?"

"It's not exactly easy, but when something's important, you find a way to make it happen."

The Marlboro College campus is an old farmstead with retrofitted outbuildings, halfway up a mountain in Vermont. Brisk air, redolent with pine trees and wood smoke and freshly cut grass. Christine and I walk from the dorm to an introductory session for the only mandatory class for incoming students: Religion, Literature, and Philosophy. When she asks what made me decide to transfer here, I tell her about the conversation I overheard in a café last spring, when I was enrolled at Richmond College in London—my third school in as many semesters.

"Two Americans were making fun of this tiny liberal arts school where you design your own course of study. All I needed to hear was 'chaos, Vermont, two hundred students.'"

Four peacocks appear on the path behind the library, strutting around, fanning their plumage. Christine says their owner, a junior, built the school's apiary. "He already has a job when he graduates," she says. "At a zoo in Singapore."

We arrive at a small, musty classroom where Jet Thomas describes RLP as "an intensive, yearlong exploration of classic literature." An older man with a small frame, he speaks with an effeminate, Foghorn Leghorn-esque drawl and rattles off a long list of book titles. Plato. Sartre. Kierkegaard. Nietzsche. Aquinas. Heidegger. Is it a joke? Nobody can read that many books in a year.

"Don't worry," he says. "If you don't see one of your favorites on the fall list, maybe we'll read it in the spring." He goes around the table counter-clockwise, asking our intended areas of focus.

I identify as a writer. So does Christine, but she adds something about postmodern femininity and Anaïs Nin. The girl next to her, with long red dreadlocks and hairy armpits, wants to explore the aesthetic theories of Kant and Schopenhauer and the problem of musical meaning. A kid with tattoos covering every inch of exposed skin aspires to preserve endangered indigenous languages in Kenya, and a guy in dark sunglasses, dressed in black, draws a connection between mathematical theology and urban architecture in modern China. The last to arrive, a blond kid who could be a J. Crew model, says he's a writer, interested in stream-of-consciousness fiction.

Jet says, "All great writers have one thing in common. What is it?"

Christine says, "They read more than they write?"

"Much more," Jet says. "All great writers read much more than they write."

A discussion about Aeschylus's *Agamemnon* breaks out. I own the book but haven't read it. I haven't actually read any book, ever. As my classmates name-drop Clytemnestra and Orestes, I'm slouched in my seat, staring at cobwebs on the faded yellow wainscoted wall.

After the intro session, I go to the registrar's office and replace my creative writing classes with film courses—I've seen entire movies.

When I return to the dorm, I hear a loud banging coming from my room. I open the door to find Christine naked, pinned against the wall next to my bed, the J. Crew model behind her, thrusting. I clear my throat. He turns his head.

"David," he says, still going. "Good to meet you. Your mom called on the downstairs pay phone."

I go downstairs and return Mom's call.

"Tell me, tell me, tell me. Is it great?"

"Better."

"So, no more *Goldilocks and the Three Colleges*? This school's 'just right'?"

"Perfect."

I'd transferred to Richmond from Franklin Pierce because of this awful, pervasive feeling—scarily similar to what I'd experienced at SUNY Purchase, which felt no different than both high schools I'd attended, where I was constantly reminded of the feeling I'd had throughout middle and elementary school, when I was plagued by the sensation of being at the bottom of the ocean, naked, surrounded by people in full scuba gear. While they glided effortlessly through the water, kicking their flippers, breathing oxygen from tanks, I was singularly focused on looking like I wasn't drowning.

Two weeks into the semester, during Introduction to Film and Video Production, I pick my fingernails until they bleed when we screen our first short films. My classmates present colorful works, with multiple angles and meticulous editing and cuts synched to upbeat music.

My piece is black and white, shot in one angle. I locked a camera on a tripod, pointed it at four folding chairs against a white wall, and sat in each and talked to the invisible me on either side. Then I spliced the footage together so I appear in all four chairs simultaneously throughout the two-minute shebang. Ambient room sounds hiss behind intentionally indecipherable dialogue: four tracks, run through every conceivable filter, which I rerecorded at half speed and then re-rerecorded in reverse.

That way, no one would hear me say, "I'm a liar and a fraud. I hate my-self and I want to die. I stole my grandfather's Darvocet a day after I left a halfway house where my friend OD'd and died. I have no fucking clue how I've managed to stay clean since then. Watermelon rutabaga. Watermelon rutabaga. Watermelon rutabaga. Watermelon rutabaga."

In International Cinema, the first few black-and-white art house snooze-fests make clear the difference between "film" and "movies." Does anybody like this crap or is the entire genre predicated upon people pretending?

A steamy, double-entendre-laden handwritten letter from Chessa arrives. Still sober, she has no desire to get high and doesn't go to meetings or believe in God. "You inspired me to pursue my dream when you started taking your writing seriously," she writes. "I'm going to school to be a pro-fessional hairstylist."

I reply with lies: "School is great. Everyone loves my writing. I never think about dope."

At the end of September, we watch *Persona*. I recognize Ingmar Berg-man's name from the Woody Allen movies Mom took me to see in the theaters, starting with *Radio Days* when I was ten.

Persona begins with a spark of light from a projector. Title cards appear and disappear, interspersed with images of a tarantula, slaughtered sheep, an old cartoon, trees, a fence, snow. A woman's blurry face comes into focus. Then a boy watching the face on a screen. Ninety-nine percent of the run time involves Liv Ullman and Bibi Anderson. The former doesn't speak.

After class, I rent a few Bergman films at the local video store. A month later, I've seen all his work, most of the films by Buñuel and Fellini, and a smattering of Ray, Goddard, Kurosawa, Truffaut, Malle. The irony isn't lost on me—a modified AA-ism is keeping me clean: one film at a time.

Later in the semester, I meet Jane, a sociology major studying the effect of war on kids. Blond, with porcelain skin and an entrancing smile. Her friends call her Glinda—as in the *good* witch.

Jane would be perfect if not for Aaron, her theater major boyfriend with a predilection for jumping on tables in the dining hall and spouting lines from plays I can't identify. There's also a timing issue. In January, she's going to the former Yugoslavia for nine months to work at a youth center in a town ravaged by war.

One night, after dinner, I stop by the cottage Jane shares with three girls. I find her in her room using a quasi-functional hotplate to cook powdered mashed potatoes from a box and corn from a can.

The unfairness hurts. Every semester, money grows in my Smith Barney brokerage account, which I didn't earn. I never have to touch it, thanks to the allowance Herbie gives me. Every semester, Jane incurs more debt while going to school full-time and working at the library for practically nothing.

Pretending not to have eaten, I ask Jane to dinner. In the car, "I Got You Babe" by Sonny and Cher plays on the radio. We sing along, laughing, and laugh our way through dinner at a local diner.

A few nights later, at a party off-campus, Jane stumbles up to me at two in the morning, asking for a ride to her cottage. I drive her home and walk her to the door. She kisses me and pulls me inside, and we make out and fall asleep on her bed.

In the morning, I pretend to be confused.

"I must've been drunk or high or . . ."

"That's funny," Jane says. "I was pretending to be drunk to get you here and have my way with you." An hour later, she breaks up with Aaron.

Over the next few weeks, much torrid, unclothed dry humping ensues, but Jane and I don't have sex. She says she's slept with only two guys. I lie and say, "Me too—except they were both girls." I find it odd when she asks about the girls. I wish I could scrub Aaron from my memory and not have to see him on campus. I don't want to know about Duane, the kid she dated in high school. Is it wrong to wish he were dead?

Jane listens to Prince and Elliot Smith and loves Woody Allen movies, especially *Stardust Memories*, which I haven't seen but claim as my all-time favorite. She describes her suburban upbringing as "vanilla." Happy married parents. Close relationships with her older brother and younger sister. Her eyes get misty when I tell her my parents divorced when I was four and I haven't had contact with my father in almost two years.

"How awful," she says, laying a hand on my shoulder.

"Nah. He's a bad, bad guy. I'm much better off without him."

We're lying in Jane's bed. I look down at our clothes strewn across the floor. One of my shoes is on its side. The leather soles, smooth and shiny tan when I bought them, are black and scuffed and worn. The insides stink. They used to be perfect. I should have been more careful.

The first time we have sex, it's strictly missionary, but there's an intensity, more meaningful than other girls I'd been with. I want to open up about my past, but I'm terrified of scaring her away. After a week of rehearsing and revising a speech, I share a picture of myself in hockey shoulder pads and tighty-whities and butterflies in my hair.

"I got a job as a promoter for Limelight, Tunnel, and USA and started doing heroin. I knew it was a mistake, so I told my parents and checked myself into rehab. Haven't looked back."

"Wow," Jane says, eyes widening. "I can't even imagine."

"You know what they say—what doesn't kill you makes you stronger. It's all about the power of positive thinking."

"I think you're the most real person I've ever met."

As the semester winds down, we don't talk about the future—where the relationship is going, or even if it *is* a relationship. Before Jane leaves for her extended semester abroad, I make a dozen mix tapes. At the end of the second side on each, I splice together hundreds of short snippets—to express the romantic feelings I can't say on my own. We agree to stay in touch via a new technology the school recently implemented: *electronic mail.*

Throughout January, I'm in the computer lab every day, checking my email, sending notes to Jane. At the end of the month, when I still haven't heard back, I resume contact with Chessa and start hooking up with girls at school.

Abby is tall and rail thin with short bleached blond hair and black horn-rim glasses. Her teeth aren't big but somehow they get in the way when we kiss. She wears men's underwear, which kind of freaks me out. In bed one night, she takes a drag from the cigarette I just lit. When she passes it back, the filter is warm and squishy and gross.

Courtney has long brown hair, wears traditional women's panties, and talks too much about hunting trips with her father. Julie tells me, point blank, that she gives the best blow jobs. I find out that she does. Then she starts showing up at my room every night. I don't want to be around her. I don't want to be around anyone.

seventeen

The letter arrives on my twenty-first birthday. Sent to the registrar, via certified mail, it was written on a typewriter in all caps:

THIS IS TO INFORM YOU THAT AS OF 3/11, I AM NO LONGER RE-SPONSIBLE FOR ANY COST OR OBLIGATION WHATSOEVER RELATED TO OR INCURRED BY MY SON DAVID. EFFECTIVE AT ONCE YOU MUST DEAL DIRECTLY WITH DAVID REGARDING ALL MATTERS CONCERNING HIS RELATIONSHIP WITH THE COLLEGE.

I try not to show emotion as I tuck the letter back into the envelope and step outside.

The sky is a smoky gray haze. It snowed a foot last night. Salt particles crunch under my feet. I want to scream but I don't. I want to cry but I can't. I get into bed and listen to Rage Against the Machine's "Killing in the Name Of."

Mom calls in a choked-up fury. She got a copy of the letter, which she refers to as "a giant fuck-you" to me.

"What kind of piece of shit does that to his own kid?" she asks. "You don't deny your kids—you kill for them. He never got it. I know you will when you're a parent."

"Uh-huh."

"Aren't you angry, David?"

"Of course."

Mom talks about hiring a lawyer. She says my grandfather will cover the rest of my education and expenses. "Your life won't change," she says. "Not one iota."

"Can I do something to help?"

"*Thrive*, David. Be strong. Otherwise, he wins."

A month after the letter, my skin is tighter, my muscles tenser and achier, my stomach queasier. I can't get out of bed and I can't sleep. With increasing frequency, I catch myself gnashing my hands together and notice little bits of skin on my bright red palms, like shards of pencil eraser on a page after rigorous use.

One sleepless night, I get into my car and drive around aimlessly on Route 9.

I've driven this stretch many times—reflective signs before Wilmington, tight curve by the Whetstone Inn, a homemade wooden cross pitched into the ground in front of a tree with a chunk of bark missing, about the height of the average car's front bumper.

Cresting the hill before Auger Hole Road, I'm thinking about Nat—a kid I knew in high school. He hanged himself from a rafter on his parents' front porch, on a Saturday night in eleventh grade. The next morning, his mom found him when she opened the door to get the newspaper. It was Mother's Day.

In the sublime calm of headlights and wind and Nirvana's "Negative Creep" cranked on the stereo, I take off my seat belt and watch the speedometer tilt right—fifty, sixty, eighty-five . . . a hundred miles per hour.

Two years sober.

When will this get easier?

Will it get easier?

An email from Jane arrives at the end of April. "I've been listening to your mix tapes, thinking about you nonstop, trying to get in touch. The internet is unreliable here."

I type a long, unabashed response: the letter from my father, the emptiness and loneliness, the urge to stick needles in my arm. I read it, then delete it and start over.

"Everything is great. I declared dual majors in film and philosophy, focusing on existentialism Ingmar Bergman and Woody Allen films. I have a summer internship at an independent movie studio in NYC. Turns out I might be in your neck of the woods soon. Any chance I could swing by?"

Jane replies the next day. "Really? You'd come here to see me?"

The day after my internship ends in early August, I take a commercial flight to Vienna and then a chartered jet to Sarajevo, where I'm greeted by a swarm of soldiers with drawn semiautomatic rifles. After searching and interrogating me, they escort me to a door that opens to the blistering midday Balkan sun and to Jane leaning against a rusted, lime green '80s era European sedan, a cigarette dangling from her lips. I've never seen her smoke before.

We run to each other. A hug turns into a long, soft, wet kiss. It's awkward at first, like we both wanted to but neither was sure the other would accept.

Jane introduces me to a tall, muscular guy who doesn't speak English. I can't pronounce his name. He drives us a relatively short distance to the youth center, but it takes four hours on cratered roads, littered with debris, lined with bombed-out, pockmarked buildings.

Jane and Muscles seem perfectly relaxed. One of my mix tapes plays on the car's shitty speakers. "Sometimes" by James ends. "Wish You Were Here" begins.

Jane turns around in the passenger seat. "Nobody here had heard of Pink Floyd until I played this."

When we arrive, I meet the staff and kids and a photographer—Frank, from Amherst, Massachusetts. Jane is working with him on a photo exhibition.

The few who speak English translate for the others. I'm peppered with questions about the price of Levi's in America, Converse All Stars color options, Pink Floyd. It's thrilling to expose Pero to *The Dark Side of the Moon*, his eyes glimmering when I point out the hidden messages.

War stories are hard to listen to. Everyone has seen friends and family shot dead, mutilated bodies piled high on roadsides. Bombs dropping and exploding. Barbed wire and land mines. Cold winters without heat or electricity. Desperation. Al lost his parents and siblings over the course of a single day.

During the war, when all the hospitals closed, the local rodent population helped themselves to whatever medicine was lying around. Rats the size of cats still roam the streets. Elvis speaks of a hunger so intense that he resorted to hunting and eating them.

I'm ashamed for not appreciating the easy life I lucked into. I decide to leave my Discman and CDs and Levi's and Converse behind when I go home.

After midnight, Jane and I retreat to a small room on the first floor. Sweat drips from the bulging plaster walls. It's a hundred degrees with the window open. We lay on a ripped sheet on a filthy, grooved wooden floor. Jane talks about living in the moment, without regret, "carpeing the diems." I think she's building to something. I'm queasy before she confesses to flings with Elvis and Al and Pero. Then I want to gouge out their fucking eyeballs.

"We never talked about us before I left," she says. "And Balkan boys are my forbidden fruit. I didn't know if you'd moved on. Are you okay?"

"Me? Yeah."

"You're not mad?"

"Why would I be?"

"Were you with anyone else?"

I say no as if I'm offended.

We have very quiet, very sweaty, very intense sex. After, Jane falls asleep in my arms. I close my eyes but can't sleep. I can't stay in this grove of forbidden fruit.

The next morning, I ask about a getaway. "You can take a few days, right?"

Jane suggests the Croatian coast. I don't want to be anywhere in the former Yugoslavia, but I don't protest. We take a bus to Split, a city with old European architecture and windy cobblestone streets, largely spared from the bombings.

The only open restaurant is in a plaza overlooking the Adriatic Sea. No menu. Two choices: spaghetti or bread with *ajvar*, a red pepper puree that functions as a sauce, condiment, stand-alone dish, and alternative to concrete.

On the other side of the plaza, a sign reads, "Ferry to Ancona, Italy." We buy tickets for the overnight crossing and lie on reclining lounge chairs on the cold, windy deck, talking, stargazing. I tell Jane about my summer internship, working almost exclusively as a courier, and then I say, "Oh, I almost forgot. My father cut me off, and my mom is suing him to pay for the rest of college."

"You say that like it's no big deal."

"Well, he wins if I fall apart, so I don't think about it. I'm just living my life."

In Ancona, we hop a train to Venice and check into a swanky hotel on the Grand Canal. Our room has silk wallpaper and gold-plated tables and lamps. I pay for everything—lodging, meals at the finest restaurants, gondola rides, city tours. Late at night, we feast on overpriced room service—crudité platters with carrots carved into flowers and crackers arranged in the shape of a heart. Jane laughs when I ask the server if he lays out the crackers in the hall or carries the trays upstairs carefully. She laughs at my TV show translations: *The Golden Girls* dubbed in Italian with Spanish subtitles.

"Oh, Rose, you big galoot. A "lanai" *is* a deck, but I call it a lanai because I'm a classy Southern ho. Hey, look at me. Thanks to a nonsensical jump cut, I'm in the kitchen, shoving cheesecake down my throat. Sofia, say something witty."

For three days, we live it up and have daily missionary sex, multiple times. Then Jane gets homesick—for the youth center. I pretend to understand while my insides burn with jealousy. We leave Venice a day early.

On my last night, the college-aged volunteers stay late, drinking and hanging out. During an impressive rendition of "Wish You Were Here" on a twelve-string, I compliment the player and mime a flick of an invisible coin in his direction. Through a translator, he asks what the gesture means. I explain the concept of busking. The guy pins me against the wall and cocks his fist and yells at me—in English.

"You fucking American mosquito. You think we're savages? Maybe we are. Maybe I'll fucking kill you right now."

A rush of people, including Al and Pero, stop the carnage before it happens. Jane yells at my attacker in Croatian. He yells back in Croatian.

In the morning, my CDs and Discman are missing, along with my Levi's and Converse. I pretend not to care. Jane is outraged.

"Everyone knows how much you mean to me," she says. "I can't believe they'd steal something of yours."

I don't point out the irony of her statement.

The guy with the muscles and the green car drives us to the airport, where Jane tries to explain her flings.

"I was lonely," she says. "And I missed you. But I didn't want to have my heart set on us, not knowing how you felt."

"It wasn't obvious? I made all those mixes and sent a million emails."

The hot air tastes like jet fuel. I breathe it in as Jane brushes stray strands of hair from her face and rubs her misty eyes.

"I don't want to be with anyone else," she says.

"Me neither."

"So can we promise to be faithful from now on?"

I nod. Jane nuzzles her head into the crook of my neck. I wrap my arms around her and pull her close and try to etch the moment into my memory.

"I love you," she says.

My mouth won't open.

"I fucking love you, David. Okay?"

"I. Love. You."

eighteen

om meets me at the baggage carousel with hugs and kisses. Then
she pulls my shoulders back.

"You're twenty-one years old, David. Don't you think you're too smart
and handsome not to stand up straight all the time? You want people to
see how confident you are, right?"

My yellow duffel comes down the conveyer. I squeeze between an older
German-speaking couple and grab it and walk perfectly, uncomfortably
erect to the car.

Rod Stewart's "Forever Young" plays on the tape deck, Mom's favorite song. She twists the volume down as I recap the trip. When I mention
Split, she says she was there with Jeffrey, her last serious boyfriend before
my father.

"We went all around Europe the summer of our twenty-first birth-
days. I don't know why we decided to go there, but I remember neither of
us knew how to drive a stick shift, so Jeffrey was in charge of the pedals
and steering, and I moved the shifter. It was hysterical. We laughed and
laughed and laughed."

To the left of the Whitestone Bridge, Manhattan's distended skyline
glows in the sun. I ask Mom if she ever wishes she'd married Jeffrey.

"Like I always tell you, everything in life is *at the time*. If I would have
known then that I'd be divorced at thirty, have cancer at forty . . ."

A pale pink marble fountain marks the entrance to Mom's condo compound. On either side, giant letters spell the name of the highly desirable,

exclusive community. The first three letters are missing from the south-facing sign. "DORAL GREENS" is now "AL GREENS." I chuckle. Mom groans.

The road curves around the fourth hole of a championship golf course, past a pool, clay tennis courts, and a spa and fitness center. As we approach Mom's unit, the suspected sign defacer appears in the road: Daniel, a brown Nat Sherman cigarette dangling from his lips. Mom pulls into the garage and we get out of the car.

"David noticed the sign right away," she says.

"I don't know what you're talking about," Daniel says, coming at me for a hug.

"It's not funny," Mom says. She goes inside.

Daniel and I smoke cigarettes on the front steps. Every other second, he flicks ash into the long, rectangular planter. A dozen plastic daisies rise from a shallow bed of bone-dry dirt. Daniel yanks one out.

"Do you think the neighbors think Mom's a crackpot?" he asks. "They have real flowers. She has *these*." He presses the stem between his palms and spins it. A petal snaps off. He lobs it at nearby shrubbery, cigarette butts scattered in the mulch.

"David, before I forget. Don't throw shit into the bushes."

"'Shit' as in 'poop'?"

"Cigarettes."

"Was there an incident involving fire?"

"No, but remember when I lit a firecracker and threw it out your window?"

"The time when the tree caught on fire and I called 911?"

Daniel lights another Sherman with the cherry of the one he's about to finish. I walk to the street, stomp out my cigarette, and kick it into a sewer grate seconds before the front door opens. Mom steps outside and glares at Daniel, a cigarette in each hand. She launches into her reformed-smoker spiel. "It stinks. It's unhealthy. It's gross." She was a heavy smoker until her first cancer diagnosis. I distinctly remember her smoking while riding a bike on multiple occasions. She smoked through both pregnancies.

"Daniel, I really wish you'd quit."

"Then I'd miss it. You say you miss smoking all the time."

"I do."

Daniel extends his pack. "Here," he says. "Smoke."

"If I took one puff, I'd be right back to two packs a day in a heartbeat."

Pointing to splotches of black ash rubbed into the light gray slate steps and the butts in the bushes, Mom says, "You've been home less than a week."

Through gritted teeth, Daniel says, "I said I'd clean it up."

"Oh, for crying out loud."

Mom turns to me, her expression softening. "I ordered pizza and salad. Do you boys want to pick it up?"

Daniel and I agree. Mom gives me twenty bucks.

"Why does David get the money?"

"Because I don't trust you."

In the car, Daniel asks, "She give you shit about smoking all summer?"

"Never."

"Urgh! That's the double standard. With me, she's—"

"She doesn't know I smoke."

"How's that possible?"

"Because I drop cigarettes in the sewer and wash my hands after."

At the pizza place, Daniel adds a meatball sub to our order. When we get home, Mom is sitting at the kitchen table, reading the *New York Times* with the TV on mute. Other televisions are audible throughout the house, each tuned to a different channel.

"Why am I an asshole for not turning off lights, but you have TVs on all the time?"

"I never said you were an asshole for not turning off lights, Daniel. I said electricity costs money. And I have the TVs on because I like to walk in a room and—"

Daniel sucks spit between his teeth while examining his sub.

Mom shudders. "Your father used to make that noise. It drove me nuts."

Daniel hurls the sub at the wall. Marinara sauce splatters. The top of the roll sticks to the matte eggshell white paint. Everything else slides down.

Mom's eyes nearly bulge out of her head. "Are you kidding? Who throws a goddamn sandwich?"

Daniel says "It wasn't well put together" as if he were merely following standard protocol.

I open the pizza box, slide three slices on plates, and serve them with a smile. Daniel storms into the living room. Mom closes her eyes and takes a deep breath, exhaling slowly. As we eat, she brings me up to date on the in-court duke-out with my father.

"The divorce agreement says he can legally cut you boys off when you're twenty-one, but it also says he has to pay for college if he can afford it—nothing about your age. He keeps crying poverty but refuses to show any proof."

Through the wall, I hear Daniel say, "Could you please stop talking about this?"

After three days with Mom and Daniel, I start packing for school. Daniel comes into my room, waving a CD.

"Radiohead. *OK Computer*. Heard it?"

"'Creep'? Those guys? Not my favorite."

"Oh, David. This is the best album of all time."

He pops the disc in my CD player. Sitting on the floor between the speakers, I fall into the distorted guitar that opens "Airbag." Halfway through the song, a car pulls into the driveway and Daniel leaves with his friends. I listen to the rest of *OK Computer*—a sonic masterpiece of glitchy, kill-switch textures and anxious, dystopian lyrics.

When I wake up in the morning, Mom is at the country club. Daniel is outside, smoking cigarettes on the deck.

"So?"

"You were right."

Daniel smiles triumphantly. "You're the guy who introduces everyone else to new music," he says. "Now I know how it feels." He flicks a Sherman over the rail and lights another.

"Mom woke me up before she left," he says. "Shook me and went, 'You don't know disappointment the way David does because you never asked your father for anything.' No 'good morning.' No 'how did you sleep?' No breakfast."

"What'd you say?"

"Same thing I say every time she brings it up. I told her it's fucked up that he cut you off. It is fucked up. But she thinks I think he's some infallible god."

"Don't you?"

"He gets me. When I'm so mad that I could kick a door off its hinges, I call him."

"And then you find some doors to kick off their hinges together?"

"He talks me down. Honestly, he's chilled a lot since the last time you saw him."

"He said my dick was going to get slammed in a window."

Daniel tilts his head from side to side. "I could see him saying that. But she shouldn't make me feel bad about having a relationship with my own father."

"I don't think she's trying to—"

"She totally is. She intentionally pushes my buttons the way she used to push his. And then when I explode, she goes, 'See? You have his temper and his impulsivity.' I think she sees him when she looks at me. I don't think she realizes that *her* ex-husband is *our* father."

The best music doesn't reveal its secrets on the first listen, or even the tenth or hundredth. But once you know it's there, you never unhear it. I don't know how many times I listened to *The Dark Side of the Moon* before I heard the spoken words at the beginning, or the sound of Glenn Gould breathing on the 1955 recording of "The Goldberg Variations," or Lindsey Buckingham's fingers sliding up the fretboard on Fleetwood Mac's "Never Going Back Again."

When I leave for school, my giant CD collection stays behind—with one exception. Eastbound on I-84, the sun shining, I roll up my windows so I don't miss a second of *OK Computer*'s nuanced sound. The last song ends as I approach the exit for I-91. I glance at the cover—a heavily obscured highway—and start the album over.

I'm living off-campus this year with another film major in a house on a dirt road. Upon arriving, I sign up for an international phone plan and call Jane. We talk for a few minutes, mostly about the hike she went on this morning.

"We took almost all the kids," she says. "And then we made ajvar."

If "we" included a girl, Jane would have said, "Alma and I took the kids on a hike." A guy was involved. My brain quickly produces a low-budget porno: Jane and half a dozen big, anonymous, uncircumcised Balkan dicks.

A week into the semester, my mom calls. The court case is over. She won.

"The judge finally subpoenaed your father's bank records," she says. "He only showed his checking account, but it had over a million fucking dollars in it."

Mom explains the sum is significant because you keep minimal money in your checking account and the majority in stocks and other investments. Before we hang up, she says casually, "Your father probably kept a lawyer on retainer this whole time to make my life miserable."

Last year in Religion, Literature, and Philosophy, we learned about Plato's "Allegory of the Cave": A group of prisoners see the shadows of passing objects on a wall in the cave only where they're chained together. These images form the basis of their reality.

When a prisoner escapes and sees the sun and the objects in their true form, he doesn't know how to process the information. Reality upended, he *returns* to the cave.

nineteen

In November, Jane returns to the States. I drive to her parents' home in Pennsylvania, and somewhere in New Jersey, I'm struck by an inexplicable fear that she'll want to have sex and I won't be able to get hard. I've never had trouble before, but the thought is so disturbing and unshakable that I stop to disprove my concern in a gas station bathroom. It backfires. I try (and fail) a few more times while driving. Why is this happening?

Jane bounds out of the house when I pull into the driveway. She comes at me and we kiss. Her lips taste foreign. Her embrace is stifling. We go inside and sit on a couch covered with sheets and colorful, rough wool afghans. When her parents ask how school is going, I lie about a short film that needs to be edited and handed in tomorrow. Jane doesn't question me. When her parents go to sleep, she kisses my neck and runs her hand up my thigh. I squirm and, feigning disappointment, say, "I don't want us to get caught."

In the morning, I leave in a hurry, repelled with a force far greater than the attraction I felt in the beginning. Why?

Over Thanksgiving break, I attempt to assuage my guilt by making a reservation at Joe's Pub at the Carlyle Hotel in Manhattan, on a night when Woody Allen plays clarinet with his Dixieland Jazz band. Our table is practically on top of the stage. Before the band comes out, Jane gives me a pen and a notebook.

"Write a note to Woody."

"No way he's going to reply."

"You're always talking about the power of positive thinking. If you think he won't, then he won't. If you think he will, then he will."

I scribble a paragraph about myself and my studies, and I've been a fan since I was twelve years old and my favorite of his films is *Stardust Memories*. I carefully remove the perforated page and fold it. The lights go down. The band enters. I pass the note to Woody and watch him stick it in the inside pocket of his blazer. When I return to school, a letter from him is waiting in my mailbox, thanking me for *my* note and giving me a few book suggestions to go with my studies. I write back immediately. A response arrives a few days later. We become pen pals.

In January, on her first day back at school, Jane comes to the editing room in the afternoon, pitching an idea for a summer sublet in Amherst or Northampton. She wants to be close to Frank, the photographer she met in Bosnia. They're collaborating on a photo exhibit in a gallery on campus—in September.

"I can work with Frank, you can write. We can get jobs and hang out. How awesome would that be?"

"Super awesome."

"That wasn't very convincing. Are you okay?"

"Yeah. Just a little stressed."

"'Cause you want to finish up and be with me?"

"Exactly."

"So finish up and come to the cottage. I'll make my famous eggplant parm. We can pretend we're an old married couple and you're coming home from work."

At eight that night, I leave the editing room with enough acid in my stomach to dissolve Jane's famous eggplant, the bane of my culinary existence. We eat while watching a documentary about the Bosnian war.

In bed, Jane is all over me like a sex emergency. Jerking off isn't a problem, so I fantasize about other girls, but the guilt is overpowering. I try to imagine I'm jerking off, but my brain won't have it. *You're inside this hot girl who's crazy for you, and you're pretending she's your hand? The fuck's wrong with you?* Finally, I let out a moan and say I came. I take off the condom, tie it in a knot, and fling it into the wicker trash basket under Jane's desk.

In the middle of the night, I panic. What if Jane inspects the condom?

I get up, take it out of the trash, and put it in my jeans pocket. In the morning, I drop it in a garbage can in the dining hall. Then I worry Jane will look in her trash and notice the condom is gone. That's worse, right?

I stop initiating sex. Jane initiates less, presumably for related reasons. I wouldn't know—neither of us initiate a conversation about it.

By March, the entire school seems to know about my correspondence with Woody Allen. He FedExes his copy of the *Deconstructing Harry* script to me—his handwritten notes are scribbled in the margins.

A rumor begins to circulate: Woody Allen is going to produce *Hypothermia*, the original, feature-length screenplay I claim to be writing, which I haven't actually begun. I don't even have an idea for the story.

For the first time in more than a year, I write to Chessa. "Sorry for being out of touch for so long. It hurts too much when we're in regular contact." She replies quickly, saying she hasn't stopped thinking about me and still has a picture of me next to her bed—I'm wearing a brown leisure suit, and my hair is purple.

As letters go back and forth, I can't decide if I'm betraying Jane or engaging in mental masturbation. Maybe it doesn't matter. I'm not going to tell her. At the end of April, Chessa mentions an abortion and a fiancé. I don't reply.

Jane makes appointments to see summer apartment options in Northampton. On the ride down, I rehearse breakup speeches in my mind. On the ride back, I seethe about the lease we just signed to sublet a bedroom in a small, dumpy apartment half a mile from downtown. Our roommate, Sol, is a transsexual man and UMASS Amherst student.

On the last night of the semester, I leave the editing room at four in the morning. Nora, a sophomore, is sitting on a rock wall by the entrance. Wearing a bulky sweatshirt and sweatpants, her bob hairdo seemingly slept on funny for a week, she's wearing the kind of glasses my sixth-grade science teacher wore—big, gray, ninety-degree uppercase D-shaped frames.

Next thing I know, Nora is on her knees in the editing room, talking about unzipping my fly with her teeth. My hand brushes against her cheek as I pull her hair back. Standing there, my jeans around my ankles, I feel guilty for not feeling guilty.

After, Nora swears not to tell anyone. "Trust me," she says, wiping her face on her sleeve. "You think I want to be the whore who made David and Jane break up?"

Dew sticks to my low-top Chuck Taylors as I walk through a field to my car. Driving home, I look at every tree and telephone pole on the side of the road. "Exit Music (for a Film)" comes on, the fourth track on *OK Computer*. Four and a half minutes of fragile vocals and delicate acoustic guitar before the electric melts in—high-gain, oversaturated velcro fuzz tearing at menacing lyrics.

twenty

Sol stands at the faucet at an angle that's clearly intentional—he wants us to see the scars on his chest, upturned half moons where his breasts used to be. He asks salaciously, "Who wants to see how I make a cock?"

Jane abandons a box of books at the top of the stairs and watches Sol fill a condom. He says something about ideal "dick water temperature," his stubby fingers struggling to tie a knot. He hands the squishy, slippery makeshift surrogate member to Jane, who squeezes it and jokes about the small size. Sol snatches it back and drops it down the front of his sweatpants.

"For your information," he sneers jokingly, "this is an 'around town' dick. If I'm going out to a bar or whatever, I have a box of Magnums."

Four hours later, the car is still filled with crap because Jane and I can't schlep boxes up three steep, narrow flights of stairs without Sol stopping us for another round of show and tell. Once our belongings are finally in the apartment, I want to rest, but Jane wants to look for jobs.

A steady drizzle pelts us all afternoon. In three hours, I don't apply for any jobs. Jane fills out one application—at Bruegger's Bagels, a crappy chain on the main drag.

"Let's call it quits," I say.

"If I don't make a certain amount of money this summer, I'll starve in the fall."

At dusk, Jane finally agrees to go home. We stop at the natural food store. She moves swiftly through the aisles, grabbing eggplant and veggie burgers and tofu while a cleaning crew preps a machine to wax the floors. When we go to pay, she asks the hippie girl at the register if the store is hiring.

"Totally. Do you both want applications?"

I shake my head.

Jane elbows me and whispers, "If we both apply, our chances double."

Twenty-four hours later, while she sprinkles shredded cheese onto layers of breaded eggplant, Sol tells me how lucky I am to be with a woman who knows how to cook such delicious food.

"David loves when I make this," Jane says.

The phone rings. Sol answers and turns to Jane. "It's Joe," he sings. "From Northampton Natural."

She takes the phone and puts it to her ear, her slight, victorious smile quickly morphing to disappointment. She hands me the phone, mouths *You got the job*, and slips into the bathroom.

Joe says, "I hope this doesn't cause problems between you and Jane." We sort out the details of my starting date and pay. When I hang up, Sol glares at me.

I wish I could be as excited about anything as Joe is about a shelf of uniformly facing labels on organic pickled beet jars. He leads me up and down the aisles with his hands clasped behind his back, comparing Northampton Natural to a Broadway show.

"You're always on. Everything has to be perfect. See how everything's lined up on the shelves?"

In his small office at the back of the store, Joe contorts his body into a backless chair and goes over employee benefits.

"Medical, dental, vision, supplemental life insurance. In a year, we'll have a 401(k). And we have this philanthropic program—you can donate some percentage of your paycheck. Totally voluntary, but just so you know, we all participate."

This month's cause is Gang Up For Good, a nonprofit that gives at-risk youth a shot at having a better life.

Joe points to a picture of birdhouses on a patio. "One of the head honchos at this regional birdhouse manufacturer donated second-quality birdhouses worth a total of five grand to GUFG. All week, the at-risk youth, God love 'em, they've been all over selling birdhouses. If you buy one, take a snapshot and bring it in."

A tall woman with heavy canvas bags dangling from each elbow appears: Matilda, the assistant manager. She drops her bags and asks Joe if there've been any new developments on *the letter*. He explains to me that an anonymous tenant at his condo compound filed a complaint about an uptick in bird excrement on the premises.

"Five bucks says it's that woman who lives next door to you," Matilda says.

"Mary?" Joe scratches his head. "Really?"

"Totally. She blamed you when a bird went to the bathroom on her last week."

Joe shrugs. I suggest he tell Mary to exact revenge by going to the bathroom on a bird. He doesn't laugh, nor does Matilda.

When Neil arrives in Birkenstocks at ten o'clock, Matilda chides him for wearing open-toed shoes. She asks him to school me on trimming a head of lettuce and reorienting it in the veggie case for maximum appeal. Walking away, she sneezes a few times. Everyone in the store, customers included, says bless you after each sneeze.

I go outside and smoke. When I return, Neil asks, "Did you get permission to take a fifteen?"

"Uh . . ."

"You can't just come and go as you please." He sniffs the air vigorously and holds his nose. "You have to wash your hands. Nobody wants food that reeks of smoke."

Northampton Natural is on the ground level of a three-story mini-mall-ish structure. After an exhaustive search for the bathroom on the second floor, I go down to the dank, windowless basement and find it in the back corner.

The floor is sticky and covered in dust. Four urinals, without dividers to prevent other guys from seeing you pee. Three toilet stalls. I notice feet on the floor. Birkenstocks. Neil. I wash my hands and turn off the light on my way out.

"Hey, not cool, whoever turned out the lights. Karma's a bitch."

Matilda tells me, "Associates eat meals together as one big, happy family, except we do it in two shifts because if we all ate at the same time, who'd be on the sales floor?" She gives me a choice between first or second lunch shifts.

"I was going to leave. I have a ton of errands."

With a frown, Matilda says to clock out anytime for my lunch break.

A drum circle of stoned hippies pound out a rhythmic noise on the village green. In front of the bike store, a Goth girl leans against a parking meter. She's dressed entirely in black, her black nail polish severely chipped. On the sidewalk next to her, a few dollar bills poke out of a coffee cup. I give her five dollars.

"Pssst," she says, "do you want to smoke a joint?"

I decline with a wave. Before turning away, I say, "If you had some heroin . . ."

Goth girl jumps and looks me over—white polo shirt, khaki cargo shorts, low-top Chucks with a hand-drawn anarchy symbol on the toe.

"I can get dope," she says. "But you have to buy me a bag."

The dealer lives in Holyoke, twenty miles south. On I-91, wind whipping through the car, I'm profoundly aware of the choice I'm making. This isn't a relapse. It's a re*set*.

OK Computer is in the tape deck. "Airbag." My new friend, Arianne, arches her back and dangles her feet out the window, her short shorts riding so high that I can see her stubbly thighs and black panties in the mirror. I think maybe she's flirting. I don't care.

"I don't do dope more than two days in a row," Arianne says. "Today was s'posed to be an off day, but I woke up thinking about it, and that's the thing about dope. It knows when you need it. *It* finds *you*."

"I thought about it when I woke up today too. And yesterday and the day before and every day for a thousand days before that."

"Yeah, you know what I mean."

"I thought about it. I haven't gotten high in more than three years."

Arianne pulls her feet in and sits straight. "Fuck, dude. I never would've done this if I knew."

I stop myself from asking, jokingly, if she wants to turn back.

We pull into a gas station at the bottom of the exit ramp in Holyoke.

Arianne calls the dealer from a pay phone. She says he's home, but we have to wait twenty minutes.

Time hangs in the humid air as we smoke on a patch of grass by the coin-operated car vacuums. I stomp out a cigarette and light another to give myself something to do, half listening to Arianne mutter about living with her boyfriend in a tent in the woods by Northampton's municipal fields.

Across the street, a backhoe digs up an empty lot. The repetitive motion reminds me of *The Myth of Sisyphus* by Camus—another book I own but haven't read. I ask Arianne if she's read it.

"Um, I dropped outta high school."

"The gods wanted to condemn Sisyphus to an eternity without meaning, so they made him roll a boulder up a hill all day every day. When he got to the top, the boulder would roll back down, and he'd start over."

In the car, Arianne calls out directions. We make a few turns and pass a playground. A few turns later, we pass the playground again.

"What if the dealer isn't home anymore?"

"Chill. He's home."

We backtrack to the gas station and start over. "Like the guy with the rock," Arianne says. "Wait. If all he did was roll some stupid rock up a hill, wasn't *that* the meaning of his life?"

Did she pick up on something nobody else has? We turn left instead of right this time and end up in a more promising-looking neighborhood.

Big, formerly single-family homes, each with eight or ten utility meters on the side and as many satellite dishes on the roof. Peeling vinyl siding. Rotted wooden columns. Webs of duct tape on broken windows with missing screens. Front yards of dirt and crispy brown grass. Empty beer and soda bottles and cans. Clothes. A giant empty cable spool. Sneakers hanging from electrical wires.

Arianne points to a space between a blue Accord and a minivan with a "Bob Dole for President" bumper sticker. "Here," she says. I coast into the spot and tell her I'll wait in the car. She asks if I'm a cop. I laugh.

"If you're a cop, it's illegal to say you're not, so say it."

"I'm not a cop. This is a one-time thing. I don't want to have access in case I get tempted later."

She studies my face. "Fine. One bag for you, one for me. Twenty bucks."

I thumb through the bills in my wallet and hand them over: a hundred dollars in twenties. Arianne gives me a long, disapproving look and takes the money. I watch her cross the street and disappear between two houses.

I turn up the stereo. Ten minutes pass and no sign of her. "Let Down" ends and "Karma Police" begins.

My stomach clenches. Something bad is happening. Arianne is getting robbed. Arrested. Or something worse? She copped and slipped away.

There she is. Finally. She looks left and right five times before running across, her arms at her side. She slides into the passenger seat and opens her hand. My mouth waters at the sight in her sweaty palm: pale blue glassine envelopes wrapped in a rubber band. Ten bags. A bundle of dope.

The sun's warmth radiates through the windshield as I pull away from the curb. Arianne rolls up a dollar bill and pokes it into the corner of a bag and then bows her head and snorts.

"Damn, dude," she says, passing the bag and the dollar to me, her pupils shrinking from the dope. "Careful. Shit's crazy strong and you have no tolerance."

I wipe the dollar on my shirt and take a quick rip, steering with my knees. A bitter mix of snot and dope runs down the back of my throat, along with three years of sobriety.

Good riddance.

twenty-one

An oscillating floor fan blows hot air at Sol lying shirtless on the couch. "Honestly," he says, "I don't know how Jane puts up with you. Poor thing's up at four in the morning, making minimum wage at Bruegger's because you took the job she wanted, and then you quit?"

I go into the bedroom, close the door, and turn on the stereo. John Frusciante. *Niandra LaDes and Usually Just a T-Shirt*. Four simultaneous guitars. Electric, acoustic, forward, backward. I keep a bag in my pocket and stash the rest in a sunglass case, which I slide into a sock, wrap in a shirt, and bury in my backpack.

I push the thin gauzy white curtain aside and stick my head out the window. Clusters of daffodils light up the small plot of land behind the house, separated from the neighbors by a tall white fence. The trees are starting to bloom. In the distance, past the old cemetery, cars chug up and down Route 5. Not long ago, dirty black snowbanks lined the road. In the crystalline eternity of this moment, winter never happened. Winter doesn't exist. This is all I know.

Wires run from the stereo on the dresser to speakers on either side of a queen-sized mattress. I lay on the bed and stare at the round, milky glass light fixture on the ceiling. A metal pull chain with fourteen beads hangs from the bottom. I lose myself in the music for half an hour—until the door to the apartment opens and Sol receives Jane.

"You're dripping with sweat. Why didn't your boyfriend pick you up, now that he's not working anymore?"

I go out to the living room, and Jane greets me with a quizzical look. I tell her I quit my job so I'd have more time to work on *Hypothermia*.

"Awesome," she says, tugging at her collar, a polyester maroon polo with the Bruegger's Bagels logo on the left breast. With the matching pants, she could be a giant blood clot for Halloween. She says something about rinsing off the bagel smell and slinks into the bathroom.

Jane makes her famous tofu stir-fry for dinner. I nurse a can of Coke while she shares a bottle of red wine with Sol. The little appetite I have disappears altogether when he says he's a lot less self-conscious about his broccoli farts now that he is officially a dude.

When Jane starts gathering the plates and silverware, I refill her glass and tell her to relax. I'll do the dishes. She continues to clear the table until Sol yanks the plates from her and drops them in the sink. "If Prince Valiant wants to clean up, let him." He dives into the futon and turns on the TV. Jane sits on the floor, and they start watching a John Hughes movie—*Sixteen Candles* or *Pretty in Pink*.

After I finish cleaning, I sit next to Jane and wrap my arm around her. "Psst. Are you sure you're not upset that I quit my job?"

"Not at all," Jane says. "You totally should if you can afford it, and honestly, in the past few hours, you've been *so much* more chill than you were all semester."

Hazelden had everything backward. Pain doesn't end when you stop taking painkillers. It gets worse. Sobriety had the healing power of a Band-Aid on a bullet wound—because life is the disease. I'm powerless *without* heroin.

I hold a bag up to the window and flick it with my finger. Tiny cakes of powder break apart and dance in the sunlight. I spill some on the back of Baudelaire's *Les Fleurs du Mal*, roll up a dollar, and snort my first hit of the day. The effect is gradual—a ramp into your bloodstream—compared to the concentrated immediacy of a shot.

Supposedly, citric acid increases the effect of opioids. I pour a tall glass of orange juice and down it in the kitchen, staring at shadows of leaves swaying on the wall. The smell of jasmine explodes through the open window. My body warms and tingles, and that cheesy '70s song by Seals and Crofts pops into my head. "Summer Breeze."

On the sun porch, I prop my feet on the desk and brainstorm ideas for *Hypothermia*. Everything revolves around the end of the world. What'll be the last flight out of any given airport? Who'll be left behind? Will they break into the nearest Lamborghini dealership and take a Diablo for a test drive, or stay put and cower in fear, washing down single-serve bags of peanuts with small plastic bottles of Jack Daniel's?

Jane comes home at three o'clock. She asks if I've been writing all day. I nod and she plants a kiss on my cheek and leaves. She comes back after dinner.

"I miss you."

"I miss *you*."

"I start working with Frank on the photo show on Monday."

"Cool."

"Think we'll see each other before then?"

"I hope so, but the way I write is like barfing on a page. Can't stop midstream."

Sometime after midnight, I get into bed and Jane rolls over and kisses me. I go along. She reaches into my boxers and feels around.

"You're not into this."

"I *am*. It's just . . . I think I'm wiped out from writing all day."

Jane groans. A minute later, her body jerks as she slips off to sleep.

Daniel calls from Mom's house.

"I can't take it here," he says. "Any chance you'll come down before I go back to school?"

"I'd love to, but my hours at work are crazy and I have to write a screenplay."

By five o'clock, the bag I opened this morning is empty. I open another. The sun sets. Crickets and birds and cicadas perform a symphony of nighttime summer music. Fuck the apocalypse. I get a better idea for a screenplay.

A former Nazi guard at Buchenwald is now a patient at a nursing home somewhere in America. He escaped Germany after World War II and maintained his secret for decades—until the nursing home director, a half-Jewish man, learned the truth and ordered his staff to torture the monster.

At the end, when the Nazi is dead, we find out he was a Holocaust survivor with Alzheimer's.

I create an outline and a list characters—nurses, a maintenance guy, a kitchen worker—and their backstories, values, and beliefs, contrasted with the edict at work. I start writing the story as a novel as opposed to a screenplay.

In the morning, Sol peers into a clear plastic bag of day-old bagels. Traces of condensation drip inside. He reaches in, separates a cinnamon raisin from an onion bagel, and takes a bite. "Eew!" he says, spitting it in the trash. "Grossy gross gross *gross*." He wipes his tongue with a paper towel.

"I guess that's why they don't make cinnamon raisin–onion bagels," I say. "Or cauliflower-pineapple. Scallion–dog food. Nacho cheese–marshmallow."

Sol laughs. Jane doesn't crack a smile, her face buried in a book about the Bosnian war with sticky notes stuck to most of the pages.

"You know," Sol says, "I thought you were a complete dick when we first met."

"Now you think I'm a partial dick?"

"I just think it's funny. You seemed all stressed and Jane was so bubbly. Now *she's* a basket case—when she's here, which is never—and *you're* totally chill."

twenty-two

open the second to last bag, take a small hit, and drive into town. Arianne is in front of the bike store, leaning against a parking meter.

"Nice day for a drive to Holyoke, don't you think?"

"What happened to 'this is a one-time thing'?"

"It is. I got a bundle and ended up with eight bags. Technically, I owe myself two."

Arianne rolls her eyes and sweeps her cup off the sidewalk. We get in the car, and *OK Computer* is playing in the tape deck. "Climbing Up the Walls."

"Y'ever listen to anything besides Radiohead?"

"My girlfriend says the same thing. With the same look on her face."

"Christ. Does your girlfriend know you're on dope again?"

"No, and she's not going to find out."

"Good luck with that." She ejects the tape and twists the radio dial to "Intergalactic" by the Beastie Boys. Tapping rhythmically on the window, she says, "I'm pretty sure that all the dope in Holyoke comes from a dealer in the Bronx."

"Aha! That's why I went through those bags so fast. It's stepped on—twice."

"Duh. And these bags are probably lighter than you're used to."

At the curb by the dealer's house, I take all the money out of my wallet—$200. When I try to hand it over, Arianne says, "What the fuck, David?"

"Equivalency matrix. I figure I owe myself eighteen bags."

"Uh-huh."

"It makes sense."

"Yep." She snatches the cash. "I'm sure it does."

Days blur together. I don't know how many bundles have gone up my nose, nor do I care. I know this can't last forever, but right now, my pain is gone.

May becomes June. The cash in my Smith Barney account dips below $1,000. Rick, my financial adviser, encourages me to sell shares of Silicon Graphics.

I give myself a budget of a thousand dollars for dope while I finish writing the book. Then I'm done.

Halfway to Holyoke, Arianne asks if I want to come in and meet the dealer.

I shake my head. "This is my last bundle."

"You've been saying that for two weeks."

"The book is almost done."

"I don't know how you can write on dope. I can barely keep my eyes open."

"I've written three hundred pages on dope."

"And you're just gonna stop when you finish the book."

"You don't believe me?"

"I'm sure you believe you."

"That's why I don't want to meet the dealer—so I can't score when I quit."

"You sound like this girl I used to know. She went to rehab, then started going to AA and got super preachy and tough lovey. 'You're powerless. It's a disease.'"

"Sure, and the only way you can go into remission is by replacing science and medicine with God and a support group—an anonymous one. That doesn't exactly scream, 'You have nothing to be ashamed of.'"

"You think it's all bullshit?"

"Experts without medical qualifications treating a medical condition? Tough love? Painkillers *cause* pain? If quack medicine and shame are bullshit, then, yes, it's bullshit."

"So why don't you come in and meet the dealer?"

. . .

Clouds part after two days of thunderstorms. Steam rises from the pavement outside the kitchen window as Sol sings to the tune of "Leaving on a Jet Plane," his early-stage pubescent boy's voice breaking.

"I'm lea-ving for my parents' place—in Virginia Beach. I *do* know when I'll be back a-gain . . . Sept-em-ber."

He peers into a container of leftover Chinese food, stabs a piece of bone-white chicken with a chopstick, pops it in his mouth, and raises an eyebrow at Jane and me.

"Not to be crass, but you two are obviously a couple of sex ninjas, doin' the nasty-nasty without making a peep. These walls are thin and I'm a light sleeper, but I see that look on David's face."

Jane buries her head in her hands.

Two days later, I can't find Arianne in town. There's an empty bag in my pocket and nothing in my stash. Someone taps me on the shoulder. I turn around. Jane.

"I got out of work early. Want to hang out?"

When she starts talking about renting a movie and snuggling, my first thought to avoid another war documentary and the possibility of sex is an excursion to the top of Mount Tom, our local mountain, which might technically be a tall hill. Jane agrees.

As we drive off, I try to think of a reason to stop at home so I can scrape the empty bag. I pull up to the house and make a point to leave the engine running and get out before telling Jane, "I'm just going to grab my Super 8 camera and some film."

"Great." She twists the key in the ignition. "I'll change out of this uniform."

The bathroom door doesn't lock. I jam my foot into the base, rip the bag open, and lay it flat on the sink. I scrape the corners with the bottom edge of a toothpaste tube and flush the toilet and snort the miniscule hit. Then I eat the empty bag and tell myself I'll be fine without dope.

We drive to Mount Tom's summit and walk around the lookout deck. On the Vermont side, sun drills into the lush, green mountains. To the south, clouds darken what is probably Holyoke. I stuff a roll of black-and-white film in the camera and ask Jane to lean against the rail and pretend I'm not here.

I burn two rolls of film and get irritated about it. Nobody makes eight millimeter anymore. Rolls are expensive—when you find them. My legs are cramping. Is the air thinner up here?

Jane natters on about the scenic majesty. "It's gorgeous," she says. "You always think of the coolest stuff." Through the viewfinder, I see the outline of her underwear through her sundress. Would I be more interested if she wore thongs?

We stop for Chinese takeout on the way home. In the car, the smell of veggie lo mein is nauseating—even with the windows down. When we get to the apartment, I tell Jane I don't feel well and I'm going to take a shower.

The claw-foot tub has one of those European-style heads at the end of a hose. The basin is against the wall, with a small window and narrow shelf with barely enough room for our toiletries. I'm still in my boxers, waiting for the water to heat up when Jane knocks on the door.

"Your mom's on the phone."

I put my shirt on and turn off the shower.

Mom says, "Your brother drove his car into the fountain in front of Doral Greens."

"Is he okay?"

"*Daniel* is fine. His car isn't. Neither's mine. He tried to pull his car out with my car by tying them together with a hose. I got a call from security. 'Uh, your son's passed out in your car by the entrance.' I ran over, and when he finally woke up and I asked him what he was thinking, he said he was going to live with your father and stormed off. David, he's out of control. He reeked of alcohol and pot. You know, the biggest difference between you and your brother is that he doesn't know how to be honest with himself. What are we going to do with him?"

I hang up with Mom and tell Jane what happened.

"Why does your mother always ask *you* what to do about Daniel?" she asks.

I shrug, make a "how the fuck should I know" face, and get in the shower. A minute later, Jane knocks on the door.

"Phone for you."

"Can you tell my mom I'll call her back?"

"It's Dave Williamson. He said it's important."

I turn off the shower, wrap a towel around my waist, and listen to Dave, a friend from Marlboro. He tells me a long story about an unplanned pregnancy with Ana, his sort of girlfriend. They're getting married in September, on the Saturday before school starts, at the college president's house. I wait for a pause to say "Okay, gotta go now," but Dave segues into some crap about Ana's old job as an au pair in New York City.

"She got to be very close with the family and stayed in touch over the years," he says. "Does the name Letty Aronson ring a bell?"

"Kinda sorta."

"It should. She produced the last few Woody Allen movies."

"Holy shit."

"She's also his *sister*."

"Holy. Shit."

"She's coming to the wedding. Guess who's sitting next to her."

"Holy. Fucking. Shit."

"Ana told her about you and your script. If I were you, I'd spank that puppy to perfection and bring it the wedding."

When I share the Letty development with Jane, she says, "It's all that positive thinking. I can barely get Frank's attention for the photo show, and you're rubbing elbows with Woody Allen and his sister."

I call Mom. "See?" she says. "Put it out there, believe you're worth it, and the universe makes it happen."

On the sun porch, I open *Hypothermia* and realize it's a stupid title for a story about a Nazi in a nursing home. I read a few pages and think the story is stupid and the writing sucks. I do a "Save As" in Microsoft Word and delete everything except the title.

For half an hour, I futz with the text. Left justified. Right. Centered. Helvetica. Times New Roman. Back and forth and back and forth. I type my name below "Hypothermia" and delete it. I type it again and delete it again. Then I type my first name and my mother's maiden name: "David Poses."

My grandfather was Herbert Pesetzky until World War II, when relatives started getting killed in the Holocaust. By 1950, every Pesetzky in America was a Poses or a Perry.

Of course Mom is thrilled when I call to tell her I'm changing my name. "David *Poses*," she says, "you bring tears to my eyes."

As soon as I say goodbye, my resolve spills like sand through the narrow of an hourglass, and a mountain of doubt rises on the other side.

. . .

I'm still sitting on the porch floor when Jane's alarm goes off at four-thirty. She stumbles in a minute later.

"You never came to bed."

"No."

"What's wrong?"

"Nothing."

I flinch as she lays her arm around me. My heart is pounding. She rubs my back and makes shushing sounds in my ear. I start to cry.

"David, what is it?"

"I told my mom I want to change my name."

"To what?"

"David Poses. Mom got all excited and I started thinking. How's my father gonna feel? Is Mom excited for me or because she knows it'll hurt him? Am I doing this for her? To honor my grandfather?"

"It's not like you have to decide right now. You'll figure it out."

"I *won't* figure it out. I won't figure anything out."

"Hey. Power of positive thinking, remember? It's gonna be okay."

"It's *not* gonna be okay. Nothing is *ever* okay."

"Baby, I'm worried about you. Do you want me to call in sick at work?"

I gulp a breath and keep it together long enough to say, "I'm just tired."

Jane returns to the bedroom. I hear her aggressively opening and closing dresser drawers. She leaves without coming in for a kiss. I light a cigarette and rock back and forth, banging my head against the wall.

"Craving" is inaccurate. Heroin isn't ice cream. Right now, I crave it the way a drowning person craves air.

twenty-three

The smell of crack pummels the early morning air in the woods across the street from the public athletic fields. In a clearing twenty yards from the trail, I spot an orange tent and Arianne sitting on a rotted-out log. She's with two guys—both look twice as old as me. One is tall, skinny, and pale, with a crew cut. The other has crispy red skin and shaggy graying hair. He raises a stem to his mouth and lights a blowtorch. When I stumble on a felled branch, he stops puffing and lowers the pipe.

"The fuck's there?" he howls.

Arianne points at me. "*That's* the guy."

"Well, well, well," the crack smoker says. "If it isn't Mr. Bundles—in the flesh."

Arianne introduces me to her boyfriend, Roy, with the pipe, and Henry.

"So," Roy says, "to what do we owe the pleasure at this ungodly hour?"

"I was hoping Arianne might take a ride to Holyoke with me."

"No shit?" Roy says. "At six in the morning?" He unzips his fanny pack and pulls out a pale blue glassine envelope. "Yours for ten bucks."

I give him a twenty-dollar bill.

"Sorry, boss, ain't got no change." Arianne glares at him. He glares back and enters the tent. "It's fuckin' impossible to find nothing in this bitch," he says, his shadow punching at the nylon from the inside. He emerges with a surprisingly shiny spoon and a sealed bag of fine gauge syringes, which he offers in lieu of change. I accept without hesitation.

"Do you have any water?"

"We're fuckin' outside, chief," Roy says, pointing the spoon at a nearby creek. "Fuckin', it don't get no fresher than that fuckin' shit." He hocks a loogie and spits.

I roll up a dollar and snort a hit. Roy fires up the blowtorch and puffs on the stem. He exhales a monstrous cloud of smoke. "Motherfucker's hitting like a banshee." He offers it to Henry, who passes it to Arianne, who eagerly accepts.

"Baby," Roy says, "you gotta really suck on it. Like a dick."

I step closer to Arianne. "Wanna go to Holyoke?"

Roy pushes Henry at me. "He'll go. She's got business to tend to."

In the car, Henry thanks me for saving him. "I been trying to get out of there since last night. But with Roy, well, you just never know." He coughs, a deep, raspy sound.

"Back in the day," he says, "before Roy mellowed out some, he picked me up this one night to go candlepin bowling, but first he wanted to go back to his place, over in Hadley, and get a buzz on—cheaper 'n paying for all them beers at the lanes. About eight o'clock, this crack whore from Greenfield come over and says she ain't got no money, but she'll suck Roy's dick for some rock. Now, Roy being Roy, at first he's all, 'Honey, if you want some rock, you're gonna have to suck my dick, my friend's dick, and five or six other guys' dicks. I don't know who all else he had in mind since it was just the three of us there, but she agrees and Roy goes 'hold on' and leaves the room. When he comes back in with Brutus, this big old German shepherd, I get this bad feeling—you know? He's got this big smile on his face and the leash in one hand and a hunk of crack the size of a beer can in the other. He goes, 'Tell you what. I'll give you all this if you let my dog fuck you.'"

"Stop. Holy . . . Oh my God."

Henry shakes his head. "Don't I know it, kid."

We ride in silence for a few minutes. I ask what happened with the dog.

"Well sir, when she agreed to go through with it, I says to Roy, I says, 'Roy, I'm going outside.' There wun't no way I was gonna bear witness to that."

"So . . ."

"Oh, she did it, all right," Henry says. "Roy come out the house later, laughing like a son of a bitch. I tell you what. To this day, I'm still not sure who I feel worse for—the girl or the dog."

In Holyoke, Henry says he knows a dealer with fatter, purer bags than Arianne's guy. I give him the same song and dance I told her about not wanting to go inside.

"Whatever floats your boat, kid." He gets out of the car.

After we score, I drop Henry at a rooming house by I-91 in Northampton. Then I go home and shoot up for the first time in three and a half years.

As I push down on the register and the dope rushes into my vein, I know this is no longer a vacation.

At noon on Mondays and Fridays, when Henry gets off work at an industrial supply place in town, we go to Holyoke to cop. I drive. He handles the transaction and gets a bag from each bundle I buy. Two weeks into our partnership, he asks why I always have money. I tell him I sold a screenplay to Woody Allen.

"Guy who played the bartender on *Cheers*?"

"That's Woody *Harrelson*."

"Your movie got a lot of explosions and shit?"

"Long on explosions, short on shit."

"Kid, you are one funny-ass motherfucker." He laughs himself into a coughing fit, pounds his chest, and rolls down the window and spits a gob of brown phlegm. It splatters on my back window. "Sorry. I'll get it when we stop."

"You've been coughing a lot lately. Have you been to a doctor?"

"Kid, I ain't been to no doctor since I was twelve years old."

"Why?"

"Too chickenshit, I guess."

After nearly a month, you wouldn't know I'm an intravenous heroin user from looking at my arms. I avoid track marks by using clean needles (ultra-fine gauge BD brand, free at a local needle exchange) and applying an occasional cold compress.

Rick from Smith Barney is more bearish about Silicon Graphics and recommends liquidating the rest of my shares.

"Take the cash you need," he says. "We'll reinvest the rest later."

As Rick explains capital gains taxes, I stop paying attention when he gets to the part about not having to pay the IRS until next April. No chance I'll be alive then.

August comes out of nowhere. I wake up in a panic on the first of the month. I still don't have a screenplay or an idea, and I'm worried about going back to school and kicking. I'm not really paying attention as I dump a bag and a half into a spoon and mix it with water. I wrap a belt around my bicep, make a fist, and push the needle in. It hurts—a skin-popped shot. A big purple bruise immediately forms. I wrap it with a cold towel and lay on the hardwood floor in the sun porch, listening to James' "Five-O" over and over.

When Jane gets home, I show her the bruise and make up a story about selling books to the used bookstore in town. "I almost fell down the stairs carrying the box to the car."

"You were distracted, weren't you? Thinking about your script?"

"You know me."

Jane looks me over. "You're way too skinny and pale. We gotta fatten you up and get you outside more."

Knowing she's meeting Frank to work on the photo show later, I propose a long walk, followed by a romantic dinner for two. She throws her arms around my neck and coos.

"Aww, you're so sweet. I feel *terrible*. I have to meet Frank later."

Henry isn't outside. I run into the boardinghouse, fully expecting a nice old lady at a brightly lit front desk to bow her head and say somberly, "Henry was a real salt-of-the-earth type of guy." But there's no nice lady or front desk.

Why did I think there would be in a building whose exterior appears to have been hit by a tornado and left to rot?

The long, dimly lit corridor reeks of pot, cigarettes, cigars, and crack, with undertones of piss. "PUSSY" is scrawled in permanent marker in multiple places on the peeling wood veneer. Halfway down the hall, two long-haired guys stand by a pay phone with no receiver. I ask if they know which room is Henry's.

"Who the fuck's Henry?" says the short, husky guy with a shark's tooth necklace.

"Forty, maybe fifty, tall, skinny guy."

"Oh, *Big Bird*. Yeah, his room's, uh, last on the right. No. Left. Second to last."

The hallway seems to get narrower, like the entrance to Willy Wonka's factory. The last door on the left is open. Henry is sitting on a twin bed, a can of Miller Light between his legs.

"Henry? *Henry?* Hennnnn-reeeeeeeeeeee."

Henry squints in my direction and waves me in. The smell of a pine tree–shaped car air freshener overwhelms the room, which is smaller than the smallest of the three closets in my childhood bedroom. A dark wood dresser has the same snowflake carvings and curved edges as the nightstand.

"Noon already?" Henry says. "Sorry, kid." He sweeps an old digital watch off the nightstand, looks at it with heavy eyes, and thwaps it against his leg. "Damn battery."

"Ready to go?"

"I can't do no more dope, kid. They're starting random drug tests at work."

He opens another beer and snickers as foam races over the lip and down the brown metal bed frame into a crack in the linoleum floor.

"How about one last hurrah before—"

"Kid, my ass is grass if they catch me."

My mind spinning, I turn and see beat-up paperbacks on a shelf. *Raise the Titanic. Dianetics. Tommyknockers. It.* Some spines have Dewey decimal numbers.

"What if I give you money instead of dope?"

"Kid . . ."

At the door, I almost stop and ask him to exchange phone numbers and addresses. But I don't know Henry's last name, and I'm pretty sure he doesn't remember my *first*.

When I reach Arianne and Roy's campsite, the tent is gone. A plastic shopping bag is stuck to a tree branch and flails in the breeze. The ground is littered with empty, crushed packs of generic cigarettes. Fuck.

Back on the trail, I follow the loop and yell out, "ARIANNE? ROY? AIRY-AAAAANNNNNE?"

I'm wearing shorts, a T-shirt, and Birkenstocks. The temperature cools as the sun starts to set. Ten more minutes and then I'll leave. An hour later, I'm still searching, my bloodied legs teeming with thorns and burrs. I can't hear cars. I don't see the trail.

Wandering aimlessly in the moonlight, I happen upon Roy passed out in a sleeping bag. I say his name and poke him with a stick until his eyes finally open. "Oh, hey, man." Sitting up, he stretches and takes a whiff of his armpit.

"Is Arianne around?"

"Bitch went back to her mom's house. Took the tent too."

"Are *you* up for a drive to Holyoke? I'll buy you a bag."

"Sheeeee-it, motherfucker. Does the Pope shit in the woods?"

Roy slides out of the sleeping bag and straps on his fanny pack. I take a step toward where I think the trail is. He laughs. "Nope. You wait here and keep an eye on my shit. Dealer's kinda skittish."

I reach into my pocket, peel a twenty-dollar bill off the wad, and hand it over.

"Won't be long," he says.

As he disappears into the dense, dark woods, I think he's not coming back. I think I knew that when I found him. I think I found him so I'd get ripped off and be forced to kick, the cherry on top of a shit sundae.

Sitting on the ground with my back against a tree, I pull my arms through my sleeves, stretch my shirt over my knees, and make a mental list of supplies for a kick. Orange juice. Nestle's Crunch bars. Vanilla ice cream. NyQuil. Hopefully the diphenhydramine knocks me out and I sleep through the worst.

Flies and gnats swarm my face, and mosquitoes feast on my ankles. All this is happening because of screenplay stress. I picture myself telling Jane my laptop crashed. In a fit of rage, I'll throw it out the window. No one will know the script never existed.

I'm about to go home when a flashlight shines in the distance. Leaves rustle. Roy appears and takes a bow.

"Ta-da. Didn't think I'd come back, did you?"

"Pffft, I trust you."

My bag, individually sealed in plastic, is stamped "Bubonic Plague." As we fix our shots, Roy brags about his God-given gift for stealing syringes from pharmacies. "You give the lady behind the counter a sob story about your diabetic grandma and they hand 'em over. Then alls you do is walk straight the fuck out without paying."

I'm high before Roy removes his sneaker, a filthy New Balance with the sole flapping off, and stabs the syringe into a vein on his foot.

"Shit, man," he says. "The fuck're my manners?" He pulls two rubbing alcohol wet naps from his fanny pack and extends his hand. I take one and wipe the inside of my elbow.

Roy pats his neck and gushes about the cooling power of rubbing alcohol. "Some spic told me about this shit on the golf course."

"You're a golfer?"

"What? Fuckin'. Man, I'm a goddamn caddy. I look like a stuck-up, golf-playing Jew bastard to you? You see horns coming out my head?"

The next morning, I return to the woods in the rain. Roy is standing on a rock, holding a garbage bag over his head and sucking his tongue and cheeks.

"You want to score?"

"Pope shit in the woods?"

We drive into town. I give Roy $200, and he drops his hands below the dashboard, fans the bills, and counts them aloud four times. "Okay, boss," he says. "Back in twenty."

OK Computer plays from start to finish before Roy jumps into the car, out of breath. "This shit's the fuckin' shiznit." He tosses me two bundles of bags stamped "In Cold Blood."

Reaching into his fanny pack, he takes out five blackened stems. "Yep, Roy hooked your ass the fuck *uuuuup.*" He bites open a small clear plastic bag of crack, loads a stem, heats it, and starts puffing.

"Would the dealer sell five or six bundles at once? I want to load up before I go back to school."

"Man, shit. This ain't commemorative coins from the Franklin fuckin' Mint, man."

Dave and Ana's wedding is in five days, and I have half a bag, no screenplay, and a date to meet Roy in town in a few hours for the big buy. I pace around the apartment while Jane is in the kitchen, shuffling through index cards. Without looking up, she says I seem stressed.

"It's the script. I wish I had more time."

"You're such a perfectionist. I'm sure it's great as is."

I open and close drawers and cabinets in the kitchen and slip a spoon in my pocket. I tell Jane I'm going to take a shower. I turn on the water and push the door until it makes a clicking sound.

As the water heats, I undress and stare at myself in the mirror until the steam obscures my reflection. Then I step into the tub and prep the shot on the edge. I load the chamber and lean out and shove the bag and spoon into my jeans pocket. I make a fist. The vein won't pop. It's there, beneath my skin, taunting me.

I pull my belt off my jeans, loop it around my arm, and hold the end with my teeth. The needle goes in smoothly once the vein is ready for business. I push the register. Blood seeps out. I bend my elbow, raise it to my mouth, and lick it.

Jane knocks. "Housekeeping," she says, in a Scottish accent.

I silently lower the belt to the rug and say "Come in" in a Scottish accent.

The door opens. "I'm so stressed out," Jane says. "I have so much work to do if I'm going to graduate in December." I watch her shadow move across the creamy white shower curtain. After a long pause, she says, "I'm so jealous of you, the way you put your mind to something and it always works out."

Blood drips down my arm onto the shower floor. I kick it into the drain.

"I'm starting to think you're a robot," she says. "If I pull this curtain back, am I going to see a bunch of metal and wires?"

Scalding hot water pelts my body, frozen with fear as Jane's fingers creep around the flimsy piece of nylon separating her—and me—from the truth. I press the needle against a shampoo bottle and close my eyes. With a sigh, she lets go of the curtain and leaves.

"Might take a little longer 'n usual, boss," Roy says. He's uncharacteristically jovial, which makes me nervous. I slip $500 in twenties and fifties into his hand and think I might have a heart attack when he tucks the cash into his pocket without counting it.

"So this is it, huh?" he says. "Last call?"

"Whaaaat?"

"You said you was going back to school. You're quits."

"I'm not . . . School's less than an hour away. I'm stockpiling in case I can't get back here so fast. I told you, remember?"

Roy wags his tongue from side to side. He knows I'm lying. He's going to rip me off. I never said I was coming back. I should have. Fuck.

"Aw, man. Shit," he finally says, knocking on his head. "You know what? Fuckin', you did say that fuckin' shit, didn't you?" He starts toward Pleasant Street and turns the corner.

Three hours later, no Roy. I go home empty-handed.

twenty-four

The feeling is at once familiar and foreign: an electric current coursing through my body as an army of ants march up and down my spine. It intensifies until dawn, when my legs start twitching uncontrollably and I'm drenched in sweat and freezing cold, sitting on the toilet with my head in a plastic trash bin, a miasmic stew of shit and piss and puke. On top of the putrid stench, a certain odor seeps from my pores. Impossible to describe, though not necessarily awful. I've smelled this way only during withdrawal.

The air is a frozen razor, slicing my tight, wet skin. I'm exhausted but I can't sleep. More ants. More electrocutions. *Zap.* My arms and twitching legs are tied to four horses walking slowly in opposing directions. *Zap.* Muscle spasms. *Zap.* My skin burns and stings. *Zap.* Legs twitch. *Zap.* It hurts when I move and it hurts when I don't. *Zap. Take that, motherfucker. And that. ZAP!*

My eyes finally close. They open when something warm and moist grazes my forehead. Jane is kissing me. How long was I asleep?

"Oh. My. God. Baby, you're so sweaty. We need to get you to the hospital. This is worse than when you got sick from sushi."

It takes me a moment to remember—a month or so ago, when I spent most of the day in the bathroom, blaming the sushi place for the diarrhea I pretended to have when I was constipated—the only time anyone ever lied about *having* diarrhea.

"Can I get you something?"

"NyQuil."

Jane turns on the TV and leaves. I see the remote, but I can't move. The sun is burning holes into my retinas while I'm stuck watching a Don Lapre infomercial. A smiley middle-aged couple in a McMansion brag about the money they're making.

"All we did was place tiny ads in local newspapers, and now we're getting checks for twelve hundred, six hundred, thirty-two hundred—thanks to Don Lapre's proven money-making system that you, too, can take advantage of right now by calling the toll-free number at the bottom of your screen."

Jane returns with NyQuil liquid capsules and ginger ale and straws. While she's in the kitchen, I free six pills from plastic tamper-resistant cells and pop them into my mouth and bite. The diphenhydramine-infused menthol goo drips down my throat.

"I thought you'd want a red straw," she says, guiding it to my mouth. "I would have stirred out the bubbles like my mom used to when I had a tummy ache, but I can't find any of our spoons. Have you seen them?"

I shake my head.

"They were my grandmother's."

I can't imagine hating myself more, wrapped in blankets heavier than concrete, curled up in the fetal position, and Jane sitting next to me, stroking my wet hair.

"Do you want to be watching Don Lapre?"

I grunt.

Jane channel surfs to *Awakenings*. Robert De Niro is ostensibly lifeless until Robin Williams shows up with the *special sauce*. Once De Niro awakens, Williams administers it to other patients. Everyone rejoices—doctors, patients, families—until we learn the special sauce isn't a permanent solution. Then it's a tearjerker as the collective faces the prospect of returning to the way things were.

Bags and boxes fill the living room. I close my eyes. When they open, most of the boxes are gone. Jane stands by the window, glistening with sweat in a loose white V-neck, an angel in the sun.

"You can't go to the wedding in this shape."

"I'll be better by Saturday."

"It *is* Saturday."

Jane helps me down the stairs and into the car. Every bump and turn is a sledgehammer to my head and my stomach. I look for Roy until the

I-91 entrance ramp. Then I close my eyes and make a silent plea to the universe. *Please, let me get through this and I'll never go near heroin again. Please help me. Save me. Take care of me. Make this all go away. I know I don't deserve it, but please get me out of this fucking hole.*

This semester—our last before graduating—Jane and I are sharing a cottage on campus with a couple of friends. When we arrive, I drag myself into the shower and crank the heat. I cough up gobs of yellow goo as the small rectangular enclosure fills with steam and water blazes toxic sweat from my body. For the first time in who knows how long, I wash my hair and lather my entire body with soap—even the spaces between my toes.

I reach for a towel and wrap it around my waist. I don't know whose it is—white with parrots in black motorcycle jackets. They're holding cans of Coors Light, except the one in the middle, whose wing is extended like a hand and he's giving you the finger. On the bottom: "Tap the Rockies and give them the bird."

My seersucker suit looks surprisingly respectable after a summer in a duffel bag. I ease my body into it, put on my wing tips, and check myself out in the full-length mirror on the back of the door. No, not the image I want to project. I take off the wing tips and put on my slightly dirty white Rod Lavers with green trim and red shoelaces. Perfect—serious and funny. Ingmar Bergman and Groucho Marx. *Woody Allen.*

I tell myself to remember to stand up straight and make eye contact. I hear Apollo Creed from the Rocky movies: "You can do this, champ. You're the champ, champ. Eye of the tiger, baby. Eye of the tiger." I throw punches in the mirror, hum-singing "Eye of the Tiger." Bamp. Bamp bamp bamp. Bamp bamp boom. Bamp. Boop. Pooka chocka, pooka chocka, pooka chocka. Risin' up. Deedle-dee-dee.

A string quartet plays Shostakovich at the top of the president's driveway while white-gloved waiters in tuxedos crisscross the lawn with silver platters, serving tall flutes of champagne and fancy hors d'oeuvres. On a small table near the bar, I find our names among all the place cards. We're table 2. I spot Letty's card and flip it open. Table 2.

When the musicians segue into Pachelbel's Canon, Jane and I file to the end of the second row on the groom's side and sit in folding wooden chairs with an unobstructed view of all twelve guests on the bride's side. Not knowing what Letty looks like, I scan the faces, and my heart sinks. She isn't here. Unless she's in her twenties.

A few minutes later, Dave and Ana are pronounced husband and wife, and they kiss to applause. I wait close to ten minutes for a Coke at the bar and then join Jane at our table as a waitress serves an *amuse-bouche* of corn chowder in a white ceramic spoon. The smell makes me sick. Across the table, a couple complain about the traffic in Hartford.

"We almost didn't make it," the man says.

"So much rubbernecking," the woman says. "Why don't people just keep going?"

"People rubberneck because they want to see a fatality," I say.

Jane smiles and squeezes my thigh under the table.

I lean over and whisper, "I'm nervous."

She whispers back, "I know. You're a rock star." She kisses my cheek.

Salad is served on chilled plates with three-tined forks. I nudge Jane. She knows they've been a bad omen ever since my father's second wife moved in and replaced his perfectly serviceable silverware with a set containing three-tined forks. Nice enough woman, but I preferred Dad's original forks—and wife.

Between courses, as the first few brave couples take to the dance floor, I get up and look for a heads-up penny to cancel the negative implications of the forks. I don't find any and return to the table.

"Letty isn't coming."

"Relax."

"She's not. You saw the salad forks, and there weren't any pennies on—"

"There's no God. The universe is run by forks and pennies."

"You make me sound crazy when you say it that way."

Through the shrubbery, I watch cars come up South Road. Letty doesn't drive a Hyundai hatchback or a rusted-out Subaru station wagon. The sun dips behind the mountain. Busboys scurry around, replacing salad plates with clean chargers and fresh sets of silverware.

Jane pokes my arm with her new fork. "Four tines."

An older couple arrives, white, possibly Jewish. Dave and Ana walk them to us. Ana looks at me. "David, Jane, Peter, and Susan, please allow me to introduce two very special people who drove a long way to be with us. Ted and Lenore, Dave's aunt and uncle from Virginia."

Fuck Ted and fuck Lenore. Fuck them and all of Virginia in its stupid fucking ass.

Eyeing the empty seats, Ana says, "Hmm. Letty and Sid aren't here yet?"

"Maybe they're stuck in Hartford," Susan says.

"Hartford." Lenore moans.

So begins another round of "why was there so much traffic in fucking Hartford?"

I lean toward Jane and open my mouth. She drills the tip of her index finger into my thigh. "She'll be here," she says through gritted teeth.

Dinner is served. Ted and Lenore and Peter and Susan and Jane have orgasms over the delicious halibut. I stare at the plates next to me—rapidly cooling slabs of fish with diagonal grill marks. I make a deal with myself to leave after the next song.

I force a few coughs as a preamble. "I'm starting to feel sick again."

Jane sighs. Balling up my napkin, I rise to my feet, but then I sit back down as a shiny black Mercedes sedan coasts into the driveway. An older couple emerges. The woman has short, reddish hair. Ana runs over and escorts them to the table.

"David, Jane, Peter, Susan, Ted, and Lenore, please meet Sid and Letty Aronson."

Sid plays the Hartford traffic game with Ted, Peter, and Susan. Letty sits next to me. My heart sinks when she asks how I know the bride and groom. Ana didn't say shit about me. I take a deep breath. "I'm sorry if this is uncouth, but it's an amazing coincidence to meet you since I've had a correspondence with your brother."

"Woody?"

"Jane and I saw his band at the Carlyle last year. I slipped him a note."

"You slipped Woody a note and he wrote back? You must have a real way with words. My brother does *not* respond to fan mail."

"We've been going back and forth for a while. He sent me his copy of the *Deconstructing Harry* script."

I'm kind of on autopilot, not really aware of what I'm saying as the conversation gets deep and eclectic in a hurry. Movies. Books. Art. Philosophy.

Judaism as a cultural phenomenon versus religion. Letty props her elbow on the table and her chin on her fist. She maintains eye contact throughout.

Toasts are made, and the cake is cut and served. As the band transitions to down-tempo instrumentals, Letty and I keep talking. She says Sid is a high school principal. They're interested in Marlboro's unconventional approach to education. I explain that the Plan of Concentration is an undergrad version of a graduate-level thesis.

"Mine is on existentialism in Woody Allen and Ingmar Bergman films. It includes an essay relating Sartre, Kierkegaard, and Nietzsche to the filmmakers, along with a few short films I wrote, directed, and edited and an original screenplay."

Letty nudges Sid and leans in close. "Tell me about your movie."

The projector in my mind flickers on. A black-and-white shot of a young man, my age, from behind, sitting on the front steps of an old house by a lake. Light snow falls from the sky. The story goes from my head to my lips before I can think.

"A young man writes a best-selling novel and then has a nervous breakdown. While he recovers, he tries to repair the relationship with his estranged father."

"Very Bergman," Letty says, nodding at Sid, who also nods.

"Two parallel arcs weave in and out. One goes forward, the other goes backward, but you don't know that until the movie's over. The last shot is the same as the first except you see the guy from the front and realize he froze to death, waiting outside his father's house all night. The audience has to decide what was real and what was a hallucination brought on by hypothermia. That's the title."

Letty says "hypothermia" slowly, enunciating each syllable. "I'd love to read it. If you're comfortable."

Eyes bugging out, I nod like a maniac. Letty writes on her place card— a phone number and address on Fifty-Seventh Street in Manhattan: Jean Doumanian Productions.

"We've been talking about finding young, up-and-coming writer-directors to make art-house films on shoestring budgets," she says. "This is really very serendipitous."

My body warms when Letty passes the card to me. I breathe. I can breathe.

After the wedding, when everyone in the cottage is asleep, I walk up the hill to the editing room with my laptop, and I write. The words flow so fast that my fingers can barely keep up. I write for almost twenty hours straight.

On Monday morning, I print the file, tuck it into a manila envelope, and write "David Poses" above the return address. Letty calls on Wednesday.

"I was delighted to see your script in this morning's mail. I'll read it this weekend and give you a call on Monday."

part three

1999

twenty-five

'm at the top of a ladder, two rungs above the one with the red line and the warning "DO NOT CLIMB HIGHER THAN RED LINE." The soundstage is an inferno. Heat rises.

When Trevor, the producer and director, calls "Action," I pour a bucket of confetti into an industrial fan above a fake fuselage. Then I remain still as Carson Daly ad-libs with mannequins standing in for celebrities.

"Madonna—may I call you Madge? Great. What's that? You're pumped to ring in the new millennium on MTV, on this private jet, in every time zone? Me too. Me. Too."

"Cut," Trevor says, and I shimmy down the ladder, pick confetti out of the rug, and return to my perch. I don't know how many times I've executed this Sisyphean task since we started shooting at seven-thirty. Ten hours later, we still haven't taken a break, but every fly on the set has sampled and shat on the nachos and wings and chicken flautas on the craft services table.

"Yo, T," Carson shouts, "some mango would be the bomb."

Trevor snaps his fingers at Annie, a production assistant on the ladder to my left. "The Talent wants mango," he says. She hustles down and out of the building and returns ten minutes later with a plastic flower-shaped platter of freshly sliced mango.

The Talent samples the offering and proclaims it "bomb-ass." He licks his fingers, says "I'm gone and this place is history," and takes off.

The rest of us stay and shoot B-roll footage until midnight, when Trevor notices some confetti in the carpet. "People," he says, "okay, people. Might

I remind you of the million film school grads who'd literally kill to work on my set. If you want to make it in this business, it takes more than hopes and dreams."

He's right. I found that out twenty-six Mondays ago, when Letty didn't call. Two more silent Mondays passed before I tried to contact her. Crickets. Ditto for Woody and Lauren. Fine.

Since graduating in December, Jane and I have been living at my aunt Jo's apartment in Midtown. Jo is in Florida on a long-term work assignment. Her cats stayed behind, shedding enough hair on any given day to make half a dozen new cats.

Jane gets up from the couch. "Hey, Poses," she says, "you're looking kinda slim. I brought food home from work."

Every refugee resettlement agency in the city wants to hire her. None have funding to offer her a job, so she's working as a hostess at an upscale Chinese restaurant. She sticks the *Village Voice* in my face and points to an apartment listing surrounded by red stars.

"Brooklyn Heights studio near the Promenade. You said you love it there."

I say a lot of things. That doesn't mean they're true. And on the emotional spectrum, the closest I get to love lately is tolerance, and even that might be a stretch. *Anhedonia*. Nothing is pleasurable. Anticipation and retrospection beat the moment every time.

Last month, I couldn't wait for a Radiohead concert. When the first notes rang out, I couldn't wait for it to be over. I couldn't just be. I can't just be. Not long after the show, while working as a temp receptionist at an accounting firm in midtown, I read an article in a psychology magazine about the ways opioids permanently change your brain chemistry. It said something to the effect that every time you put dope in your body, your receptors multiply to accommodate the flood of dopamine and serotonin, so the more and longer you use, the bigger the field you have to saturate to feel "even."

In other words, I was miserable before dope, and that's the happiest I'll ever be.

My so-called disease, in remission since Northampton, is no less ravenous. I light a cigarette and open the window. Leaning into the freezing air, ten stories above the sidewalk, I spit and watch my saliva come apart—a straight shot down between the balconies. From this height: quadriplegia or death? Head-first would be a challenge. I never learned how to dive properly. Jumping out a window isn't the answer. It's too tough to make it appear accidental.

Maybe tomorrow I'll get hit by a bus or be pushed in front of a subway. Pianos and safes and anvils fall from pulleys in cartoons—why not in real life? Are there random acts of cyanide poisoning? Why am I so nonchalant about life and death? Why is "nonchalant" a word but "chalant" isn't?

I call it elevator roulette. Waiting in the hall before the bank of elevators, I press the down button, my back to a floor-to-ceiling window overlooking Manhattan. The leftmost door opens. The elevator is full. I pat my pockets, turn, and mutter, "It's in the apartment."

What percentage of the building's upper-floor population thinks I leave something in the apartment every morning?

Outside, a vague hint of early spring is stifled by bus exhaust and subway fumes rising from grates in the sidewalk. I descend the steps to the Thirty-Third Street station. On the platform, commuters jockey for a position. A female voice crackling out of a loudspeaker is too muffled to understand.

I think about Chessa and her new husband in Kansas. She told me about him in a letter she sent to my mother's address in December. It was on my bed when I came home after graduation. I still haven't responded.

A packed train pulls in. Nobody makes an effort to get on during the brief, awkward moment when the doors open and some passengers look out, somewhat apologetically. On the other side of the tracks, a Tylenol PM poster gives me an idea.

LETHAL SMOOTHIE FOR ONE
Ingredients:
   Tylenol PM—1 fuckload (approx.)
   Vanilla ice cream—¼ pint
Directions:
   Combine Tylenol and ice cream in blender. Mix to desired
   consistency. Pour concoction into a plastic cup. Clean blender
   thoroughly. Discard all evidence in public trash receptacles.

Consume beverage in a subway station and discard cup.

Board a train, find a seat, fall asleep.

When my mother's face appears in my mind's eye, I know I won't do it. The day I stop caring about the pain my death will inflict is the day I die—unless I get lucky and something kills me first.

Every five minutes for an hour, Trevor says, "The Talent will be here in five minutes." He gets a phone call at nine-thirty and announces a slight change of plans. "People, okay, people. We'll shoot on Saturday instead of today."

The crew groans in unison.

"I don't know why you're complaining, people. This is literally the most gorgeous day ever, so take a hike. Scat. Scram. *Vamanos. Au revoir. Arrivederci. Auf Wiedersehen.*"

I'm on the loading dock smoking a cigarette with most of the crew when Trevor leaves in a chauffeured Town Car.

Annie waves. "Bye," she says through a smile. "You condescending prick."

"I hate to make generalizations," I say, "but every Trevor's a condescending prick."

"I hate how he says literally: 'litch-ruh-lee.' And he says it a hundred times a day."

"And it's an adverb that, literally, means without exaggeration. But he only uses 'literally' hyperbolically, figuratively."

Annie laughs, guttural and sincere. Waifishly thin, with medium-length brown hair, she stuffs a cigarette in her mouth and leans over. "Hey, cowboy, got a light?"

I take out Herbie's old Zippo, spin the wheel, and hold the flame to her Marlboro. She cranes her neck and blows smoke toward the sky and waves it away.

Geoff, a production assistant who is very particular about everyone knowing his name doesn't start with "J," drapes an arm around Annie's shoulders.

At the other end of the loading dock, Will, also a production assistant,

sucks on a Newport like it owes him money and complains about the recent seismic shift in New York City's drug-dealing paradigm.

"Fuckin' Giuliani made the city too clean. And the beepers and cell
phones. It used to be you go to shitty neighborhoods to buy weed from
shady individuals. Now, they come to you—if you know how to get in
touch with them."

"I have a guy," Geoff says.

"Not that asshole from the mp3 website?" Annie says.

"Fuck that. He only had fucking *heroin*."

I drop my cigarette and run to the subway. Over the past few months,
I've downloaded thousands of albums from hundreds of mp3 websites.
They're all bookmarked on my laptop.

When the train stops at Thirty-Third Street, my feet refuse to move. I
ride to Eighty-Sixth Street and wander into Barnes and Noble, to a display
table in the fiction section: "Books about Armageddon."

Scanning the titles the way a froufrou woman looks at designer purses,
I wonder how I'd be perceived with Nevil Shute's *On the Beach* in hand or
The Drowned World by J. G. Ballard. I pick up *Cat's Cradle* by Kurt Von-
negut. The chapters are short.

One of my favorite lines is from Vonnegut's novel *Mother Night*: "We
are what we pretend to be, so we must be careful about what we pretend
to be." Keith Gordon directed the film. He played Rodney Dangerfield's
son in *Back to School*. Vonnegut had a cameo.

I park myself in an overstuffed, coffee-stained chair and start reading. I read and read and read. Save for a few smoke breaks, I devour the
book in one sitting. In *Cat's Cradle*, Vonnegut writes about a made-up
religion—Bokononism:

We Bokononists believe that humanity is organized into teams that
do God's Will without ever discovering what they are doing. Such
a team is called a *karass* by Bokonon . . .

"If you find your life tangled up with somebody else's life for
no very logical reasons," writes Bokonon, "that person may be a
member of your karass."

. . . The first sentence in *The Books of Bokonon* is this:

"All of the true things I am about to tell you are shameless lies."

My Bokononist warning is this:

Anyone unable to understand how a useful religion can be founded on lies will not understand this book either.

So be it.

Late in the afternoon, I leave the store, somewhat disoriented—similar to going to a matinee that ends when it's light outside.

Under a streaky orange sky with polluted, pale pink cotton candy clouds, I feel the presence of a force. Not some dude with a beard in a robe. A well-intentioned, precisely timed blowing of wind at my sails. The Talent didn't show up and Trevor would dismiss us. I'd hear about a heroin dealer on-line, resist temptation, and read *Cat's Cradle*, which, for all I know, Kurt Vonnegut wrote to keep me clean.

When I return to Jo's apartment, the first thing I see is Sunday's *New York Times* Help Wanted section on the table by the door. My eye is drawn to a big ad for an advertising headhunter. Get paid to make shit up? I call the number in the listing. A woman with a Long Island accent and a gravely, five-packs-of-cigarettes-a-day-for-two-hundred-years voice answers.

"Stella Weintraub and Associates. How may I help you?"

"I need to make an appointment as soon as possible."

"Hon, I got *bupkes* till the middle of next month. You want morning or afternoon?"

As I try to decide between morning, afternoon, or fuck this—maybe I read the sign wrong—the receptionist says, "Whoa. Beep beep beep. Back up. Today must be your lucky day. I just got a cancellation, first thing to-morrow. Can you be here at nine?"

I take the appointment and turn on the stereo and connect my laptop. I dance in the living room to Eurythmics' "Love Is a Stranger."

Jane comes home. I tell her about the incredible stroke of good fortune.

"This is what I mean about your magical abilities," she says. "The big-gest headhunter in the city happened to get a cancellation for the next pos-sible appointment at the exact moment you called? You think that happens for everybody?"

We roll scotch tape around our fingers and remove cat hair from my nice pants and blazer. I try them on and like what I see in the mirror.

Normal. Normal people get real jobs and dream of getting a house with a picket fence, not of being impaled by a fence picket.

Jane gets in bed. "You're looking mighty cute in that suit." She pats the covers. "But why don't you take it off and let's go to beddy-bye."

Kissing leads to touching leads to sex. It feels good and familiar. I stay hard until the finish line. Afterward, breathing heavy, Jane says, "You should read more Vonnegut."

A framed faded print of Van Gogh's *Sunflowers* from an '80s exhibit at the Met hangs on a beige wall. The paint is peeling. Mountains of folders rise from the floor—some with coffee cups at the summit, mauve lipstick on the rim. There doesn't seem to be a corollary between the size of the help-wanted ad and the size of the office. I'm not sure who the "Associates" are in Stella Weintraub and Associates, but I know who answered the phone last night.

In smoky Long Islandese, Stella says, "Take a seat, hon." She taps my resume with a chewed-up pencil and reads it aloud.

"Nightclub promoter in high school? Dual majors? Film *and* philosophy?"

I make an aw-shucks face.

An old-fashioned radiator gurgles. Stella tells it to "shut up. Mama's in an interview." She swivels in her chair and clasps her hands together.

"You graduate. You temp for a while, but when you get the call from MTV, it's a no-brainer. You're thinking, *This is it. Look out world. Here comes David.*"

"Basically."

"But now you're here."

"Uh, yes."

"S'okay. Seen this movie before. How many headhunters you met with?"

"You're the first."

"Swear to God?"

"Cross my heart and hope to die."

"Dating anyone? Girlfriend? Boyfriend?"

"Girlfriend. Jane."

"So while you're running around like a chicken with his head cut off, Jane figures out that if you divide your pay by the hours you're working, it's *bupkes*. One day she says, 'I've had it up to here with this cockamamie horse manure. I want to settle down and make babies, so get a real job or else.' You call Stella. Am I right or what?"

"She didn't say 'manure' but—have you been spying on us?"

Stella peers at me over her glasses and lowers her voice to a near-whisper. "Let me tell you this—99.99999 percent of the people I place are artsy-fartsy types. They work in movies and TV for years before they realize artsy gets you nowhere and fartsy pays the bills. But you graduated three months ago, and already you figured it out."

I think that was meant as a compliment.

"What about computer proficiency? You're proficient, right?"

"Totally."

Stella lists hardware and software. I claim to have "extensive experience" with everything, including QuarkXpress, which I've never heard of.

"You're a likable guy. You know that? You know you're a likable guy?"

"My mom says I'm handsome too."

"Mom also tell you you're a little bit of a wiseass?"

Stella pulls a card from her Rolodex. "You'll fit in great at Saatchi. You'll love it. Downtown. Young. Fresh. Hip. And entry-level positions don't open up there every day." She says to stand up and twirls her fingers. I do the same with my body.

"Eh—what's with the—don't have a blazer with matching slacks?"

"I spilled coffee on them."

Stella tilts her head from side to side and returns to the Rolodex. "You know what—you're more of an Ammirati guy. You'll like it better there. Uptown. Established. Sophisticated. Great client roster."

Twenty minutes later, I'm in the Ammirati Puris Lintas lobby, sitting on a low black leather sofa with chrome fixtures. On a matching sofa across from me, two girls whisper about interviews they've had at other ad agencies, referring to them as "safeties" and "reaches" the way high school seniors talk about colleges. I stare at the floor. Carrara marble. Why do I know that?

A woman in a gray suit steps off the elevator and goes for the blond girl, who rises with impeccable posture and makes eye contact while shaking hands. On the way to the elevator, she backhands lint off her skirt and mouths *Good luck* to the other girl.

Another woman in a gray suit comes at me. "Kara," she says, extending her hand. I grab it awkwardly, the knuckle of her ring finger and pinky—the way a serf greets the queen.

In the elevator, she asks, "Is it warmer than when I left my apartment this morning?"

"Probably—if your apartment's in Saskatoon."

"Ha! Stella said you were funny."

In a large conference room, the firm's work is plastered on the walls. BMW, Burger King, Club Med, UPS, GMC, Four Seasons, Iridium. Sitting across from me at a long table, Kara explains the position I'm applying for.

"We call it a floater," she says. "The person supports all the creatives, designers, copywriters, producers—all that jazz." She breezes through the benefits: paid sick and personal days, bereavement time, maternity leave, stock options, 401(k) with match, medical and dental coverage, life insurance. "If you work past 6 p.m., the company pays for dinner. If you work past 7, you'll get dinner and a cab home. After 9, it's dinner plus a car service."

"Wow." I hope my enthusiasm is believable.

Kara glances at my resume. "I went to Tunnel once," she says, the way you'd name a restaurant that gave you food poisoning. "I saw Michael Alig there. Before he got arrested for killing that guy, obviously. You didn't have to work with him, did you?"

"Never met him," I lie.

"Thank God."

"I never actually went to the clubs. My job was advertising."

"Come on, you didn't want to party with the Club Kids every night?"

"Do you want to eat Burger King every day?"

"Touché."

After the interview, I imagine the conversation between Stella and Kara.

"Did I tell you or did I tell you? The worst candidate I've ever met in my whole entire life, ever, period. End of story."

"He totally lied to me. 'Never went to the clubs.' There are pictures of him in the clubs in magazines and newspapers and that book."

At Jo's apartment, the light on the answering machine is blinking.

"Hi David, this is Kara from Ammirati. We'd love for you to join our team."

I call back and accept the offer.

twenty-six

Jane and I sign a lease on an apartment in Carroll Gardens, Brooklyn. It has a terrace and views of the Statue of Liberty. I use the remaining funds in my Smith Barney account to cover the first month, last month, security, and realtor's fee.

Our historically Italian neighborhood has a small-town feel: brownstones and row houses with impeccably manicured lawns on tree-lined streets. "Coming soon" signs hang in the empty storefront windows on Clinton Street. We're getting a bike shop, a bookstore, and various eateries. On Henry Street, between a bakery-café and an Italian "social club," a new gourmet food store offers an impressive selection of meats and cheeses.

The vibe changes on Smith Street, where a Mediterranean restaurant is the only business amid blocks of abandoned, commercially zoned nineteenth-century buildings.

My mom takes us shopping for furniture, kitchenware, and other essentials. In Fish's Eddy, she recalls the time when she was nine years old and my grandfather drove her across the Brooklyn Bridge, just because. "You remind me so much of him," she says, blotting her eye with a tissue. "So smart, so talented, so capable."

Jane gets a job at a refugee resettlement agency in Brooklyn. Combined, our monthly pay will just about cover overhead. We open a joint checking account, and I volunteer to manage our finances—paying the bills and balancing the checkbook.

We move into the apartment before any of the furniture is delivered.

On the first night, we have sex on the bedroom floor. It feels good for half a second. Then I get soft and slide out in defeat.

"Sorry."

"Oh, baby, it's okay. Don't worry."

At three in the morning, I'm huddled in the corner, swollen with regret, watching Jane sleep. Sticky snores drip from her open mouth. In the morning, she takes a shower and emerges from the bathroom, naked, drying her hair with a towel. She slides her arms into a peach-colored bra, fastens the strap, and makes coffee in a *jezba*—a small, hammered copper pot, given to her by someone in Bosnia. Looking at the view of New York harbor from the living room, she blows into her mug of strange-smelling coffee.

"Well," she says. "This is where our life begins. Right here, right now." She sighs and, under her breath, says again, "Right here, right now."

Kara meets me in the lobby. "Hope you enjoyed your last days of freedom," she says, laughing. She takes me to a conference room and introduces me to Bill, a junior art director who started as a floater last year, and Patrick, a senior creative manager.

"Technically," Bill says, "you report to Loretta. She's out today. But actually, the entire creative team is your boss. Don't let that intimidate you—everyone hovering over you. Think of a floater as being at a buffet."

"No, no," Patrick says, shaking his head. "'Floater' is a metaphor for 'a piece of shit.'"

I want to say, "If I'm a piece of shit, then the creatives hovering over me are assholes, which makes the entire agency a toilet. So fuck you." Instead, I smile.

Bill takes me on a tour, running through taglines in the elevator. BMW's "Ultimate driving machine," Club Med's "Antidote for civilization," GMC's "Do one thing, do it well."

"They're all Martin's," he says.

On the thirty-eighth floor, Bill introduces me to Marge, a plump, middle-aged woman who sits in a double-wide cubicle across from a closed door with a placard: Martin Puris. She smells of grocery store sheet cake. Beanie Babies occupy the top of a file cabinet behind her. "Welcome aboard," she says with a warm smile.

As we walk away, Bill says, "You'll know you're doing something right if Kara asks you to fill in for Marge one day." He lowers his voice. "If you've been here six months and you haven't sat for Marge yet, start looking for another job."

Back in the elevator, we head for the fortieth floor. Even before the doors open, I can hear loud classic rock pumping out of the offices. Two foosball tables face a wall of windows with commanding views of Lower Manhattan. A mezzanine with a kitchen and a lounge connects to the floor below via staircase. Bill shows me to my desk in the hall by the elevator bank, across from a wall of offices.

My new bosses introduce themselves and give me things to do. Nobody asks. They say, "I'm going to *have you* . . ."

It doesn't take me long to learn how to scan in stock photos and mount storyboards. Photoshop is tougher, but no one seems to notice or care that I'm retouching images with a user manual in my lap. My bosses dictate lists of research materials (CDs and DVDs) and have me fetch them. They give me receipts and *have* me fill out expense reports. I go online for instructions on how to itemize hotel taxes and tip allocations at restaurants.

On Saturday, Mom calls. "How's your job? Great, right?"

"Uh-huh."

"It's nice to have one kid I don't have to worry about."

Mom recalls an incident some years earlier when Daniel refused to get out of the car in Greenwich and then yelled at us when we got back twenty minutes later.

"At fifteen, how did he not know how to unlock a car door from the inside?"

My recollection, which I don't tell her, is that Daniel chose to remain in the hot car because he didn't want the alarm to go off if he opened the door.

Mom asks for my phone number at work. On Monday morning at nine, she calls. "Still loving it?"

"Yeah," I say, with Jimmy Connors, fist-pumping, 1994 US Open enthusiasm.

"I hope you're remembering to stand up straight and make eye contact."

The next day, Mom calls again. It becomes a pattern—every weekday at nine.

"They know you're hot shit, right?"

"Uh-huh."

"I'm telling you—you're going to be running that place soon."

A relatively new client files for bankruptcy and terminates its contract with the agency, which, in turn, terminates every employee on the account. A parade of my newly unemployed, now-former, coworkers lug boxes of personal effects past my desk. Some speak in halfhearted idioms you'd hear at an AA meeting—"one door closes and another opens." Others talk of doing tequila shots.

Dan, a floater and aspiring graphic designer, says, "Mass shitcannings are common at ad agencies." He predicts another round in the near future. "It's always been my dream to be a stay-at-home wife, so if I get shitcanned, it'll be a sign for me and Jim to take things to the next level."

Bill urges me to put together a portfolio. "We work in teams of two," he says. "Decide if you want to be a copywriter or graphic designer. Then find a counterpart and start pumping out campaigns."

"Who and what am I making them for?"

"Anything. Doesn't have to be one of our clients. In fact, it shouldn't be. You want to think outside the box. Take risks and do the unexpected. But have fun with it. Unless you get to be creative director someday, this is the last time you'll call the shots."

I make a campaign for Ducati Motorcycles. Full-bleed images of heavily blurred roads to show the perspective from the bike. Each ad has a date and time in the middle of the page in a small serif font, along with marketing copy: "Life is a short, warm moment."

Amy, a floater and aspiring copywriter, stops at my desk and looks at my ads. "Who did the graphics."

"Me."

"Then who wrote the copy?"

"Me."

"We have rules for a reason," she says, her eyes bulging. "You can't design *and* write copy. And PS: when companies advertise something, they want it in the ad."

Patrick shuffles over. "Jeez, Amy. Who took a dump in *your* breakfast?" He flips through the ads and shouts "Bravo!" as Amy slinks away. He says she probably shat on your work to discourage me from showing it to others, so she could steal my idea. "Be careful, David. There isn't a person in this entire insidious industry who wouldn't kill their own mother for a three percent raise or a fancy title."

My face is buried in a pillow. For two minutes, the only sound is pounding flesh. No kissing or eye contact, no fondling. As I start to slide out, Jane grabs my ass and pulls me close.

"Stay," she says.

I force a yawn and say I'm tired. Then I lie perfectly still with my eyes closed, which makes my body more restless.

"David?"

I don't respond.

"Are you still attracted to me?"

I don't respond.

"Do you still love me?"

I sit up and tilt my head, putting a look on my face that says, "How could you possibly think I don't love you?" Jane's smile is unconvincing. My smile back is probably the same.

In the morning, she points to a stack of unopened bills on the kitchen counter. "Do you want me to take care of this stuff?"

"Not at all."

I bring the bills to work, and they sit on my desk for a few days. Then I throw them into a drawer.

From the bottom of the staircase, Herbie looks up as if he's at the base of Mount Everest. Nana says, "Come on, Herbert. Let's go see David's apartment."

He plants a hand on the banister and lets out a heavy breath, shifting his gaze to the floor. Jane and I walk up with Nana. In the apartment, she peers into every room and flashes an unimpressed grin. "Okay," she says, and heads for the door.

We drive to dinner at the Mediterranean place on Smith Street. Once his drink is served, Herbie gives me an envelope. "Get some furniture."

Nana tsks. "We should have seen the size of their place before you wrote that check."

"I said *some* furniture—and a decent set of clubs and a couple thousand golf balls."

"They don't play golf, Herbert."

"Then blow it on booze and whores for all I care. Whatever makes you happy."

A disapproving look from Nana when Herbie orders another drink. He takes a sip and leans close, reaching for my arm. "How's the writing going?"

"I haven't written anything in a while."

"Taking a corporate job doesn't mean you have to stop being an artist. When you have the soul of an artist, you always find a way to create."

After graduating from college with a degree in textile design, Herbie joined the army, then opened a supermarket with his twin brother, Ralph. When they retired, weeks before their fiftieth birthday, they had built the biggest chain of supermarkets in New York City at that time. My mom used to think he opened new stores because he saw the walls as giant canvases.

A waiter offers dessert menus. We decline. He says, "The calories won't matter if the Millennium Bug kills everyone on New Year's Eve." We decline again.

Nana brings up my aunt Cathy, my mother's brother's second wife. "Always a shrimp cocktail appetizer, tiramisu for dessert, and a cappuccino at the end. And the drinks." She glares at Herbie. "But she stopped drinking."

Nana asks if I'm still "being good"—as in "clean."

"Four years."

After dinner, my grandparents drive off, and Jane and I walk home.

"It's sweet how protective she is of you," she says. "She doesn't want him to drink in front of you so you won't be tempted."

"That's not it. My mom's told tons of stories about my great-grandmother stopping my great-grandfather from smoking cigars. Nana comes from a line of women who deprive their husbands of any vices."

"Still, she obviously thinks he has a drinking problem."

"He doesn't have a drinking problem."

"Doesn't he drink every day?"

"Yeah."

"Then he's an alcoholic."

"Alcoholics get belligerent and beat their wives and crash cars. He's not an—"

"But he drinks every day."

"It relaxes him. He's funnier after a few drinks. It makes him more himself."

"Don't you think that's sad—he can't be himself without alcohol?"

twenty-seven

Mom calls on Sunday morning. "You're on the front page of today's *New York Post*," she says. "Same picture they used in that nightclub book."

I grab Anthony Hayden-Guest's *The Last Party* off the bookshelf and flip to the photo taken at Tunnel when I was seventeen. I'm wearing Mom's leopard print tights, a Western string tie, my face slathered in makeup, a pile of powder on a flier on my lap.

Jane asks what's going on. I explain. She's seen the picture before.

"I wouldn't have known it was you," she says. "All that makeup and the outfit."

Mom says, "Remember when you showed up in that magazine and I called the photographer? I think I need to call him back and buy that negative. And this one."

"Those guys are pretty well-known."

"It's not about the money, David. I've had a horrible pit in my stomach all morning."

"Sorry."

"It's not your fault. It's . . . you remember what they told me in Hazelden."

"That was a long time ago."

Jane and I walk to the deli on Henry Street. Outside, a metal rack displays today's major newspapers. The *New York Post* headline reads, "Club Drug Blitz: Gatien Hotspot Faces Padlock after Cops Bust 'Ecstasy Supermarket.'"

Of all the pictures they could have used, why this? Why now? I grab every copy and go inside to pay. When I reach into my pocket for my money clip, the check from Herbie falls out. Ten thousand dollars.

At home, Jane lays the *Post* on the kitchen table and opens to the feature spread.

"They mention Michael Alig," she says. "That must've been crazy for you, being friends with—did you ever think he'd be a murderer?"

"Never."

"And you were really close, right? He was the one who gave you heroin the first time."

"That was Rob."

"I don't think I've heard that name before."

"He's probably dead."

"Why did I think Michael was a heroin addict?"

"Not when we met. He used to make fun of Rob and me for—"

"But then he got hooked?"

"A lot of people got hooked."

"So you and Rob got them addicted to heroin."

One bag. Maybe two. That's all.

At work, I spend the day scouring mp3 websites for the dealer Geoff mentioned. The next morning, I find a link to a Yahoo forum: *Opiates212: For Connoisseurs of Dope in the City.*

Hundreds of posts by hundreds of users, all referring to somebody named SWIM. SWIM is selling pot. SWIM is looking for heroin, Vicodin, Dilaudid. SWIM took a ton of Imodium because the active ingredient, loperamide, is an opiate receptor agonist. SWIM didn't get high, but it helped SWIM's PAWS. SWIM, I soon realize, is an acronym for somebody who isn't me. PAWS is post-acute withdrawal symptoms.

Scrolling down, I see a thread started by Chickenbone_77: "Can't find dope? SWIM knows a spot in Brooklyn." I set up a dummy email account on Yahoo and send a private message to Chickenbone_77 via the forum's internal mail feature. "I'm interested. I don't check my PMs often. Please reply to my Yahoo address."

For ten minutes, I refresh my Yahoo inbox incessantly. Then Kara comes by. "Congratulations," she says. "You're filling in for Marge today."

She walks me to Marge's desk and gives me a list of names and numbers and instructions for every conceivable request Martin could have, from coffee to private air travel. He strolls in fifteen minutes later and enters his office without acknowledging my existence.

Refresh refresh refresh refresh refresh refresh refresh refresh refresh refresh.

The intercom buzzes. "Get me Phil," Martin says.

The lone Phil on my cheat sheet is Geier, CEO of Interpublic, the publicly traded company that owns Ammirati Puris Lintas. I connect Martin with Phil and *refresh refresh.*

The intercom buzzes. "Turkey powerhouse."

According to the cheat sheet, this is a sandwich, attainable at the crappy restaurant in the lobby. I call in the order and tell the woman on the phone it's for Martin.

Refresh refresh.

I pick up the sandwich. How is the handoff supposed to go? Do I knock on Martin's door and give it to him? Buzz him and say, "Your turkey powerhouse is here?" Should I ask if he wants a plate and a napkin? Assume he does? Where are they?

Martin is in the hall when I step off the elevator, a disappointed look on his face as he snatches the sandwich neatly wrapped in wax paper. He pivots on his heel and sits on the couch in his office and inhales his lunch with the door open. I keep one eye on him and one on the computer screen.

Refresh refresh refresh refresh refresh refresh refresh refresh refresh.

Martin wipes his mouth with a cloth napkin, balls it up, and tosses it on the couch.

Refresh refresh refresh refresh refresh refresh refresh refresh refresh refresh.

Martin leaves his office with the *New York Times* under his arm. "I'm going to the washroom," he says.

Refresh refresh refresh refresh refresh refresh refresh refresh refresh refresh refresh refresh refresh refresh. I have to pee. *Refresh refresh refresh refresh refresh refresh refresh refresh refresh refresh.* I really have to pee. *Refresh*

refresh refresh refresh refresh refresh refresh refresh refresh refresh. I really, really have to pee. *Refresh refresh refresh refresh refresh.*

Martin returns. *Refresh refresh refresh.* I run to the washroom. On the way back, I see a gaggle of executive administrative assistants in the lounge, all eyes on the TV.

CNN is broadcasting live from a school in Colorado, where two students shot and killed a dozen of their classmates and then committed suicide. The screen is split between looped footage of the school's exterior and talking heads.

"Not only did the alleged attackers have guns—they had bombs too."

"They wore all black. They referred to themselves as the trench coat mafia."

"The massacre appears to have been meticulously planned over a period of months, as evidenced by information discovered in the alleged assailants' diaries."

The executive administrative assistants chatter.

"It's the parents' fault. How could they not know what their kids were planning?"

"It's society's fault. We're obsessed with violence."

"It's Marilyn Manson's fault. The shooters listened to that sick bastard's music."

"Marilyn Manson should be locked up."

A picture of two smiling boys appears on TV—it could be a Gap ad.

"The assailants have been identified as Dylan Klebold and Eric Harris."

An administrative assistant throws a crumpled tissue at the screen. She says, "I hope those vile creatures *and* their parents rot in hell for all eternity."

A lump forms in my throat. I go back to my desk and *refresh refresh refresh refresh refresh refresh refresh refresh refresh refresh refresh refresh refresh refresh refresh refresh.*

Intercom. "Decaf cappuccino."

I run to the coffee shop on the cheat sheet—on Second Avenue and Forty-Fourth Street. The news is on TV.

"Klebold and Harris are thought to have been drug abusers."

Hitting your wife is domestic *abuse.*

Unwelcome groping is sexual *abuse.*

Shooting dope to ease the pain of existence is drug *abuse*?

Martin peels the lid off the cup and gives a satisfied nod and retreats to his office.

Refresh refresh refresh refresh refresh refresh refresh refresh refresh refresh refresh refresh refresh refresh. Clap of thunder. *Refresh refresh refresh refresh refresh refresh refresh refresh refresh refresh refresh refresh.* Rain pelts the windows. Long, beaded strands come together and stretch across the tinted glass, a liquefied spider web.

Refresh re—

A new message appears from Chickenbone_77: "I can meet after work if you're still interested."

I reply, and we go back and forth via email, coordinating a 5:45 rendezvous outside the Bowling Green subway station.

I call Kara. "I'm so sorry. I need to leave early. My grandmother had a stroke."

"Oh, David, don't apologize. *I'm* sorry. Please—go be with your family."

twenty-eight

On the subway, I fixate on the possibilities. Chickenbone_77 could rob me and beat me within inches of my life. He could be a cop. Is this a sting? It'd be entrapment but I'd still be fucked. A million bad scenarios and only one good one.

The train stops at Bowling Green. Going through the turnstile, I see buckets of rain flooding into the station. When I get to street level, clouds part and a rainbow appears in the sky. Sharp, vivid colors. A perfect fucking rainbow arching over lower Manhattan. It's gone in ten seconds.

A guy in a crisp blue suit pauses on the sidewalk and looks me over. He's older but not by much. Thirty maybe. Close-cropped hair and clean-shaven. Carrying an umbrella with a Chase Manhattan Bank logo. A normal dude. Unremarkable.

"David?"

"Chickenbone_77?"

"Grant," he says, shaking my hand. On the train to Brooklyn, he describes himself as a functioning junkie. He has a good job on Wall Street as an analyst and occasional consultant for venture capitalists.

We talk about the racist catalysts for US drug laws—beginning in the 1870s, when a bunch of white dudes in San Francisco got opium smoking banned by complaining that white women were sleeping with Chinese men who owned the city's opium dens. Cocaine was outlawed in the 1920s—after newspaper articles described black men as "impervious to bullets" when on coke. Pot became illegal in the 1930s when Harry Anslinger, head of the newly created Federal Bureau of Narcotics, started referring to it as "marijuana" and associating it with Mexican immigrants. In propaganda, marijuana was said to cause insanity and was blamed for bizarre murders and sex crimes.

Grant pulls a tattered issue of *Harper's Magazine* from his backpack and reads a quote from an interview with John Ehrlichman, Nixon's counsel and Assistant to the President for Domestic Affairs. About the origins of the War on Drugs, Ehrlichman says:

> We knew we couldn't make it illegal to be either against the war or black, but by getting the public to associate the hippies with marijuana and blacks with heroin, and then criminalizing both heavily, we could disrupt those communities. We could arrest their leaders, raid their homes, break up their meetings, and vilify them night after night on the evening news. Did we know we were lying about the drugs? Of course we did.

On Myrtle Avenue in Bushwick, oil slick rainbows appear in lake-sized potholes. I follow Grant down a side street to a restaurant with a filthy red-and-black-striped awning.

By the door, a dry-erase sign says, "Please seat yourselfs." We pick a table next to a glass partition. Ceiling fans whir. Hanging on the wall opposite me, two speakers play Yellowman's "Nobody Move, Nobody Get Hurt." All the patrons have plates in front of them, but no one is eating.

A waiter in a dirty apron uses a dishrag to wipe two laminated menus. Grant orders spicy pumpkin soup, which isn't on the menu.

"Bowl or cup?" the waiter asks.

"Two bowls."

The waiter nods and shuffles into the kitchen.

"Check this out," Grant says, pointing to the window.

A black Vespa screeches around the corner and pulls onto the sidewalk. Two guys in black leather pants, jackets, and helmets with tinted face coverings hop off. One stands at the door while the other is directed by the waiter to our table. I can already taste the dope as Grant makes the deal and passes a bundle to me under the table. I start to get up.

"Wait," he says. "There's a catch."

I freeze, expecting a SWAT team to pounce.

"We have to order food and sit a while. What do you want?"

"I don't care. I'm not hungry."

"I'll handle it," Grant says. He gestures to a narrow hallway by the kitchen. "Bathroom's over there—if you want an appetizer first."

The sticky tiles in the hall are riddled with cracks and gouges. I duck into the small, windowless bathroom, lock the door with the flimsy hook-and-eye latch, and examine the off-white glassine envelopes. "Noise Gate" is stamped in red. I roll a dollar and shove it into a bag, careful to avoid the corner as I snort the hit. Then I gaze into the foggy, scratched mirror until my giant black pupils shrink.

While Grant is in the bathroom, I stare at the place mat. Ads for a vacuum cleaner repair service, real estate, a company that will advertise your company on a place mat. The waiter with the soiled apron serves a bowl of red beans and rice, a wicker basket filled with slices of white bread, and two dishes: thinly sliced gray meat slathered in a thick orange sauce and half a rotisserie chicken.

A cook steps out of the kitchen, wiping his face on his shirt. He points a remote at a busted receiver on a refrigerator, and Bob Marley's "Natural Mystic" begins. Grant closes his eyes and slaps the table, drumming along and singing in a whisper.

I breathe deep and let it out slowly. This isn't a relapse. It's a resuscitation.

The next morning, I lock myself in the bathroom, run the shower, and snort a hit. I take off my clothes and stand under the water for fifteen seconds, long enough to rinse my body.

Jane is getting dressed in the bedroom. Facing away from her, I step into a pair of boxers and pull them up my legs, holding my towel in place.

"Why don't you ditch the towel and undies and let's have a quick one."

"I can't. There's a big meeting at nine."

"When you were running around in tights and platform shoes and doing drugs, did you ever think you'd end up here?"

"I don't know if I thought I'd end up here, but I *wanted* to."

"Shack up with some goody-two-shoes girl and have a real job?"

"Not *some* girl. *You.*"

"You didn't know me."

"I knew you existed. I knew I found you when I heard people call you Glinda."

"Because I was a good witch?"

"Because you were Glinda."

"I'm so confused."

"I told you about the fifth grade DARE assembly, right?"

"The cop said a kid took acid and peeled off his skin."

"He said something about every drug. When he said heroin came from poppies, I thought of the scene in *The Wizard of Oz*. Heroin is evil, poppy, wicked-witchy business, and you were Glinda—the exact opposite."

"How come you never told me that before?"

None of my bosses protest when I refuse assignments under the auspice that another boss has me on another task. Nobody asks what I'm so busy typing all morning. It feels good to write. I think this story could be a novel:

Second Chances™ revolutionary new product, The Save As®, helps you realize your full potential™ by doing the Microsoft Word equivalent of a "Save As" to your life. You designate the changes you would like to make, and Licensed The Save As® technicians execute them by performing a Hippocampular Trituration (aka hippo scrub), a minimally invasive procedure that replaces old memories with new ones in your hippocampus and the hippocampi of your family, friends, and acquaintances. Second Chances™ then consigns your original life to their Certified Preexisting Existence Marketplace. Once the process is complete, the world around you shifts to reflect the changes. No one—not even you—will remember how life used to be.

Wednesday afternoon at three-thirty, a bar cart winds its way around the office, as it does every week. Snacks are served. In the lounge, Loretta, my supervisor, dressed in her usual beige, performs surgery on a glazed doughnut with a plastic knife. Dan swirls a martini glass, and I sip a small bottle of Coke.

Dan bites an olive off a plastic cocktail sword and points it at my drink. "What are you, ten years old?"

"I prefer heroin, but the company only provides legal drugs."

"You are too funny," Loretta says, snarfing a fraction of doughnut.

Patrick joins us with a tall, clear effervescing beverage in hand.

"So, Patrick," Loretta says, "what's your poison these days?"

"Club soda," he says. "Seventeen years. Since we were at McCann together. Remember?"

Loretta sucks air through her teeth. "I was going to ask, but . . ."

"It's a disease, Loretta. No shame in that."

There's an awkward silence.

Loretta snaps her fingers. "Patrick, I've been meaning to tell you. I saw Barb at Barney's last year. We just waved but she was with—I'm so sorry. Remind me."

"Rebecca. My daughter's name is Rebecca."

"Rebecca. That's right. She got big. How old is she these days?"

"Twenty-one."

"And how's she doing?"

"I wouldn't know. She hasn't talked to me in years."

twenty-nine

In the bathroom Friday morning, I stick a rolled dollar in my nose and hesitate. Holding the bag upright, I look down and consider the physics. Tilt my arm slightly and the dope spills into the toilet. I snort the hit and get dressed—jeans and a flannel shirt. I look at myself in the mirror and change into a suit and tie.

F train to Forty-Seventh Street. I stop at a drugstore and reach into my pockets and frisk myself at the pharmacy counter.

"I wrote everything down—it's here somewhere. Ugh. Grandma and I were at baggage claim at La Guardia for an hour before anybody talked to us. Thank God her medicine was in her purse, but everything else was in her suitcase and . . . I'm sorry. I have a huge presentation in half an hour and a jerk of a boss who'll fire me if I'm late and . . . I think Grandma said they're orange? Super fine? Does that make sense?"

I lift my head and meet the pharmacist's pitiful gaze. She reaches for a box of BD brand syringes. Thirty-one gauge. Orange cap. Jackpot.

"Most diabetics use these," she says. "Ultra fine. See, the box is orange."

"You. Are a saint. Bless you."

"I know how it is. My husband's suitcase went missing on our flight home from Hawaii last year."

I run to work and take the elevator to the fortieth floor. Dan stops me in the hall.

"Are you coming from or going to a job interview?"

"Huh?"

"Puh-leezze." He twirls my tie. "Like you dress this nice every day."

I put a spike in my pocket and lock the box in my desk and ride the elevator to the fifth floor. In the handicapped bathroom, I shake a hit into a spoon, add water, and suck it into the chamber. I roll up my sleeve and make a tight fist and hammer the needle into my vein. Relief comes fast. I drop the uncapped syringe on the floor, bend my knees, and slide down with my back against the wall.

My sweaty palms melt into the cold tiles. I close my eyes and see a scene from the movie *Lean on Me.* High school principal Joe Clark (played by Morgan Freeman) drags a student to the roof and yells at him for smoking crack and getting expelled. As the kid cries and begs for another chance, Clark gets in his face and tells him to jump.

"I don't want to jump," the kid says.

"Yes, you do. You smoke crack, don't you? Don't you? Look at me, boy. Don't you smoke crack?"

"Yes, sir."

"Do you know what that does to you? Huh?"

"No, sir."

"It kills your brain cells, son, it kills your brain cells. Now when you're destroying your brain cells, you're doing the same thing as killing yourself—you're just doing it slower. Now I say if you want to kill yourself, don't fuck around and do it expeditiously. Now go on and jump."

In April, my Smith Barney account balance: $9,800.

May: $9,100.

June: $7,900.

July: $6,700.

August: $5,400.

September: $4,100.

As usual, the phone rings at nine.

"I bumped into your old friend Rob yesterday," Mom says. "I told him you're clean and working at Ammirati and you're going to be running that place soon."

"What's *he* up to?"

"David, he looked terrific. He's been clean for two years, runs fifteen miles a day. He's training for the New York City marathon. When he asked for your number, I figured . . ."

Rob calls on Saturday. He sounds good, healthy. "Your mom said you stayed clean. What's that, four and a half years?"

I hesitate for a beat.

"David, please tell me you're not on dope."

"I had a couple slips—very early on. I'm fine now."

"Thank God. I'll never forgive myself for turning you, of all people, onto that shit."

Rob fills me in on his life, from the four-hundred-day orgy of heroin and crack that began when he left me at my mother's house to multiple arrests for burglary, shoplifting, possession, and check forging. He got sober in jail two years ago.

"The things I did near the end. I'm just so relieved you never . . . I had no idea what I was capable of until I got to that point."

Early fall air creeps through the bedroom window. My throat stings. My eyes burn. My body aches. Is today the day? I ask myself every morning. I know how this will end: a bundle in my arm at once. I'll do it before the money is gone.

In the bathroom, I stand on the toilet seat and grab my works from the top of the vanity, between the mirror's high beveled edges and the wall. I prepare a hit, draw the liquid into the chamber, and make a fist and drive the sharp into my vein. My muscles and joints get loose and limber. My throat cools. The opening lick from "Airbag" plays in my head. Six notes.

No, today is not the day.

October: $2,600.

November: $1,000.

The hit starts to wear off before I leave the handicapped bathroom. At this point, I use to stave off withdrawal. Some fleeting semblance of "even" is the most I can hope for.

By the time Grant gets to the restaurant, I've already dealt with the moped guys and ordered two dishes of disgustingness.

"My friend," he says, taking a seat. "When was the last time we saw each other?"

"August or September, I think."

"Yeah. Well, between then and now—you look bad, dude."

"Work is killing me. I'm getting plowed in the ass by a giant, commercialized dildo every day."

"Did you ever send your shit to an agent or a publisher?"

"No."

"Why not?"

"I don't know."

"*I* do. It's called fear of failure."

A waiter brings two plates of empanadas with a small white ramekin of orange liquid and the customary bowl of rice and beans and basket of bread. Grant tears the crust off a slice, dunks it in the sauce, and stuffs it into his mouth.

"If you hate your job and you're obviously too much of a pussy to be a writer, why don't you invent something? I know a ton of VCs who'll throw money at anything halfway intelligent."

"Actually, when I first got into mp3s, I had an idea for a Walkman but with a hard drive. You could fit thousands of albums on something the size of a pack of cigarettes."

"Not to be a dick, but nobody's buying that."

"I would."

"I meant no normal person is. Music's a tactile experience. People want to touch covers and liner notes and shit. That's why vinyl's coming back."

"Okay, then how about a custom kayak made from a mold of your vagina, or the vagina of someone you love?"

"Do you come up with this shit on the spot?"

"Don't want to spend the money on a custom model? Imagine yourself paddling around in something from Vayak's Deluxe line. The Simone de Beauvoir, perhaps, lined with genuine imitation fur."

"I should hook you up with my friend Sara. You need to get laid."

"She a kayak enthusiast or a person with a vagina who might want to order?"

"She's a whacked-out artist-type who writes poetry and listens to Radiohead. Her grandpa has terminal emphysema. She said when he dies, she'll grab every fentanyl patch and lollipop in his house. I should call her and see how Gramps is doing . . ."

December. One bag left. Only $1.13 in Smith Barney. I push my Chase card into the ATM. The joint account balance is $3.28.

Today is Tuesday. Jane gets paid next Wednesday, and I get paid next Friday.

Across the street from the office, kids in plaid and khaki school uniforms sell candy bars to raise money for hurricane relief. Their upturned watercooler jug teems with tens and twenties. I stare for a minute before going inside.

Dana is by the window on the fortieth floor, waving a twenty-dollar bill. "Free candy for whoever'll get me a candy bar from those cute little kids on the corner."

I volunteer. I think I'm going to Bushwick, but when I get outside, my feet go across the street and my hand gives the money to a cheery boy, who gives me two Hershey bars, a ten-dollar bill, and five singles. I shove the ten into my pocket, ball up the singles, and give them to Dana with a Hershey bar. She puts the money in her wallet without counting it. I return to my desk and call Grant.

"Do you think the moped guys would come to the restaurant to sell one bag?"

"Dude. You need to control dope, not the other way around."

"I lost my ATM card."

"You know you can go inside a bank and get money from a teller, right?"

"It's Smith Barney—no branches."

Fax machines and people yelling on Grant's end. "I'll front you a bundle," he says. "Of course, you have to blow me first." He laughs. We agree to meet at the restaurant at six. "Oh. Good news. Sara will be there. Gramps is on his way out."

Dana laughs when I return her money and apologize. She stops Loretta in the hall and tells the story of how I robbed her.

"You gave it back?" Loretta says. "I would have kept it."

"David's weird," Dana says, running an impeccably manicured finger along the crease of the ten-dollar bill. "Since Patrick left, he's the only one here who doesn't drink."

A thin, semi-frozen mist falls on Myrtle Avenue. I pass a liquor store and a convenience store with bulletproof glass partitions at the counter. I get to the restaurant ten minutes early and smoke a cigarette outside.

An NYPD cruiser creeps by. When the streetlight turns yellow, the cruiser's sirens start flashing and it blazes through the intersection. A short Latina woman approaches. She gestures for me to take off my headphones.

"Hey Papi. You got a cigarette for me?"

"Sorry."

"You here for coca or crack?"

"Neither."

"Oh," she says, nodding salaciously. "I know why you here. I could tell you where to find some mean-ass puta. Tear that pussy up all night, son."

"I'm okay."

"You okay? Yeah. You okay, fag."

By six-thirty, the mist has turned to sleet, the moped has come and gone half a dozen times with military precision, and Grant still isn't here. My face is frozen, my ears stinging. I dig a quarter out of my pocket and try three different pay phones before I find one with a dial tone. Grant's answering machine picks up. I don't leave a message. I walk back to the restaurant and stand under the awning, listening to Radiohead on my Walkman, trying to lose myself in Thom Yorke's ghostly vocals on "Paranoid Android."

When the song ends, I enter the restaurant and make a beeline for the bathroom, waving to a waiter in a way that—to me—means "I'm meeting a friend, going to pee first." I latch the door, scrape the remnants from my last bag, and snort the hit off the flattened glassine envelope. Then I throw it in the trash and turn to leave. Wait. The trash is probably nothing but empty bags. Maybe they're not all scraped. I tear the lid off and root around and find fourteen empties.

· · ·

Hot, wet, tiny daggers shoot out of the shower head, drilling my skin. I get out and dry off and put on my jeans and open the bathroom door.

Jane's jaw drops. "Baby. Oh. My God. I can see your ribs."

I stick my hands in my pockets to hold up my jeans. I've been meaning to go back to the shoe repair place and get another hole punched in my belt.

"I'm going to make you lunch. You need to eat. There's plenty of egg-plant parm—"

I say "Great," knowing I'll give it to a homeless person.

On TV, a meteorologist reports a hurricane forming in the Caribbean. "Local law enforcement in towns along the eastern seaboard are urging residents to evacuate before the Category-4 storm makes landfall."

Footage of rain and wind, battering a beach. I fantasize about sitting on a beach, letting the surge carry me away. If I disappear, will everyone forget I existed?

"*David.*"

"Uh-huh."

"I just said your name like fifty times."

"Sorry."

"Did you hear what I said?"

"Uh-huh."

"*David.*" Jane lets out an "are you fucking kidding me" laugh. "I said that Kathy and Valon were talking about going to South Carolina and helping."

"Cool."

"Cool?"

Jane gives me a Tupperware container and comes at me for a goodbye kiss. Our lips barely touch. She says, "We got a second notice from Con Ed."

"I paid the bill."

"Are you sure? I'd hate for our credit scores to get messed up."

I don't know how credit scores are calculated or what's considered good or even what my score is.

At work, cheesy classic rock blares in the hall as my bosses prepare for a big pitch. Steve Miller's hits. Peppier Elton John. Billy Joel's *Greatest Hits* disc two. "Pressure" plays on repeat for more than an hour. Everyone speed walks and sings along, pausing midstride to belt out the chorus. "Pres-sure."

I put on my headphones and listen to Mahler's Piano Quartet in A Mi-nor—possibly the saddest music ever composed. After a quick look around me, I tilt my computer monitor to the side and read about suicide methods on an online forum called *Catch the Bus*. Most are messy or obvious or both. I click on a thread with the subject "Exit Bag." You tie a plastic bag around your head and run a hose from a helium tank. It seems quick and painless—not that anyone posts with firsthand experience. Evidence would be a problem. Forget it.

Bill charges toward me. I close the browser window before he pulls me out of my chair and shakes me, screaming, "Are you psyched?"

I nod.

"I said, 'ARE. YOU. PSYYYYYYCHED?'"

"I'm psyched, okay? I'm psyched."

"GRAAAAAAHHHH!"

An exit bag chain could work. A cleans up after B. Then C for B. No. There'd be geographic obstacles. And I wouldn't trust a stranger.

Grant calls and says he got arrested last night for buying crack from an undercover cop in Washington Heights. I think he's lying. If the situation were reversed, I wouldn't have been so eager to help him.

"It was insane," he says. "Plainclothes pigs hopping out of this beat-up Maxima on the corner of St. Nicholas and 149th after I gave the money to the supposed dealer."

"Can you meet tonight? I still don't have a replacement ATM card and—"

"Are you kidding? The amount of crack was just above the threshold between casual smoker and dealer. If I get caught with *anything* before my trial, I'm fucked. So until further notice, I'm out."

One hit left. At five in the morning, I'm in the bathroom. The door is closed but not locked. I stab the needle in hard, pushing until it hurts, until the plastic at the base feels like it's puncturing my skin. Blood rushes to the surface. I raise my arm and lick it clean, and then quietly get dressed in the kitchen.

A wall calendar is inches from my face. December 29 has a big star— Daniel's birthday. I still have a couple of weeks to send him a gift, but not if all goes to plan. I fill a moving box with CDs and write his address on the top. In a cabinet, I find a roll of packing tape on the stack of *New York Posts* featuring me on the front page.

The office will be empty. I don't know where else to go.

A security guard and three cleaning women argue in Spanish around a wet vac in the lobby. I drop Daniel's box in the mail room and take the elevator to the fortieth floor. At the end of the hall, I press my face against the cold glass window. Morning light sprays across Manhattan—my last sunrise. A feeling of calm envelops me.

thirty

At the top of a poster-sized file in QuarkXPress, I type "PLEASE GIVE," and underneath, I place images of hurricane-ravaged landscapes. Then I go to the lounge and remove the jug from a watercooler, spilling most of the contents on the way to the sink. I tape the poster to the jug and swipe a box of Three Musketeers bars from the pantry. My plan: I'll raise however much money, go to Bushwick, and bang every bag into my arm in one shot. *Game fucking over.*

The exercise in legerdemain commences outside Grand Central Station. It can't hurt that I happen not to look like a complete slob—corduroys and a clean peacoat. Nobody knows there's blood on the inside of my elbow, sticking my shirt to my arm.

Commuters look at me and the jug and reach into their pockets and drop money in. A cop approaches, cupping his gloved hands to his mouth, huffing steamy breaths. He reads the sign aloud and asks in a heavy Brooklyn accent, "This a con?"

I shake my head and unintentionally affect a faint Southern drawl. "No, sir. Father McKenzie was just helping a blind gentleman inside, and Sister Eleanor's over there somewhere. Our church is raising money for the victims."

The cop kind of chuckles and nods. Did he get the "Eleanor Rigby" reference? Why did I do that? He slides a black leather wallet from his back pocket, flips through bills and receipts, and donates a few singles. I offer a Three Musketeers bar. He takes it and mutters about his ex-brother-in-law's rental properties in the Outer Banks.

"I told him a hundred times, I says, 'Mikey, not there. What you wanna do is you wanna go farther south.' I says Vero Beach. I says Lauderdale."

An older Black woman ambles over with a cane. "Bless your heart," she says. "This here's what I call the Lord's work."

Head high in her pastel purple coat with matching hat and dress and satiny gloves, she fishes a fat bank envelope from her pocketbook, removes a crisp twenty-dollar bill, and drops it into the jug with a satisfied nod. "There. Now I can say I done did my part."

I hold up the Three Musketeers box. "Please take as many as you want."

"Ever since I got the diabetes, doctor's been telling me to lay off the sweets—if you can believe that." She shakes her head and then turns to the cop.

"*You*?" he says, as if he's known her all his life. "*Diabetes*? Nuh-uh."

"Yes indeedy. It's dreadful is what it is, just dreadful."

She takes a few steps toward Madison and comes back. "My late husband, God rest his soul, he used to tell me, 'Virginia, you'd lose yo head if it wun't screwed top yo shoulders.'" Walking away in the other direction, she says, "I'll tell you another thing—when you go, it's much harder for the living than it is for the deceased."

Close to the subway station with almost $400 in my pocket, I think I hear my name. I turn around and see Dan shivering, his lips chattering. "Coldest day of the year," he says. "Care to warm up in Barnes and Noble?"

I follow him into the store and through the departments as he grabs items for Loretta: *Breathless* on DVD, a Marshall Tucker Band CD, and a heavy, expensive French cookbook.

"What do you wanna bet that none of this has anything to do with a Burger King campaign?"

In the checkout line, the guy ahead of us argues with the cashier about an expired coupon. Dan drops Loretta's stuff into my hands. He says not to move and runs off. He returns with a handful of Kurt Vonnegut books.

"You're a bookworm, right? Which is the most famous?"

"*Cat's Cradle* is the best book I've ever read."

Dan abandons the other titles on a table of discounted hardcover biographies and rolls his eyes as I start to summarize the book.

"It's not for me. I'm just gonna wait in the lobby for Kurt to show up and—bam—I'll have an autographed copy of *The Cat's in the Cradle* for Jim for Christmas."

"Right, because Kurt Vonnegut hangs out in our lobby so much."

"You're a bookworm and a smoker, and you don't know Kurt Vonnegut lives in one of those townhouses on Forty-Eighth Street?"

"Kurt Vonnegut. Lives across the street from the office."

"Amy barely leaves the building and she's seen him hundreds of times. Practically every morning he has breakfast in that—ahem—restaurant in the lobby."

Is this actually happening?

As we walk along Forty-Seventh Street between Sixth and Fifth Avenues, I hear a loud thud and rattling change or a tambourine. The sounds repeat rhythmically. Halfway down the block, I see a homeless woman sitting on an upturned milk crate. She's pounding a ratty coffee cup against the pavement. A stoic expression on her frozen face, she's wearing nothing but a big, dirty garbage bag with holes cut out for her head and her arms.

Dan elbows me, side mouthing, "Scam city. Cover your wallet."

I drop the proceeds from my fundraising endeavor into the cup and walk faster. Dan chases after me, yelling, "She's gonna use that money to buy crack. You know that, right? She probably sold her clothes for a hit."

Selling her clothes is the least awful reason I can think of for her circumstances. I don't care if she buys crack with the money. I don't care if she burns it to get warm for a minute. She needs it. And I don't.

The first battalion of ants arrive in the afternoon. Then the electrocutions begin. I don't want to be at work when my body starts systematically ridding itself of everything besides vital organs, but I really don't want to be in transit. It's freezing in the office, and I'm sweating like a fat guy in a sauna. My boxers and shirt are soaked. I don't have other clothes to change into.

Loretta comes down the hall with her head bowed, untying a scarf from around her neck. Once it's off, she uses it to fan herself. She stops abruptly, five feet from my desk.

"Holy hell, Dave. You look awful."

"I think I'm coming down with something."

"Go home before you give it to the rest of us."

I put my computer to sleep and ease out of my chair. The ants fall to the base of my spine and start over. Loretta sits on the unoccupied desk next to mine, speed dials the car service company, and arranges a pickup for me.

For three days, the ants and electrocutions intensify, and everything hurts. I piss and puke and sweat and shit and squirm and writhe and cough and sneeze. I'm hot and cold simultaneously, saturating sheets and blankets with foulness when I'm not in the bathroom. I alternate between thinking I'm dying and wishing I were dead.

By Saturday, I'm able to ingest liquid without my body acting like a sieve. Jane holds cans of ginger ale and guides straws to my mouth and makes toast. She pats me with wet washcloths and dry towels. On Sunday, we lay in bed and watch *Mother Night*. Does Kurt Vonnegut really live across the street from the office or did Dan tell me in a dream?

On Monday morning, my thinking is just clear enough to know it's not quite clear. My throat is raw and sore. My bones hurt. I get out of bed and smoke a cigarette by the window, and I feel a vague pull drawing me out, the invisible thread of karass. I take a shower and get dressed for work.

ATMs are everywhere on Forty-Eighth Street between Sixth and Second Avenues. Passing each one without so much as a pause is a major victory. A poster for the Lincoln Center Ballet shows a time-lapse photo of a ballerina in the different stages of a pirouette. She's crouched at the far left, midair in the middle three, and on squared toes on the right. That's how it works—you have to get really low before you can soar.

Instead of going straight into the office, I wander up Second Avenue for the first time since I started working at Ammirati. Wads of black gum stain the sidewalk, and trash clogs the gutter. A sign in a gallery window reads, "Exclusive Worldwide Dealer of Kurt Vonnegut Art."

The small, dark shop has low ceilings—not what you'd expect from the exclusive worldwide dealer of anything. Nearly every inch of wall is covered with originals and limited-edition prints. Mostly drawings, but also a few quotes. All are signed.

"What can I do you for?" the proprietor asks.

"Just poking around. I'm a big Vonnegut fan."

He asks where I'm from. I think he thinks I'm a tourist.

"I work across the street—in the building where Mr. Vonnegut eats breakfast every day."

"Ammirati?"

"Yep."

"Copywriter?"

"Yeah, but what I really want to do is—"

"Write novels?"

At the end of the narrow space is a framed quote in Vonnegut's handwriting: "Peculiar travel suggestions are dancing lessons from God—Bokonon."

Walking back to work, I remember what my grandfather said when he and Nana returned from two weeks in the Pacific Northwest. "Never go to Vancouver. You won't want to leave. Nowhere else on earth has mountains and ocean so close together."

Loretta dispatches me to the production studio to mount storyboards. I crank them out and listen to John Fahey and briefly consider getting back into therapy, but there's no reason for me to pay to hear what I already know. I need to stop pretending to be someone else and stop worrying about making everyone else happy. I need to make some changes and accept that all I can control is how I react to what I can't control.

In a few hours, I'll have another clean day under my belt. I resign myself to not stopping in Bushwick on the way home, and I leave tomorrow open for discussion. Hopefully I'll resist, but there's something freeing about reserving the right not to.

At six-thirty, achy and exhausted and probably high on toxic fumes, I finish the last board and gather cans of spray adhesive and paint brushes. I open the closet and see a quote handwritten on a picture of Albert Einstein taped to the inside of the door.

"'The definition of insanity is doing the same thing over and over again and expecting different results.'—Albert Einstein."

I wait in the lobby until seven so the company will pay for a cab home.

On the corner of Forty-Eighth Street and Second Avenue, five minutes pass without a taxi sighting. Weird. I start down Second with my hand in the air. I'm almost at Forty-Third when a taxi screeches across all four lanes of traffic to pick me up.

The driver turns his head and greets me with a warm smile and a "hello" in an accent that sounds kind of Jamaican but not really. On his ID badge, his first name is Ali and his last name is crazy long, with very few vowels. Taxi drivers generally don't talk to me, and I don't talk to them, but this guy is gregarious.

"New York City, such a wondrous place. Don't you think, mon?"

"I think it's a hellhole. I need to get out of here."

Ali looks at me in the rearview mirror. "Move to Camden, Maine."

Before I take another breath, before Ali says another word, before I get home and launch a full-scale online investigation, I know I'm moving to Camden.

"I been there only once, mon. And I get out of the cab for just one minute, but it was breath-tak-ing."

"You were there for only a minute?"

"My dispatcher gave me a special fare on my first day driving a cab. I had to turn around right away."

"But if it's so breath-tak-ing, why haven't you gone back?"

Ali laughs. "Twas three weeks ago, mon. I just move here from Senegal, but oh! Camden was mountains, right next to ocean."

The first result on an AltaVista search for "Camden Maine" is the chamber of commerce's website. A picture on the home page shows a dark blue ocean against a backdrop of lush mountains. "Breathtaking" is an understatement. I click on the photo gallery tab: images of high-masted wooden sailboats in a picturesque cove. Islands. A lighthouse. Old, Federalist-style houses. An archetypal New England fishing village. Small and peaceful. The website pegs Camden's population at five thousand year-round residents, tripling in the summer.

A list of places of interest includes restaurants, shops, art galleries—and Maine Photographic Workshops, "the world-renowned learning center for photography, film, and multimedia." I click the link. A new page opens. I recognize many of the photographers' names: Mary Ellen Mark, Arnold Newman, Joyce Tennyson. Impressive.

The Workshops operates out of an old grange hall on Rockport harbor, one mile south of Camden. The About Us page says the founder is a former *National Geographic* photographer. I click a link at the bottom: Employment Opportunities. My heart races as the page slowly loads. Long load time means mucho content, right? I'd move to Camden to wash dishes in the Workshops cafeteria. I'd do anything to live and write there. The page finally finishes loading. There's one job:

> The Maine Photographic Workshops seeks an experienced in-house graphic designer/copywriter to produce materials for our internationally acclaimed programs in photography, film, video, and multimedia. Qualified candidates must be comfortable on a Macintosh, with proficiency in QuarkXpress, Adobe Photoshop and Illustrator, and related software. Send resume, cover letter, and portfolio to Kevin.

The salary is $5,000 more than I make at Ammirati, plus medical and dental. I draft a letter, spiff up my resume, and attach PDFs of my portfolio to an email.

First thing in the morning, Kevin calls. He tells me about the job: producing every shred of Workshops' marketing material—their course catalogs, promotional pieces, print ads. While he describes the process and flow, everything is "You'll be doing (this or that)," as opposed to "Whoever we hire will be doing . . ."

He asks if I have a computer. I claim to own a brand-new Mac G4 and list the specs from J&R Music World's full-page ad in the *New York Times* tacked to the corkboard behind my desk. Since I'm already lying, I tell him I have licenses for all the software in the job listing, as well as a license for Adobe's nine-thousand-font suitcase package.

"Outstanding. When can you come for an interview?"

Before I can think of how and when I'll get to Maine, Kevin says the Workshops will pay for my flight. We settle on next Wednesday. He says to expect a call from Stephanie once the arrangements have been made. Holy shit!

Looking at pictures of Camden and Rockport online, I strategize about telling Jane. Break up with her now? Wait until I get the job? I will get this job.

Grant calls. A family friend with ties to the Manhattan DA's office might be able to get his charges dropped. He sounds hopeful. He says he'll know soon. Then he hums the riff from "Another One Bites the Dust."

Maybe he wasn't lying to me after all.

"More news. Sara's in Florida for her grandpa's funeral. This time next week, when she's back in town, I'll know if I'm free or fucked. Either way, I think it's cause for a celebration."

My brain starts churning out excuses to reschedule my interview. I go outside and smoke a cigarette and tell myself that this job is a matter of life or death. It sounds cheesy in my head, but I know it's true. I call Jane at work.

"Is everything all right? You never call me at work."

"The craziest thing just happened. I was looking for places in Maine for a GMC trucks shoot, and I found the Maine Photographic Workshops. It's on the ocean, surrounded by mountains, and they're looking for a graphic designer/copywriter."

"You want to move?"

"I mean, I saw pictures and thought it'd be amazing to live there. Then I found the Workshops, and you know, the whole 'everything happens for a reason' thing."

"What about the whole 'I can't wait to move to the city' thing the whole time we were in Vermont?"

The line is silent for a beat. Jane says, "It sounds interesting, but can we take it one step at a time? Who knows if they'll even call if you apply."

"I applied and they called. I have an interview next week."

thirty-one

Stephanie's short, bright orange-dyed hair is impossible to miss at baggage claim. I wave and she runs over and hugs me. "I'm so happy to meet you."

In the car, Stephanie describes the Workshops staff as a family of artists. "Everyone's totally unpretentious and laid back. As long as the work gets done, you can pretty much come and go as you please—no set hours, no dress code, no corporate hierarchical BS. And when you see this place . . . my God. It's magical."

"I just can't believe how lucky I am, the way everything fell into place."

"Things don't just fall into place, David. You make things happen."

"I didn't know Camden existed until a taxi driver told me about it last week."

"And you decided to look into it, and you found the Workshops, and you decided to apply. So give yourself some credit. And you impressed the hell out of Kevin, who, by the way, isn't easily impressed. He hasn't stopped talking about you. Do you know how long we've been looking for—I'll be stunned if he doesn't hire you on the spot."

Driving through a desolate, snow-covered landscape of trailers, rusted-out cars, and junk piles on Route 90 in Warren, I start to have some doubts. Stephanie mentioned the length of the search, but not the volume of applicants. Do the locals know something I don't? My brain concocts a story of a grisly murder. Everyone knows Kevin did it, but he can't be charged because the evidence was destroyed in a mysterious fire.

Stephanie turns on the radio. "Carnival" by Natalie Merchant crackles in and out as we take a detour through Camden. On the east side of Bay View Street, Penobscot Bay's choppy water stretches past dozens of ragged islands, with a faint mirage of the Blue Hill peninsula in the distance. To the west, tall mountains with snow-covered trees. Most of the structures in town were built in the 1800s or earlier. At any second, the frame in my line of sight could be a postcard.

Kevin opens a drawer, hauls out a stack of fliers and pamphlets and collateral materials, and drops it on his desk as if letting go of a bag of dog shit.

"For the past ten years, the guy who started the Workshops and still runs it—Lyman—has been paying a local freelancer to design this hideous crap."

"I guess he's big on pastel, two-color gradients, and not much font variety—unless somebody told him to only use Arial and—is that Garamond?"

"I'm no designer, but look at the formatting. Something is wrong everywhere."

"Paper stock's flimsy too. That doesn't help the ink saturation. And it's so flat. How about some die cuts? Or maybe a satin aqueous coating on the images? Something to make it pop. You could reverse emboss the logo or use thermography—you know—when the ink is injected with—"

"I don't know what any of that means, but you'd do better in your sleep than this yutz on his best day."

Kevin leaves the room to find Lyman. I stare out the window at Rockport Harbor and replay the conversation, certain that I came off as an arrogant, egomaniacal know-it-all. *Of course, let me tell you about thermographic ink.*

Lyman has scraggly white hair and male-pattern baldness. Without introducing himself or shaking my hand, he turns a chair around, plops himself down, and rests his hands on the seat back. He draws a deep breath and exhales in three quick bursts—a weird yoga thing?

"*He* wants to hire you," Lyman says, thumbing at Kevin standing behind him. "He thinks your work is good, but he forgets who's in charge here. *Me.* And if there's one thing I absolutely loathe, it's minimalist design."

"I can be less spare with my aesthetic."

"You'd better. When I pay to have something printed, I want ink on every inch of the page. White space is throwing money out the window."

Lyman talks like Mr. Howell from *Gilligan's Island*. I hear the "h" in "white." He runs his hand along the top of a chair as if smoothing the wood grain. "Fine." He gets up and trudges toward the door. "Hire him. But no white space."

Kevin listens to Lyman descending the staircase. When the creaking stops, he says, "It's okay if you want to think it over."

"Nothing to think about. I'm in."

We talk about a start date and how to find a place to live. Kevin recommends a realtor, saying I can stay in Workshops housing for as long as I need. He tells me about his wife, a filmmaker and occasional instructor at the Workshops, and says they moved here last year with their young sons to escape the rat race in California, where he worked as a marketing director at Silicon Graphics.

"Funny. I used to own their stock."

"I'm happy you said 'used to.' It's not worth the paper it's printed on right now."

A girl around my age enters the room. Long brown hair, big brown eyes, perfectly shaped, perfectly proportioned breasts under a tight black tank top. She twirls her hair with her index finger and pulls it to her nose. I can smell the jasmine in her shampoo from across the room. What's her story? Is there a reason to get in touch with her before I move?

My heart pumps unicorns and lightning and magnets. I want to kiss her. I think she feels the same, when she momentarily glances at me. I'm here because of her. I'll tell her the story of Ali someday, and she'll think I'm crazy. And someday, she'll tell the story to our kids.

"This is David," Kevin says. "Our new graphic designer. David, meet Andrea. She runs the photo program."

The fan in my hotel bathroom grinds like a jet engine with a bird trapped inside. I run the shower, squirt half a trial-size bottle of Paul Mitchell Awapuhi Shampoo on a washcloth, and place it where the water hits. I hope that by the time the housekeeper cleans the room, the awapuhi smell will have overpowered the Camels I've been chain-smoking since Stephanie dropped me off an hour ago.

For dinner, I eat two stale bags of vending machine pretzels and a Nestle Crunch bar. Then I call my mother and break the news.

"David, I'm thrilled for you. Thrilled, thrilled, *thrilled*." She bombards me with questions. What'll I do about a car? Where will I live? What's Jane going to do in Camden?

"She's thrilled, right? She must be."

"She doesn't know I got the job yet."

"I'm sure she'll be thrilled. Don't you think?"

"Yeah."

"You think she won't be thrilled?"

"I'm sure she will be."

Mom offers to take me shopping for clothes or anything else I need for the move. Staring at J&R's ad ("Power Macintosh G4s starting at $2,999.99. Add a professional-quality display monitor for only $1,299.99"), I tell her I don't need anything.

The plane slices through the cloud line, and Manhattan comes into view. I'm in the window seat, next to a middle-aged woman who spits a wad of gum into a napkin and tucks it into her seat-back pocket as we land. She takes forever getting her stuff out of the overhead compartment.

New York says welcome home with a blast of frozen polluted air. I light a cigarette and get in the long taxi line. A guy in a reflective vest blows a whistle and waves drivers forward, his eyes absent of patience as tourists ask him for restaurant recommendations and Broadway musical opinions.

"Keep it moving," he says. "Keep it moving."

When it's my turn, the guy in the vest asks where I'm going. I tell him, "Carroll Gardens." A cab pulls up. Vest guy opens the door and says "Brooklyn" to the driver. I get in and close the door. We lurch forward.

"Where in Brooklyn?"

"Carroll *Bushwick*. I'm going to Bushwick."

At an ATM on Myrtle Avenue, I withdraw fifty dollars from the Chase account and tell myself it doesn't count. The moped guys come. I snort a small hit in the bathroom and then swing by the office. Good thing I didn't chuck the needles.

Loretta is in the hall talking to Robert and Rog, the co-creative direc-tors. They're looking at me. I can't hear what they're saying because Dan and Amy are at the Foosball table, yelling about the Millennium Bug.

"There's no computer glitch," he says. "It's a ploy to sell bottled water."

My voicemail light is blinking. I play the message. Grant. Yesterday at 4:02 p.m. "Free at last, free at last. Hallelujah, free at last—and home girl came through."

Loretta approaches. "I thought you were out for the rest of the week."

"I am. Just picking up my Filofax."

"Ah. Well, since you're here, got a minute?"

I follow Loretta to her office, thinking she's going to fire me. Before she closes the door, I give her two weeks' notice.

"Really? We were about to promote you and give you a raise."

"Really?"

"When I showed Martin your book and told him you did all the graph-ics and wrote all the copy, he said, 'Fast-track him before he goes some-where else.'"

"Shit."

"Yeah. Still want to quit?"

I explain the situation with the Workshops. Loretta says she under-stands and gives me a hug. She makes me promise to call if I ever move back. I return to my desk for a couple of needles, take the elevator to the fifth floor, and shoot up in the handicapped bathroom. *It's okay. There won't be any heroin in Maine.*

Climbing the stairs, I hear a male voice with a Balkan accent booming from my apartment and Nina Simone's cover of Bob Dylan's "Tom Thumb's Blues." I open the door. Jane is on the couch next to a skinny guy with dark hair. Valon. She sighs in an I-just-laughed-really-hard way and takes a sip of wine. A girl with an unpronounceable Balkan-sounding name sits cross-legged on the floor. She says something in Bosnian.

Jane says, "I feel bad for the animals—and I haven't had meat since I was fifteen."

"Come on," Valon says. "You never smell bacon cooking and think, *Hmmm*?"

"I really don't. At this point, I think it'd make me sick."

"That's the problem with Americans. Don't know how good you have it. When you've lived through war, you don't take anything for granted."

Did I kill the party? I hold my sides as if I'm in pain. I want Jane to ask if I'm okay so I can tell her I feel sick, and when she offers to throw her friends out, I tell her not to. Then she'll feel guilty and we won't talk about it.

I see the way Valon looks at Jane. The glint in his eye repulses and excites me. Maybe she'll cheat on me with him and make this easier for me. I slip into the bedroom and close the door. I hear muted voices and laughter with increasing frequency.

In the morning, Jane says, "I want to hear about Maine, but I have to get to work early." For the first time since I've known her, I think she's lying.

When she leaves, I shoot up and unfold J&R's ad and read the fine print at the bottom. "Purchase any Apple products by 12/31/99 and get low-interest financing. See store for details." I call my mom and tell her about the computer and monitor I need to buy.

"Could you give me and two large boxes a ride to Brooklyn?"

"Sure thing, honey. I'll leave right now."

At J&R, Larry punches numbers into a calculator and sticks it in my face. "My best price for the G4 and the monitor. The whole nine, out the door. Bam."

I nod. Larry hands me a clipboard with a J&R Music World credit application. As I fill it out, he tells my mom to get the car. He twists the small diamond stud in his left ear and runs a hand over his head—balding with a ponytail. When I finish the paperwork, he gives it to a manager and skips to the back of the sales floor. He returns a minute later with two giant boxes strapped to a hand truck.

"Hold on," the manager says. "You only qualified for $800." He twirls a finger. Larry does an about-face. I start toward the door, my head down as I work on a story to tell Kevin about my brand-new G4 and monitor getting destroyed during the move.

Mom comes back. "What happened?"

The manager tells her.

"But he needs that computer. He just got a new job. In Maine."

"Unless one of yous wants to pay for the difference."

Welling up with tears, Mom takes off her red leather gloves and reaches into her pocketbook. Without asking how much, she gives the manager her AmEx.

"Mom, you can't—I'm supposed to buy that. It's going to be like $5,000."

"This is what I've always said to you about being a parent. You kill for your kids."

Mom wipes her eyes and signs the sales slip without hesitation, spending money she doesn't have, on equipment I lied about owning, to a guy who hired me to do a job I'm not qualified for, in a place I don't deserve to live, probably with a girlfriend I can't seem to break up with.

Larry parks the hand truck at the front of the store. I lug the computer and monitor to Mom's car, overwhelmed with gratitude and wracked with guilt. We drive away, commercials on the radio as we cross the Brooklyn Bridge, and Mom reminds me—again—that I remind her of her father. "David, you are one unbelievably smart, handsome, talented, creative guy."

A commercial for a car dealership ends. Rod Stewart's "Forever Young" begins.

"There are no coincidences," Mom says, choked up. "Everything happens for a reason."

She raises the volume, not needing to say another word as her favorite song plays. One teary eye on the road, the other on me, she sings along.

After Mom leaves, I call Grant at work. A woman answers. She says he's not available. I ask to leave a message. She sniffles. I hear papers shuffling.

"Uh, could you please tell him David called?"

"I'm so sorry. He passed away on Wednesday night." She hangs up.

I run to the bathroom, dry heave into the sink, and splash water on my face. I bring my head up and force myself to look in the mirror.

This, you fucking asshole. Take a long look and remember.

I don't want to be alone or in the apartment. I can't think of anywhere to go or anyone to be with. I put on my headphones and go outside.

Without thinking, I walk up Court Street and take the subway to Manhattan. I get out at Grand Central and walk up Second Avenue to the exclusive Vonnegut art gallery. The guy in the shop remembers me and the piece I was interested in.

"Sorry," he says, "sold it last week." He points to other Bokonon quotes on the far wall. None are as applicable as the one about peculiar travel suggestions, but I stay and look. As I'm about to leave, the bell above the door jingles.

An older man in a brown tweed overcoat and newsboy hat enters and greets the proprietor with a jovial wave. As if surprised, he says, "You've got a customer."

"This young man was interested in *Peculiar Travel Suggestions*, but it sold."

"Oh? That's a real shame."

"He said he's a writer—maybe you could give him some writerly advice instead?"

Vonnegut scratches his chin and walks toward me. Looking me dead in the eye, he says, "Get yourself a whole mess of pennies and put 'em in your socks. You want to make sure you fill 'em real good so your feet are always on the ground."

part four

2000

thirty-two

A month of smoke hangs in the air, trapped behind double-paned storm windows. My reflection appears in the glass—grim and sober. I step back and the view comes into focus: overcast sky, cars crunching down Sea Street, spraying compacted chunks of salty, sandy snow from the tires. Waves thrash in Camden Harbor.

The phone is going to ring. Jane is going to say she cheated on me. I don't know why I know or how I know, only *that* I know. I light another cigarette and pace the wide-pine floors.

I revise and rehearse a breakup speech. Another hour passes. The sun explodes behind Mount Battie, an orange haze over the tree line. Streetlights flicker on. The phone finally rings.

Jane is crying about last night. Half a dozen coworkers at a bar in Queens. Valon drove her home. "Baby," she moans, "I made a bad mistake."

I don't ask for details.

"I'm so, so sorry."

I don't respond.

"Do you think you can ever forgive me?"

"I think I need to think."

In the coming weeks, Jane will quit her job, pack everything in the apartment, reserve a U-Haul, and research places to work around Camden. She'll call at every turn and ask if I'm sure. I'll lie every time. "Yes. I want this to work."

She arrives at the house on the first Saturday in March, late in the afternoon. I meet her at the front door, my arms hanging at my sides as she hugs me.

"What's wrong?"

"I can't do this."

Jane crumples to the floor and starts bawling. I stand over her and unload, my body vibrating with rage. "There's no way Valon was the only one or it happened only once with him. Balkan boys are your forbidden fruit. Remember? I can't trust you. I can't even look at you."

"Baby . . . you're scaring m-m-me."

"Good. *Leave.* I'm done."

"I . . . don't have anywhere to . . . Where am I supposed to . . ."

"You want *me* to figure that out? FUCK YOU."

Sweat pours down my face and my chest. I want—need—to destroy everything around me. I storm outside and throw a chair off the deck. I kick the side of the house and stomp up and down the driveway and stand in the road and light a cigarette. My sticky sweat starts to freeze. I hear Jane crying. I flick the cigarette and it breaks in half. I drop it and rake it with my heel. Wind carries bits of tobacco to a filthy snowbank.

When I go back in, Jane is upstairs, sitting in the corner in the hall. Head bowed, holding herself, gulping breaths, choking on tears.

"I called Kate," she says, slow and quiet. "She's coming from Bar Harbor."

"Fine. *I'll* go." I grab my keys and start down the stairs.

"Wait."

"What."

"Can we talk?"

I turn and face Jane's moist red eyes. "There's nothing to talk about." I jump down the stairs and open the door.

Jane howls, "I'm so fucking stupid. I ruined the best thing in my life."

Every cell in my body tight and twisted, I drive across the street to the boatyard. James in the tape deck. "Five-O." I roll down the windows and breathe. I try to think about Andrea—traveling around Cuba with a friend since I moved to Camden. I want to imagine a future with her, but I'm stuck on the past. It takes all my energy not to go back and hold Jane.

I remember this story she once told me. For months before her seventh birthday, she begged her parents for a Strawberry Shortcake bicycle. They said it was too expensive and couldn't afford it, but she didn't stop asking and prayed every night. She woke up on her birthday to a giant, gift-wrapped box. The bike wasn't assembled. After two hours, her father, who can put anything together, started screaming and cursing. Her normally patient, soft-spoken mother started yelling at him. "Why did you spend so much on something so frivolous?" The bike was still in pieces when Jane went to bed that night. The next morning, it was gone. She didn't ask where it went. No one said a word about it.

A green Volvo pulls into my driveway and then backs out. I watch it disappear at the top of Sea Street. Then I go home, surprised to feel nothing—as if the relationship with Jane never happened. Or maybe I'm just numb.

The day Andrea returns from Cuba, Kevin abruptly quits his job, and Lyman fires me during lunch in the crowded dining hall.

"Your design is atrocious," he says, raising his voice. "*Uh-trocious.* And I'm out of patience for it." He keeps yelling. I half expect him to shoot a revolver at my feet and tell me to dance.

Driving home, I think the universe (for lack of a better description) is trying to send a message. "Careful what you wish for. We gave you a taste of good so you'd know what you're missing when we yanked it away."

I get an idea for a story about the making of an amateur adaptation of Sartre's *No Exit*. I scribble an outline of the story and the show within. Instead of a hotel, it takes place in a giant shopping mall. Instead of "hell is other people," hope is the most brutal form of torture. Instead of a straight-up play, it's a disco musical. Instead of *No Exit*, the director, a flamboyant, middle-aged elementary school music teacher, calls it *Exit*. I write character descriptions and backstories for the actors playing the characters. I hit a wall when I start to write the actual story. It's a comedy. I don't feel funny.

Hundreds of miles from anyone or anything that might provide a modicum of comfort, I'm hard-pressed to imagine I'm not in hell. I hang towels over the curtainless windows and crawl into bed. As I try to think of my next move, the freedom is overwhelming and terrifying. I'm accountable to nothing and no one—for the first time ever.

For three or four days, I subsist on graham crackers and Miles Davis mid-'70s doom funk era albums. *Agharta, Get Up with It, On the Corner.* Acidic street jams that don't belong in the jazz section.

After the graham crackers run out, I eat nothing for two days before dragging myself to the supermarket. I fill a basket with bread and Campbell's tomato soup and cheddar cheese—and a dozen pints of vanilla ice cream to coat the acid in my stomach.

In the checkout line, the guy ahead of me asks the cashier for two bottles of coffee-flavored brandy. He's thirtyish—scruffy face, matted hair, dirt under his fingernails, a Leatherman strapped to the belt loops of his double-kneed work pants. In his cart, amid TV dinners and cases of Mountain Dew and blocks of Velveeta, two young boys beg for quarters to buy stickers from a vending machine.

"What, you think I'm made of money?"

A manager retrieves the bottles of brandy from a row of locked cabinets at the front of the store, the cashier puts them in a plastic bag, and the guy sticks it in the seat of the cart. After paying, he pushes the cart only two feet before the bag falls and the bottles break.

Thick brown liquid spreads across the scuffed floor. The guy gapes as if he's watching a friend bleed out. The manager steps over the spill and unlocks the cabinet. Calling to someone to get a mop, he grabs two more bottles and tries to give them to the customer, but he says "I'm all set" and trudges out of the store.

In the next lane, two women coo at boxed items in the cabinet o' vice: a Frisbee with a bottle of Cuervo, Jack Daniel's and a flask, two martini glasses and a chrome shaker with Bombay Sapphire.

"We should totally put on ball gowns and make martinis."

"Totally."

"Shaken, not stirred."

The double standard is maddening. Alcohol can shut down more of your organs than all other substances combined, and alcohol withdrawal can kill you. No other drug is that addictive or dangerous.

Illegal drugs are involved in more overdose fatalities because potency is unknown. If those drugs were legal and regulated, potency would be measured and printed on labels—and heroin overdose would be as easy to prevent as alcohol overdose.

Alcohol isn't legal because it's safer. Alcohol is safer because it's legal.

thirty-three

M om leaves a dozen messages before I call back and tell her about the firing.

"Everything happens for a reason," she says. "First it was Jane and now this. I'm sure you'll find someone and something else up there. You're too smart and handsome and capable not to. I keep hoping Daniel will go to Maine and work at Hyde School after he graduates. That place was so good for him."

"Is he thinking of doing that?"

"He's not thinking. That's why he needs to be back there. Your grandparents said he reeked of alcohol and got up to go to the bathroom twelve times when they took him to dinner for his birthday. When was the last time you talked to him?"

"I don't remember."

"The other day, I was thinking—you've been clean for five years. He can't stay clean for five minutes. Maybe you can talk some sense into him. Will you call him?"

"Sure."

If I don't do it now, I won't later, and I don't want Mom nagging me about it. I hang up with her and call my brother.

"David, I'm doing bong hits with Jason on my new glass six-footer. Listen."

I hear the buds ignite and water bubbling in the chamber and coughing. Although I've never been there, I can see the cloud of pot smoke in

Daniel's apartment in Deerfield Beach. When he gets back on the phone, I tell him what Mom said about his birthday dinner with our grandparents.

"Jesus Christ. I went to the bathroom twice to smoke cigarettes."

"I'm just telling you what she said."

"Well, not to be a dick, but—"

"Dick butt."

"I'm serious. If you called to give me a speech."

"Have I ever given you a speech?"

"No, but you did make me order a douchebag at a Chinese restaurant in front of Nana and Poppa, though. How old was I? Five?"

"Young enough for me to hornswoggle into ordering a douchebag."

"You loved torturing me. But then you gave me all those CDs for my birthday. Did you stop listening to music or something?"

"I switched to mp3s. I found a ton of Radiohead bootlegs. And now that Jane's not around, I can listen to them anytime."

"That's one way to look at it."

"What do you mean?"

"If I had a girlfriend for three years and she cheated on me and we broke up, I'd be lying in bed, completely depressed—but you're all upbeat and shit."

"Nah. It happened for a reason. Everything happens for a reason."

"You sound like Mom."

From the kitchen, I hear rain pinging on the metal lawn chairs and pouring from the gutter downspout. I grab the last pint of Häagen-Dazs from the freezer and force ice cream down my throat, staring at my keys, thinking through the route to Brooklyn—I-95 to 295, to something else, then Framingham Service Plaza, the weird bookstore in Tolland, 84 to 684 to the Hutchinson River Parkway. I see bridges over highways, cylindrical concrete structures holding them up, steel guardrails surrounding them—in place, I assume, to stop a person like me from plowing into an immovable object.

Long days of nothing intensify the pain. I cycle through other ways to off myself: hanging, drowning, overdose on over-the-counter medication. I end up dialing into AOL, looking at guns and gun store websites. My life isn't going to get better.

I type "Maine methadone clinic" in the search bar. Two results. Bangor, two hours away. Portland, same distance. I call the Bangor clinic.

The guy on the phone says to make an appointment for a urine test. "If there's dope in your system, we'll put you on a program and taper you down. You'll feel better once you're off the smack."

"I'm *off* the smack. I could piss heroin if I could find it around here, but if I could find it around here, I wouldn't need to drive to fucking Bangor every day."

"Ayuh," he says. "I hear ya, but them's the rules."

Though I'm more restrained with the woman on the phone at the Portland clinic, the result is the same. "I understand," she says, not exactly brimming with understanding. "But it's the *law*."

Methadone is a safe alternative to heroin. If I can't get on the former, I have no choice but to track down the latter. In Switzerland, heroin can be dispensed at clinics. The government calls it harm reduction. We'd do that too—if US drug laws had anything to do with health or safety. Drug use isn't a moral failure. Punitive drug policy is.

Would Andrea have invited me to the party if we hadn't bumped into each other in town? Her backyard is teeming with drunk Workshops employees, celebrating the illicit bounty she smuggled from Cuba. Rum. Coffee. Cigars. I watch from a distance at first, where the grass meets Lake Megunticook's shoreline, staring at the rippling reflection of a waxing gibbous moon.

A little before midnight, the crowd starts to thin. I summon the nerve to approach the hostess.

"Great party. Thanks for the invitation."

"Well, we didn't really get to hang out." Andrea smiles and says something about a Workshops job fair tomorrow and all these people to interview. She takes a swig from a bottle of high-proof rum. "You should come to dinner after. We'll make sushi."

"Okay."

"Okay," she says with drunken seriousness. "But only come if you wear something made of Q-tips."

"Will you also be . . ."

"I'll wear a skirt that rustles like chiffon."

In the morning, I pick up a fruit smoothie and write a note, wishing her a speedy recovery from the hangover I assume she's nursing. I leave it on her desk at work and spend the rest of the day fashioning hundreds of Q-tips into a necktie. When I show up at her house for dinner, Andrea runs a finger over the cotton swabs of my labor.

"Wow. You actually did it."

"I aim to please."

"And you're so nice, bringing me a smoothie."

"My mom says I'm handsome too."

Andrea laughs and shows me to the kitchen where her two housemates are cursing at an uncooperative sheet of seaweed. As we attempt to construct California rolls, Andrea mentions an upcoming photography book contest in Manhattan. The books are in her office. Lyman is making her drive them to the city.

"I keep telling him my Jetta's too small," she says. "Wait. You have a Cherokee. Wanna take a road trip this weekend?"

I accept with muzzled enthusiasm and offer my mother's condo as a lodging option—she'll be in Florida.

Over the next few days, I craft the perfect mix tape for the drive. "Olsen Olsen" by Sigur Rós, "Everyday I Write the Book" by Elvis Costello, "Into Temptation" by Crowded House, "Everloving" by Moby. The tape is in the deck on Friday morning when Andrea hops in the passenger seat.

"So," I say, backing out of her driveway, "tell me everything about yourself."

"What do you want to know?"

"Everything. Your past, likes and dislikes, secrets, sexual fantasies—just kidding!"

Andrea tells me about growing up in southern Maine in an achievement-oriented family and falling in love with art in college. With a fire in her big brown eyes, she describes her work across a variety of media: a desk covered in cake frosting with "blow jobs from a dirty virgin" in icing; a wall in a gallery, with hundreds of pieces of chewed gum stuck to it—pussy goblins, she calls them. She moved to Brooklyn after graduating without ever visiting New York City before. She spent a year there working at the Brooklyn Museum. Then two years ago, she applied for a job at the Workshops.

I immediately drop the heroin bomb—the version of the story everyone else in my life believes. Five years sober. Don't look back. Positive thinking. Mind over matter. Blah blah blah.

At a gas station in Connecticut, Andrea gets out of the car to stretch while I fill the tank. Her tight gray sweater rises up, revealing a sparkly green thong at the top of her jeans. I look at the books in the back of my Jeep and think they could have fit in her Jetta, easily. She knows that, right? She wanted me to go to New York with her.

Within minutes of arriving at my mom's house, we tear each other's clothes off and have the most intense, most explosive sex in the history of the world. Lying in bed, we stay up late and compare notes on art and movies and books and music. We share our dreams—what we want to be, where we want to travel.

In the morning, we fulfill Andrea's photo book mission and I take her to the city's finest magical and secret locations—the twenty-five-foot waterfall on Fifty-First Street; the arches outside the Grand Central Oyster Bar, where we can hear each other whisper from opposite sides of the crowded hall; Track 61; Tomoe Sushi; frozen hot chocolate at Serendipity.

We can't keep our hands off each other, and I can't get enough of the passion in her voice, the sparkle in her eyes, the way she laughs to the point of hiccupping. Everything about her turns me on.

High on the newness of love, I don't give heroin a single thought.

thirty-four

As spring turns to summer, we're together all the time. Andrea shows me her favorite photography ("there's Nan Goldin and then there's everyone else"), and her favorite painter, Ida Applebroog. I introduce her to my favorite music, Radiohead and Sigur Rós, and filmmakers, Bergman and Buñuel.

We explore Maine's coast, cook decadent meals, and have lots of kinky sex. Andrea teaches me to drive a stick shift, and I tell her about Ali the cab driver. I give her my copy of *Cat's Cradle*, and she gives me Knut Hamsun's *Hunger,* which I read cover to cover. We write love notes back and forth. Every glyph is a work of art in her confident, lowercase block print.

I can't afford an original Nan Goldin for Andrea's birthday, so I write a passionate plea to her: "If you have any scraps lying around, your trash would be Andrea's treasure." When I can't track down her address, I find a way to reach Applebroog and repurpose the letter. Soon a FedEx package arrives containing a note and a small original painting.

I make a Jell-O mold with cigarettes and dismembered Barbie dolls, and present it with the Applebroog on Andrea's twenty-fifth birthday.

"No fucking way," she says, misty-eyed, studying her Applebroog. She wraps her arms around my neck. "I can't believe you made this happen."

"Power of positive thinking."

Every day, Andrea takes photographs and paints while I embark on a new novel, *Pilgrim,* a dark comedy:

Lying on the couch, unable to find the TV remote, and unwilling to get up and change the channel, David watches a documentary on plate tectonics. When the narrator speaks of the San Andreas Fault and California's inevitable detachment from the mainland, our protagonist experiences an epiphany. Some divine force wants him to buy property on the California-Nevada border, and dig down to the earth's crust and jump-start a geological event that'll dislodge California.

Hilarity and high jinks ensue as David moves to Pahrump, Nevada, and assembles a crew of misfits and dignitaries. He encounters other oceanfront property prospectors, including the Van Dorsten brothers, Keating and Kipling, fresh off their discovery of 3,200 acres of Minnesotan land in southern Manitoba. They have experience, corporate sponsorship, and the support of Dudley Baumgartner, amateur podiatric surgeon, mayor of Pahrump, and father of Lolita, a middle school geography teacher, who schools David on the ways of love and the irrefutable fact that state lines aren't perforated.

By the end of summer, Camden feels too small for our big dreams. We fantasize about moving to far-flung places and living as artists. I'm going to be a writer. Andrea is going to be a painter. We call ourselves "an unstoppable force."

One night, as we're flipping through an oversized *National Geographic* world atlas, one of Andrea's friends calls. He's looking for a roommate to share his Brooklyn apartment in the nice part of Sunset Park. We agree to split the rent.

Before the move in September, Andrea secures freelance photo-editing opportunities with several magazines. I get a job at as an art director/copywriter at a boutique ad agency. These gigs are temporary. They won't stop the unstoppable force.

We spend one night in the loud, sweltering Brooklyn apartment and start planning our escape. Soon we find a place in Piermont, a small town twenty miles north of Manhattan, on the other side of the Hudson River. It's much more conducive to our artistic leanings—except that after eight months, I am still not writing and Andrea is still not painting.

On a Monday in May, my mom calls before her usual nine o'clock. She says my grandfather was rushed to the hospital with chest pain.

Mom takes the next flight to Florida. She tells me to stay put until we find out more. The next day, as he lies unconscious in a hospital bed, Mom says not to come. "He won't know you're here. And who knows when he'll wake up."

Looking out the window, I see leaves on the trees, flowers, birds. Life is everywhere. Life is strong. Life endures. He'll be okay, I tell myself.

Twenty-four hours later, "when" becomes "if."

On Thursday, Herbie is moved to hospice. Mom pleads with me not to get on a plane.

"You don't want to see him this way. His body is filling with fluid and . . ."

"I need to see him."

"David. He wouldn't want this to be your last memory of him."

I start to cry and can't stop. I drive to Tower Records and buy a Discman and Mahler's Eighth Symphony on CD. I ship them to Florida via overnight express. He'll wake up when he hears Mahler.

Andrea comes home and holds me. I tell her about the hundred-degree movie theater with the broken air conditioner, where Herbie and I watched *Amadeus* on opening night. We turn off the air conditioner and close the windows and watch *Amadeus* in the sweltering apartment.

Mom calls in the morning. "Your package came. He has the headphones on and the music playing."

"Is he awake?"

"David."

Reality is a wrecking ball through Sheetrock. It winds up and swings and doesn't stop. Over and over and I'm hollow inside—nothing to absorb the blow. There is no next time with my grandfather. There's only a wrecking ball. A few hours later, while listening to Mahler's Eighth, he takes his last breath.

Herbie used to complain about cemeteries. He thought the land should have been used for something happy—a golf course or playground. Per his instructions, there is no funeral or obituary.

Weeks after his death, I'm still choking on tears. When I catch myself thinking about heroin, I can't remember the last time I thought about it. The urge is a *craving*: an intense want, not need. I don't tell Andrea. She still believes the lie. It bothers me, but I'm too afraid of losing her to come clean.

As cravings come and go, with increasing frequency and intensity, I think about moving farther north. Andrea and I take day trips around the Hudson Valley and fall in love with a cosmopolitan village surrounded by mountains and the Hudson River. I'm not sure it's far enough away, sixty-five miles north of the city.

In August, we make an impulsive decision to rent a small oceanfront house—sight unseen—in East Blue Hill, Maine, for $400 a month. Two hours northeast of Camden, the town has eighty-three year-round residents. We'll get part-time jobs at a coffee shop and live like royalty. I'll write. Andrea will paint.

Our friends think we're crazy when we share the plan. Days before the move, two planes crash into the World Trade Center. Nobody thinks we're crazy anymore.

I print a resume and a few short stories and hand-deliver them to R. Nathaniel W. Barrows, publisher of Blue Hill's local newspaper, *The Weekly Packet*. He speaks with an underbite, wears the same hat as the Captain from the Captain and Tennille, and reads my stuff in his office of mahogany, brass, and leather, and old paintings of sailboats in gilded frames and ships in bottles.

"This is a well-educated town, but if I print articles with 'corybantic' and 'alacrity' . . ."

"In high school, I sometimes used 'Cory Bantic' as a pen name."

"Point is, folks will be offended if they need a dictionary to read my paper."

"Got it. No gimcrack—don't be a sesquipedalian."

"And don't be so extreme. Your writing is big words or slang. Serious journalism is centered."

R. Nathaniel W. assigns an article about an old farmhouse that burned down last week. He says to contact firemen, police, and the property owner, and then write the piece and give it to Betty, the editor and lead columnist.

No one at the fire station or police station will talk to me. The property owner won't talk either. I write the article anyway and give it to Betty, who takes off her glasses, puts on another pair, and makes a popping sound with her lips while reading.

On the wall above Betty's desk, next to a framed journalism degree from Barnard, is a picture of Betty on a novelty *Time* magazine cover. "1990 Pulitzer Prize for Literature: Bette Britt."

With a warm smile, she pops the story into a wire basket on her desk. "Very good work. When did Nat give you the assignment?"

"Ten o'clock."

"This morning?"

I nod. Betty calls to Nat in the hall. "When'd you assign the Sedgwick piece?"

"Sometime this morning. Why?"

"Never mind."

Running her finger along a blotter calendar on her desk, she says, "There's a PTA meeting tomorrow night. Get there early, take minutes, and write a summary."

The morning after the meeting, I hand in the piece, and Betty dispatches me to an away junior varsity wrestling match in Ellsworth. Then an eighth-grade band performance, a school budget meeting, the science fair. I don't complain when she wordsmiths the shit out of everything I write, but I beg for more variety. Betty responds by giving me nothing.

Andrea gets a full-time job at the Blue Hill Land Trust and a part-time job milking goats at five in the morning every day. I think they pay her in cheese.

I reach out to every business on the peninsula, offering my services as a graphic designer/copywriter/website builder. No one responds. I make follow-up calls. Only one person will talk to me: Marvin Lebowitz, founder of a small local private school, self-proclaimed Manhattan refugee, and Jerry Garcia's doppelgänger.

During our first meeting, Marvin quibbles about the public education system in America for two hours before telling me he needs pamphlets and a website. He says he has no money and plies me with promises of karmic rewards and networking opportunities. I commit to the projects pro bono, and we schedule standing meetings on Tuesday and Thursday afternoons. They always involve long walks.

Starting from East Blue Hill's one-room post office, Marvin leads me along the rocky coastline—an expanse of ocean and islands and fishing boats. The crisp autumn air is an intoxicating mix of salt water, damp leaves, and wood smoke. Work is typically discussed for two minutes.

Marvin often stops midsentence to kneel down and examine a particularly smooth rock or drying jellyfish carcass. He's full of stories of young couples who tried to make a go on the peninsula—the burned-out Wall Street executive who wanted to start a bank, the people from Philly who thought a bike shop was just what the town needed.

When Marvin is late, I wait in the post office and smoke cigarettes with the postmistress.

"This job would drive anyone to drink," she says, thumbing the cap off a fifth of cheap whiskey. She takes a long pull, her weathered face scrunching as she swallows. "Sort the mail. Deliver it. Clean up. Dun't nothin' gets done less I do it." She pokes an iron into the wood-burning stove and kicks a pile of dirt into the corner.

"If you need some help, I'm looking for a job."

She laughs with a two-packs-a-day wheeze.

Andrea reads *The Good Life* by Helen and Scott Nearing, whose homestead is on the Blue Hill peninsula. Their simple lifestyle inspires her to learn more about sustainable living. She makes a deal with a local farming family: in exchange for shoveling cow shit in a barn on Sunday nights through the winter, we get space in their greenhouse.

"They have only thirty cows," she says.

I worry we're growing apart. Organic farming and sustainable living displace her interest in provocative art and hard-core fucking.

Daylight hours dwindle. The air gets that "it's going to snow any second" smell.

Marvin's pamphlets and website fail to yield any networking opportunities much less new business. Nana sends a check for $11,000, continuing my grandfather's tradition of gifting me the maximum amount a family member can give in a year.

For the first time in I can't remember, I open *Pilgrim*. The writing sucks. The content is entirely peripheral—like watching Batman vacuum the Batmobile at a gas station.

"Bat dammit, Robin! It's going to take a lot more quarters to clean the mess from that super-interesting shit we're intimating but not showing our audience."

After deleting hundreds of pages, my skin tightens and my muscles tense when I try to write. Soon, I stop fighting inertia and lie in bed all day, sleeping, jerking off, reading *Infinite Jest*, wishing I'd started reading books when I was younger, wishing for a fast-acting terminal disease.

thirty-five

Before dawn on my twenty-sixth birthday, Andrea wakes me with a cup of coffee. A lit candle is taped to it. After I blow it out, she gives me a card—on the front is a drawing of me at a desk in a cabin overlooking the ocean.

"I was thinking about the way Frida and Diego lived," she says. "Having their own spaces for art. When we buy a house, I'm going to get you a writing cabin."

I open the card to a love riot of handwritten words and line drawings. It's too much. We bundle up and go to the beach as the sun crests the horizon. Purple and orange and red and yellow streak across Mount Desert Island's mountainous silhouette.

Andrea wraps her arm around me. "Our lease ends in a couple of months. We should probably start looking for a place soon."

"Here?"

"You don't want to stay?"

"I do. It's just—it's going to be ten times the price during the summer."

"What happened to the power of positive thinking and mind over matter?"

"I'm not sure they apply to financial—"

"They totally do. And we're an unstoppable force, remember?"

Andrea says she'll talk to Jim, her boss at the land trust. "There have to be donors with spare cottages, right?"

I say yes and hope the answer is no.

Jim's pessimism doesn't tamp Andrea's belief that the power of positive thinking will manifest a spare cottage out of thin air. I try to psych myself up to tell her I need (in addition to more sex and less cow shit shoveling) to leave here when our lease ends.

While Andrea waits for a benefactor with a spare cottage to appear, I secretly look for rentals in Camden and Rockport. At the beginning of May, when we're on the brink of homelessness, I sign a monthly lease on an apartment in Rockport with a terrace overlooking the harbor.

"Why'd you do that?" Andrea says. "This is our home."

"Think of it as insurance in case our home burns down."

The next day, Andrea hears about a rental on a farm in Surrey.

At the top of the peninsula—half an hour from the ocean—we cross Route 1 and venture into a landscape of untamed woodland, punctuated by small, cleared patches with double-wide trailers. We pass crumbling rock walls and "No Hunting" and "No Trespassing" signs nailed to trees.

The pavement ends and we turn onto a narrow, horse-ribbed road. Beams of sun pierce a canopy of leaves overhead. Deer prance by, seemingly unconcerned for their safety, and chickens cross the road. Andrea rolls down the window and inhales. I hum the banjo lick from *Deliverance*.

"This isn't East Bumblefuck," she says.

"Yeah, I think it's Northwest Bumblefuck."

In a few miles, a bucolic gentleman's farm appears. I think it's a fluke until we pass another and a small cluster of immaculate Federalist homes at the end of half-mile, tree-lined driveways.

Fuck. The farm is going to be fucking awesome. It probably has a name, something with joy or happiness. I picture a row of tall, evenly spaced oak trees leading to a perfectly round pond and an archetypal white farmhouse with green shutters, and barns and outbuildings with weather vanes. Andrea will fall in love. What will I do? My neck stings and my shoulders tighten.

Andrea points to a big red mailbox in the distance. "There it is."

I see a small shed and a patch of grass fenced in with chicken wire. I turn onto the driveway and slam on the brakes to avoid crashing into a double-wide trailer. Good.

A woman steps out of the trailer, a baby slung to her body, and a man strides over from the garden. "You must be Andrea and Dave," he says, dirt all over his face. "I'm Carl. This is Erin." He leads us to a small windmill that I think used to be the obstacle on a miniature golf hole. It has a single octagonal window with a square screen stapled to the outside.

"No running water or electric," Carl says, peeling back his fingers as if he's keeping a tally of the missing features. "Oh, no gas and no phone, neither."

I'm tempted to point out the double negative and ask if it means there actually is phone service and gas.

"It's real cozy," Erin adds. "And nice and quiet." She kisses the baby's forehead and says in baby talk, "Yes it is. Yes it is. Isn't it?"

Behind the windmill, heads of cabbage poke through the ground. Carl says he also grows spinach and tatsoi. Rent is $125 a month if we help with the harvest. Otherwise, it's $150.

"We grew tatsoi over the winter," Andrea says. "We'll totally help."

Driving home, she proposes we split our time over the summer between her—ahem—house and my apartment and look for a permanent place in Blue Hill.

I reach across the console and slide my palm into hers. "Perfect."

It's my first night in Rockport, one in the morning. I'm on the terrace, smoking cigarettes, reading Plato's *Republic*. Moonlight reflects off the calm ocean.

Plato said, "To know the good is to do the good." I think the context is our actions—awareness of the right thing in a situation means we'll automatically do it. My awareness of what I should do and my inability to do it proves how hopeless I am.

The door opens, and Andrea comes in, tears streaming down her face, swollen and red with bug bites.

"I can't live there," she says. She strips off her clothes and gets in the shower. I join her. We have intense, pre–Blue Hill sex and sleep naked in my bed, our bodies intertwined. She leaves before dawn, drives two hours to work, and returns at night with all her belongings.

I cobble together freelance graphics and copywriting projects with local clients, as well as with a private equity firm in New York—a former client of the boutique agency I worked for. The money is good, but it feels empty and I'm inside for days on end in a purple bathrobe and boxers, pacing around the house, taking clients' feedback by phone.

Andrea commutes to Blue Hill on weekdays through the end of June, when she gets a job at a gourmet deli in Camden. She cultivates friendships with her new coworkers, going for drinks after work. I'm always invited but seldom go.

One night when I'm at home alone, it occurs to me that Andrea has tons of friends and I have none. She maintains contact with former coworkers and her old crew from college and high school. I can't remember the last time I hung out with a friend or connected with one via phone or email.

At the end of summer, my old house on Sea Street is available to rent. Andrea and I snap it up and celebrate the symbolism, returning to the first place we lived together. My old shower curtain, which I bought when I moved to Camden two years ago, is still here, now ripped and slightly moldy.

After New Year's, I get a part-time job as a line cook at a decent restaurant in Rockland. The objectivity of working in a kitchen is a refreshing contrast to the subjectivity of advertising. Orders come in and food goes out. No ambiguity about my performance. Every day is a fresh start.

In April, my responsibilities increase when Ken, the chef, breaks his arm. The details change every time he tells the story. Usually it involves a fall from a tree. Alcohol may or may not have been a factor. He tries to help, but there's only so much a one-armed chef can do.

On a Monday, as the lunch rush winds down, Ken pulls a prescription bottle from his backpack and waves it at me the way you'd offer gum to someone.

"Vicodin," he says. "Want some?"

I say yes without thinking and twist off the cap and tip a white capsule-shaped pill into my hand. Eight or nine remain. The label reads, "Vicodin 2.5/300." Each pill contains 2.5 milligrams of hydrocodone and 300 milligrams of acetaminophen.

"Have them all," Ken says. "They make me nauseous."

I pop two pills in my mouth and open a bottle of Pellegrino to wash them down. My body immediately warms and loosens in psychosomatic anticipation. The effect fully kicks in half an hour later. No customers, the front of the restaurant awash in sunlight. Outside, small trees on the sidewalk sway in a gentle breeze. Life is good.

When my shift ends at four o'clock, I take two more Vics and drive home with the windows down under a cloudless sky. Penobscot Bay on my right, flecks of gold and silver dancing across the water. Sigur Rós on the stereo. *Ágætis Byrjun.*

I turn onto Sea Street and pull in the driveway behind Andrea's car. The sight of my pinned pupils in the rearview mirror triggers a wave of guilt, but that's all it is—a wave. Cold water laps at my ankles and pulls back, my feet melting into warm sand on the shore. *This is a fluke. I wasn't looking. Dope found me. It's okay. You're okay.*

Andrea is lying on the couch in the living room, reading E. B. White's *One Man's Meat*—essays about his saltwater farm in Brooklin, Maine, near Blue Hill. I greet her with a kiss and jump in the shower to wash away the raw onion smell.

I'm drying off when Andrea comes into the bathroom. "I miss my job milking goats," she says. "Do you think we'll ever live someplace where we can have goats?"

The slideshow projector in my brain flickers on with a carousel of scenic locations on the Blue Hill peninsula: the path on Little Deer Isle abutting Eggamoggin Reach, Naskeag Point in Brooklin, pretty much all of Cape Rosier, Parker Point, and Lighthouse Beach in East Blue Hill. I imagine an apple orchard with old wooden ladders that narrow at the top and goats cavorting about. Yeah, I could get down with that.

"By 'someplace we could have goats,' do you mean Blue Hill?"

"Actually, I was thinking of somewhere around here since you hate Blue Hill."

"I don't—"

"Come on, David. You think I don't know you by now?"

Late in the afternoon, Camden has the light of an Edward Hopper painting. I propose a walk to French and Brawn, an upscale grocery store, to pick up dinner supplies. Andrea agrees and we take the extra-long way: Bay View Street to the loop at Beauchamp Point in Rockport. We buy lobster, asparagus, and fresh greens with nasturtiums. When we get home, I stage a trial for the lobsters.

"Claws McLobsterpants and Lobstey McTrousenheimer, the jury finds you guilty of being lobsters on a Monday. You are hereby sentenced to death by boiling in lightly salted water. Bailiff, the *fleur de sel*, please."

Andrea laughs. Van Morrison's *Astral Weeks* is playing on the stereo, and there's a nice cross breeze in the kitchen. Andrea makes salad dressing in a coffee cup, whisking Dijon mustard with olive oil and Herbes de Provence and lemon. She licks the whisk and offers me a taste.

"I wasn't a mustard person until I met you," she says. "Or sushi or . . ."

"I didn't know how to drive a stick shift until we met . . ."

Andrea pours a glass of wine and takes a sip. My gaze travels from her lips to her shoulders, her black bra straps poking out from behind her ribbed, form-fitting tank top. I get caught on her breasts for a beat, then move to her legs, smooth and muscular from running up and down Mount Megunticook every day and working out at the gym.

As we eat, I think about coming clean—the Vicodin and the whole shebang. Between field hockey and lacrosse and wisdom tooth extraction, Andrea must have taken some kind of painkiller in her life, right? I write a script in my mind: *Opioids are a category the way alcohol is a category. If you've had beer, you know how moonshine feels. If you've taken codeine, you know how heroin feels. Oh, you had codeine when you broke your toe? And you liked it. Drugs are legal in Portugal. We should move.*

After dinner, I duck into the bathroom, take two more Vics, and decide it's too risky to come clean, and besides, I don't have enough pills to share. We snuggle on the couch and watch *Being John Malkovich*. I take two more before bed and fall right asleep. In the morning, I take the remaining pills, brush my teeth, and go to work.

Ken looks at me with a crooked smile. "Bet somebody had fun last night."

"Actually, I opened the bottle at home and all the pills fell into the toilet. And I'd just told a friend I had some Vics and—can you get more? He'd pay you."

Ken studies his cast poking out of a blue sling and then raises his eyes. "I'll ask my doc. If I can get 'em, buy me a beer one night. I don't want to be a drug dealer."

· · ·

Two days pass. Ken doesn't say anything about the Vics. I don't bring them up.

I'm too distracted to work. In a period of ten minutes, I reach into the pizza oven and grab a steel plate without a mitt three times. When it happens again, Ken laughs and gets Bacitracin from the first aid kit. He points to scars on his hands and non-broken arm and tells the story of each burn, knife mishap, and mandolin malfunction.

Nell, a baker and co-owner of the restaurant, complains about her back and all the painkillers she had to take when she slipped a disc last summer.

"Vicodin, Percocet, Oxycontin. You name it."

I start to look for ways to injure myself with minimal pain and maximum visual impact. My eye keeps wandering to the knives on a magnetic strip above the prep station. Once a week, Nell pays a guy to come in and sharpen them.

When Ken steps out to make a phone call, I pick up the meat cleaver, surprisingly heavy with a cold, smooth, contoured wooden handle. I lay my left hand on the cutting board, palm down, and raise my right arm. I hold the position for a few terrifying seconds. Then I hear Ken's voice in the back of the kitchen, and I return the cleaver to the strip.

The phone rings after midnight. Daniel says, "I just spent my last four bucks on a lukewarm Bud Light. Now I'm thinking of walking into the ocean."

"Are you kidding?"

"I have no job, no money. I just . . ."

"Did you ask Mom for—"

"I'm not asking her."

"Why?"

"Because."

"Because?"

"David, she knows how fucked I am, and she's not offering to—I'm so sick of this. The other night, I drank all this beer and ate a big bag of Oxys, Xanax, Vicodin and passed out. Next thing I knew, I was in a hospital getting my stomach pumped."

"Ugh."

"The worst part is when I got out and asked my friends who called 911 or took me to the ER, nobody had a clue and . . . I don't want to keep doing this."

"I know."

"You don't. You just woke up one day—seven fucking years ago—and decided to stop like it was nothing. I just want someone to tell me what to do."

"I'm at my computer. There's a 6 a.m. flight from West Palm to White Plains."

"So?"

"It's past midnight. The plane probably boards at five. Go to the airport and—"

"I can't."

"You can. Just go to the airport and I'll meet you at Mom's."

"I feel so weak."

"All you have to do is—"

"I know. Get to the fucking airport."

I hang up with Daniel and call Mom to tell her to pick him up. "I'll come down for a few days. He needs treatment."

"He's been to rehab. He needs somebody to sit him down and say, 'Daniel, you have to decide how you want to live your life. When you choose to do drugs—"

"He's not *choosing* to. He can't control it."

"David—you said so yourself. Addiction *isn't* a disease."

In the morning while I pack, Andrea comes behind me and slides her arms up my chest, pulling me close. "It must be so hard for Daniel," she says, "knowing how easy it was for you to quit and stay quit all this time."

I drive to the restaurant and find Nell kneading focaccia dough in the back of the kitchen. I ask if we can talk. She drops the dense wad on the chrome table and looks up as it lands with a dense, sticky thud.

"Please don't tell me you're quitting."

"I'm not quitting."

She exhales slowly and reaches for a canister of dried rosemary. "I need to get these in the oven. Can you give me two minutes?"

I hear "Psst" and turn to see Ken nodding at the walk-in refrigerator. I follow him inside. He wedges his foot in the door and pulls a prescription bottle from his pocket. I wait for him to leave and then swallow two pills and call my mom from the office.

As the phone rings, I look at the label on the bottle. Vicodin 10/300—four times stronger than the last script. Twenty-five pills. Mom picks up.

"I'm so sorry—the chef broke his arm last night. If I leave, the restaurant will have to close."

Mom says not to worry. "Daniel needs to learn that not everybody can drop what they're doing when he's having a hard time. And he's goddamn lucky you were there for him last night, and so am I. You are one extraordinarily remarkable man. When anyone asks how my kids are, I say I never have to worry about David."

When the Vicodin is gone, I try to distract myself by putting in more hours at the restaurant and asking my freelance clients for more projects. The guilt and shame are inescapable.

I go shopping for an engagement ring. The selection in and around Camden is brand-new, gaudy crap, so I investigate estate jewelry stores in Portland and take a day off to check them out. At the first one, my eye is immediately drawn to a princess cut diamond set in a thin hundred-year-old platinum band.

The woman in the shop removes it from the glass cabinet and places it in my hand. She says it's so petite that it can't be resized and warns me not to buy anything until I've measured Andrea's finger. "Can you imagine the heartbreak if it doesn't fit and there's nothing you can do?"

I buy the ring. I know it'll fit like I know the sun will rise tomorrow morning.

Driving back to Camden, I hatch a scheme to make a picnic and propose at the top of Mount Megunticook—Andrea's favorite place. I stop for supplies at French and Brawn and tell the cashier about my plan.

"Today?" she says, jabbing her thumb at the window. "It's cold and rainy."

At home, I shine the ring on my shirt a hundred times and arrange and rearrange everything in the picnic basket until Andrea's car pulls in the driveway. When she comes through the door, I'm on my knee, holding the ring, holding my breath.

"Will you marry me?"

Andrea says yes and wells up with tears. I slide the ring on her finger. It fits perfectly. I breathe.

Later that fall, the private equity firm in New York offers me a full-time job, building and running a marketing department. Andrea and I don't want to leave Camden, but this opportunity will never exist here.

We move from our harbor-view house to a small apartment in Greenwich, Connecticut, facing a vacuum cleaner repair shop. The moment my shiny new Prada loafers hit the office's soft carpet, I feel out of place.

I'm an animal in designer clothes, pretending to be a person, surrounded by guys in pleated gabardine slacks and blue blazers with gold buttons. They call me Dave and practice their golf swing with invisible clubs while talking football and all-inclusive Caribbean resorts.

I'm the only one who's ever used heroin. I can tell. There's something really sad and lonely about that. I worry it's obvious. I worry they know who I really am. They're going to fire me.

Every morning, I'm in the office before everyone else. At night, I'm the last one out. One by one, I rebrand every company under the corporate umbrella, negotiate better prices with media partners, and consolidate hundreds of print and promotional vendors into one resource. At the holiday party, I receive a generous raise and an unexpected bonus. It feels empty and unearned.

Andrea gets a job as a visual manager at Anthropologie. The hours are long, and she misses Maine.

A year passes. Slowly.

thirty-six

At least once a month, I drive to a local print production facility to sign off on a press check with Greg, my sales rep. Afterward, he always invites me to a large conference room, where he fills up on free snacks and pitches all manner of satin aqueous coatings, die cuts, and promotional materials.

One morning in early 2005, he closes the door to the conference room and settles into his usual seat. "You party?"

"Uh, not really. No."

"But you might know where to get some blow?"

He reaches into the pocket of his suit jacket and pulls out a small Ziploc bag of pastel Skittles-like pills. "Oxycontin," he says. "Took 'em from my grandmother's place after she passed. My buddy is having a bachelor party this weekend. I figure you're artsy, you'll know someone who'll trade an eight ball of blow for this. If you can do something by Friday, great. If not, I'll flush them."

I don't know where to get coke or how much an eight ball costs, but no price is too high if it means the Oxy comes home with me.

"I'll see what I can do."

In the parking lot, I smoke a cigarette and scroll through the contacts on my cell phone. The only possibility is Susan, a freelance graphic designer, who once alluded to being a pothead. She picks up on the first ring and agrees to meet at a nearby coffee shop when I plead for help with an emergency project.

For forty-five minutes, I listen to every idea in Susan's thick spiral notebook. When she's finished, I sputter about my cousin's upcoming bachelor party.

"I know you know *I* don't do drugs but . . . he's pretty desperate for an eight ball of coke . . . the party's this weekend so . . . if you happen to know anyone who might—"

"Say no more," Susan says, whipping out her cell phone. She places a call, asks for "a thing," and hangs up and blows on her phone like a cowboy with a six-shooter.

"Twenty minutes," she says.

Fifteen minutes later, a black Lexus SUV with chrome rims and dark-tinted windows screeches into the parking lot, blasting "Nuthin' But a G Thang" by Dr. Dre and Snoop. A short, skinny girl in an LA Raiders hat hops out and flings a brown plastic shopping bag at Susan, who hands it to me. After paying her, I wrap it in my blazer, bury it in my trunk, and drive back to Greg's office.

"My man," he says, leaning back in his chair, ogling the powder. He licks the tip of his index finger, dips it in the powder, and runs it along his gums. "You sample the goods?"

"Nope."

"It's okay if you did."

"I really don't—"

"Bull. Shit."

"I'm serious."

"Not even weed?"

I shake my head.

He smiles and hurls the bag of Oxycontin at me. "I hope your guy is happy with the trade."

"I'm sure he will be." I put the pills in the inside pocket of my blazer and drive back to work. In my office, I grab a pen and folder and hurry to the bathroom.

The farthest stall from the door is empty. I pull down my pleated gabardine slacks and sit on the toilet to examine the haul. Most of the pills are mint green stamped with the number "80." Must be milligrams. The other colors are stamped "20," "40," and "10."

I MacGyver the ballpoint pen into a snorting vessel and use a quarter to

pulverize a forty-milligram pill on the back of the folder. The rough powder burns with a nasty chemical taste. I wait in the stall until a familiar
warmth begins to envelop me. Twenty minutes later, I feel the full effect
at my desk—much closer to heroin than Vicodin.

I crank the thermostat for noise, slip into the bathroom, and crush an
eighty-milligram pill on the only usable surface: a save-the-date postcard
for our wedding, a stodgy maroon damask pattern with "Free Booze &
Cake" in big gold letters. Placing the pen in my nose, I flush the toilet and
snort. The burn and taste are no less unpleasant. I check my nose in the
mirror. No residue around my nostrils, no chunks in the hairs.

Andrea is lying on the couch. I get behind her and tilt my head back,
so the dope juice drips in the right direction. Without thinking, I take a
hard snort.

"You've been very sniffly," she says.

"Yeah. I think it's allergies."

The next morning at work, I'm sitting on the toilet in the far stall about
to snort an eighty and a twenty when shiny burgundy leather tasseled loafers enter the bathroom. I watch them point at the sink and mirror and
hope this guy is like me—if I come in for non-illicit sit-down purposes
and anyone is in any of the four stalls, I'll take a moment to look in the
mirror or wash my hands and then leave.

Tasseled Loafers strides into the stall next to me. Pleated slacks drop
to the floor. I can't snort the pill, I can't leave the bathroom with a pile
of powder on a folder, and I sure as hell am not going to flush it. For ten
minutes, I breathe sparingly and try to block out the sounds.

The toilet finally flushes and Loafers whistles "Zip-a-Dee-*Fucking-
Doo-Dah*" for fucking ever while washing his hands. The automated paper towel dispenser makes a "gaddunguh" sound and then the door opens
and stays open.

Loafers face navy blue Docksiders at the threshold. Two unfamiliar
voices. I stick the pen in my nose, hold the folder carefully with one hand,
and flush and snort simultaneously. I start to get up and realize I can't leave
without checking my nose. Docksiders shuffles into the second stall, the
slacks land on the floor, and I hustle out.

This becomes a pattern—negotiating bathroom traffic at work. I'm relieved when the last specks of Oxy dust burn up my nose in the men's room in the far stall next to black wing tips. Hours later, I feel desperate and selfish and hopeless.

As the wedding approaches, I try to neutralize my guilt by surprising Andrea with dates at fancy restaurants, day trips to new places, mix CDs with elaborately decorated covers. But I can't do anything without questioning my own motives.

Walking down Greenwich Avenue, I take her hand and give it a squeeze. She deserves to know the truth before entering into a legally binding agreement to be my wife till death do us part. Halfway down the block, I tell myself she's better off *not* knowing, not being burdened with concern. I know it's bullshit. I don't want the burden of *her* concern.

A couple of weeks before the wedding, I'm at a flower shop, buying a dozen Gerbera daisies—Andrea's favorite. In a bucket behind the register, I see dried poppy pods on stems.

"Oh, I've been looking for poppies for an art project. How many do you have?"

"Forty-eight," the florist says.

"I'll take them all. And another three dozen Gerberas."

I get home before Andrea and crush a few pods and brew them into tea with a French press coffee maker. The effect is milder than any other opioid I've tried, but it lasts longer.

The next day, I leave for work earlier than usual with the press and remaining pods. I begin a ritual of brewing a fresh batch of tea every morning. The press stays in my drawer. Nobody asks about the liquid in my mug.

Five days before the wedding, while sipping the last cup at my desk, I'm struck by the pathetic irony: everyone believes I've been clean for ten years, but I can't honestly say I've been clean for ten *seconds*.

The day after my twenty-ninth birthday, Andrea and I are married by our friend Amie, who signed up to be ordained for twenty-four hours by some bullshit online ministry. The ceremony is a religious smorgasbord with elements of Judaism, Buddhism, Hinduism, Islam, Zoroastrianism, astrology, and a pinch of Catholicism to appease Andrea's mother.

We write our own vows. I'm in a tuxedo with tails. Andrea's gown is from a gas station that also sells guns and ammo and beer. Daniel is my best man. He hasn't had a drink in two years. He lives in Manhattan and works in reality TV. Rob, still clean, is a groomsman. Sprigs of rosemary are placed on guests' chairs—a symbol of love and happiness. Our first dance is to "I Can't Give You Anything but Love" by Django Reinhardt.

We honeymoon at Le Sireneuse in Positano, Italy, in a room with a balcony overlooking the Tyrrhenian Sea. Not long after we return, we find out Andrea is pregnant. At our first ultrasound, the technician says our baby is healthy and lets us hear the heartbeat and gives us black-and-white screenshots of a jelly bean.

Andrea loads up on books about parenting and researches the shit out of breast pumps, rocking chairs, and this product called a diaper wizard or a diaper genie, something that supposedly eliminates the smell of baby poop. She's especially thorough when investigating things that will touch or be ingested by the baby. Organic cotton onesies, organic food, cribs, and foam wedges you put in cribs.

"These wedges are expensive," she says, "but with SIDS, you don't fuck around."

"Is that like AIDS? I don't think our kid's going to be getting laid so soon."

"It's sudden infant death syndrome."

"So spontaneous combustion for babies? Did the wedge company invent that?"

"David, google it."

I google SIDS and read the first paragraph of an article on a parenting website. I tell Andrea to please order multiple packs of the deluxe wedges.

If we don't buy a house right fucking now, there won't be anything available later in our desired location and price range, and when all the good stuff's gone, we'll end up in some tiny shit box in the middle of nowhere. This isn't a bubble. Real estate is finite.

On a Saturday morning, Andrea and I take a drive to our favorite village on the Hudson River. Drenched in sun in the passenger seat, she talks about quitting her job when the baby is born and starting a line of kids' T-shirts with whimsical line drawings. An elephant on roller skates. A frog holding an umbrella. A gorilla playing a ukulele.

"I'll be your sugar mama," she says. "You can quit your job and write full-time."

The windows are down, and the smells of early spring whip through the car. My brain switches off the thrashing, gnashing, racing panic long enough to picture us living the dream. It feels possible—no—*definite*. We're an unstoppable force.

We park on Main Street and skip down the sidewalk to a real estate agency, where a nice woman informs us that no homes are for sale in the village at this time. She advises us to check the national database listings every day.

"The village is always a seller's market. Supply and demand. When something comes up, you need to make an offer on the spot—*above* asking price."

Weeks pass. Nothing is for sale. We return to the village on a Sunday just because and happen upon an open house half an hour before it's scheduled to begin and the listing will go live on MLS. The realtor hasn't arrived yet. Beth, the owner, offers to give us a tour.

The 1,350-square-foot house was built in the mid-1800s. It needs a ton of work. Decades-old carpet covers every inch of the original pine floor. Wallpaper galore, floral in the living room, illustrations of butter churns (the word "butter churn" is printed on the butter churns) in the kitchen and dining room.

The price is steep—more than a reach when you add the cost of stripping the place down to its bones. But it's in the village, with a major serendipity factor.

Beth opens the basement door and says the old steep wooden stairs are perfectly safe, but we have to go one at a time as we follow her down. I see antique cobwebs and think the floor looks dirty. Beth says, "It's a dirt floor." She pulls strings attached to light bulbs screwed into industrial ceiling fixtures. Maybe she should have kept the lights off. The phrase "money pit" comes to mind. Maybe this isn't the house for us.

"Well," Beth says, deflated. "That's it."

Andrea points to a stack of old horseshoes on a rotted wooden work-bench. "One of your good omens," she says.

We inch our way to the back of the musty, scary space. "HOPE" is carved into the wall. Andrea takes my hand. I look up and notice an old *New York Times* front page glued to the ceiling. Standing on my tippy-toes, I squint and read the date. March 12, 1905. Exactly one hundred years before our wedding.

"Beth, we want to make an offer."

thirty-seven

We close on the house in June, on Andrea's thirtieth birthday, and spend the night holding paint swatches to walls, peeling back carpet, and looking at furniture online. We make a bed of blankets on the dining room floor under a window. I drift to sleep feeling safe and secure. In the morning, I wake with tight skin and a sour stomach.

The first contractor arrives at eight o'clock. A floor guy. Then a painter, another floor guy, an electrician, a carpenter. They take measurements and give estimates. We're looking at two months of construction before we can even think about moving in. Rent plus mortgage, plus the cost of moving and all the furniture we need, plus accoutrements for the baby, plus bills for things we never had to pay for: water, sewer, electricity, oil, propane. Plus, plus, plus. I'm going to lose my job. We're going to be homeless—with a baby.

I experience this weird phenomenon—it's as if my life were an '80s comedy and I'm watching it in fast-forward. I can see Andrea's water break and then the two of us sloshing through a sea of amniotic fluid on the kitchen floor and racing to the hospital. I see a caravan of squad cars chasing us, along with a parade of gimmicky characters driving gimmicky vehicles—a pizza guy with a handlebar mustache in a chef uniform, shaking his fist out the window, screaming Italian obscenities, unable to see past five pepperoni pizza pies plastered to the windshield of his van, whose hubcaps detach and fly toward the cops, who shimmy and shake out of the way and, in the process, accidentally fire their guns at the clowns getting out of the

VW Beetle behind the pizza guy's van. That's typical in the moments before everyone's kid is born, right?

One night, I have a dream about getting high. I'm in a room with red walls and a red velvet sofa. An antique syringe with a huge glass chamber and steel rings around the plunger goes into my arm. My brain floods with the warm feeling of relief. I wake up with the taste of dope in my mouth.

A week later, on three consecutive nights, I dream about almost getting high. In one, I'm alone in an unfamiliar car with white vinyl everything. In the passenger seat, I hold a spoon and suck the medicine into a syringe. I make a fist, and as I push down on the plunger, I wake up, gasping. Andrea is asleep, lying on her side, the baby bump visible. *The baby. Think about the baby. You're a father. Keep your shit together.*

I recognize my father's unmistakable loopy cursive handwriting on an envelope in the mailbox. A decade has passed since we've seen each other, eight years since I've heard from him—the letter on my twenty-first birthday. This one is very different.

Dear David,
It's been a while. I hope you're well. I'd love to see you and catch up
if you're up to it.
Love, Bob

At this point, Bob is some guy I once knew, not my father. My first instinct is to throw the letter in the trash and forget about it. Seconds later, I think about the baby. Someday, he or she will ask about his or her other grandfather. Bob.

The letter sits on my desk for a week before I type twenty pages of stream of consciousness, recapping the past ten years. Then I delete it and start over. Then I pick up the phone and call.

"David, my son. It's a pleasure to hear your voice."

The conversation is quick, just the particulars of a date we make for the following afternoon at Starbucks in Rye.

Andrea says, "How do you feel about seeing your dad again?"

"I don't really feel anything."

"Are you nervous?"

"No."

"Excited?"

"No."

"Nothing?"

"Nothing."

"Really?"

"Really."

I find it odd, feeling nothing. When Bob strolls into Starbucks, and I see his weathered face and completely gray hair, he is just a guy and that, I realize, is not nothing. It's huge. He's just a guy—not my fearsome father.

We sit and talk for half an hour. I tell him about Andrea, his unborn grandchild, Maine, my job. He listens and occasionally drops a subdued "That's terrific." He doesn't tell me what I'm doing wrong or point out ways my dick will end up in a windowsill. These absences come as a relief and a reminder that he never offered fatherly advice. He commanded, decried, and scared. My kid will have a different kind of father.

When Bob asks if I'm clean, I stick with the lie.

"Ten years."

"Good for you, Dave. That's terrific."

No hug at the end. We shake hands. In the coming months, we talk on the phone periodically and see each other once or twice. I wouldn't say we buried the hatchet—more like we made a nonverbal agreement not to unearth the hatchet. As long as it's inaccessible, no one can get hurt.

On December 14, 2005, Ruby Grace Poses is born. In an instant, I know I'll never touch another opioid for the rest of my life. I've never been so clear about anything.

The umbilical cord is cut. A nurse rolls black ink over Ruby's foot and then plants it on a birth certificate and on my shirt, which I'll keep forever and never wash. In these first few minutes of my daughter's life, every cliché about parenthood becomes a fact. This kind of love didn't exist before. It couldn't have.

After thirty-six hours in the hospital, Andrea and I strap Ruby into her car seat and take her home. I made a CD for the occasion, starting with "Beautiful Child" by Rufus Wainwright, followed by "First Day of My Life" by Bright Eyes.

Traffic is light on the Taconic Parkway. Clear skies and the temperature well above freezing. I always thought the speed limit was too low. Now it seems irresponsibly, criminally high. I see danger everywhere. Every driver is a drunken, bloodthirsty maniac.

Ruby keeps odd, unpredictable hours, waking at all hours of the night, hungry, screaming like a maniac in a language Andrea and I don't speak but understand fluently. *Wake (the fuck) up. I'm hungry.* Andrea is exhausted, but she has this indescribable glow and an ear-to-ear grin while nursing our child. We make a pact not to refer to ourselves in the third person or talk baby talk to Ruby, even when she is a baby.

Most mornings, I lie in bed and read the *New York Times* while Ruby naps on my chest. Were there always this many articles about pedophiles and kidnappers? I realize Mom's old saying—"you kill for your kids"—is figurative and literal. I think of buying a gun. Then I worry about a gun in the house with a baby.

I take every opportunity to impart valuable life lessons as things pop into my head. "Technically, Reggiano is Parmesan cheese, but don't call it Parmesan. Boys are evil. *OK Computer* is the best album ever recorded. Don't park on the street in Manhattan if your inspection is expired."

Ruby's birth announcement is a CD. Every song has her name in the title, save for Rufus Wainwright's "Beautiful Child." The stereo is always on. I introduce Ruby to Cat Stevens, Nick Drake, Radiohead, Van Morrison, Charles Mingus, Bob Marley. We dance together for the first time to "Is This Love?" Holding her in my arms, I sway back and forth and tell her to "take a mental snapshot so you'll never forget this." I catch myself saying that a lot. Ruby doesn't understand English yet. I know she won't remember. I will.

Between Christmas and New Year's, the house swells with friends and family. My parents take great pains to visit when the other isn't here. I didn't consider the multi-generational impact of their war. How will we deal with Ruby's birthday parties? When Daniel visits, I ask him.

"Fuck 'em," he says. "Invite them and say, 'If you have a problem, don't come.'"

I've spent my life contorting, conforming, concealing, and operating from a place of fear. Daniel is, and has always been, unabashedly honest and unapologetically himself. My little brother, my hero. Sober, happy, healthy.

The day before I return to work, we strap Ruby in the stroller and give her a tour of the village. It's sunny and warm. Water drips off snowbanks and races down Main Street, passing antique stores and crap marts en route to the river.

I carry the stroller down the stairs to the tunnel below the train tracks. On the other side, Storm King Mountain rises, making the Hudson look like a fjord. The tide pushes icebergs toward Manhattan. To the north, Breakneck Ridge and the crumbling Bannerman Castle and Civil War–era arsenal on Pollepel Island.

Wreathes and Christmas lights stretch between telephone poles. We follow Church Street to the Tiny Tots' Park and meet a woman and her baby daughter—the first parent we've met as parents. As we compare notes on sleep habits and local day care options, there's no doubt in my mind that when she looks at me, Heather sees another parent—not a junkie.

We take the scenic route home, past the elementary school—an old brick building on a hill with panoramic river views. Ruby begins to whimper and stir. Andrea makes soft shushing sounds in her ear.

"We made this person," she whispers. "Can you believe it?"

Everything I ever wanted and never thought I'd have. I bend and kiss Ruby's soft, chubby cheek.

thirty-eight

The inertia is overwhelming. I don't know when this started or why or how to make it stop. It takes all my energy to keep everything inside. I've cobbled together stretches of sobriety, but I haven't begun to recover.

Sleep is elusive. I have practically no appetite. I can't drive anywhere without looking at every tree and bridge support, gauging their potential for a fatal crash.

On a Saturday, Andrea waves me out of a trance at the bottom of the snow-covered hill.

"It's the weekend," she says. "You're sledding with your wife and daughter in the most beautiful place in the world."

I turn and force my frozen lips to curl into some approximation of a smile.

Ruby shimmies and shakes in a long red plastic sled. "Bees," she says. "Dada. BEES!" She's two years old, but she can't quite say "please." I pull her up the hill and we take another run. Up and down and up and down and up and down, doing everything in my power to appear in the moment.

At dusk, I pull Ruby home in the sled on unplowed roads. Andrea walks alongside and teaches her to catch snowflakes on her tongue. They giggle, and I wonder why I get to raise my family in a real-life Norman Rockwell painting, but other people live in the apartments you see from the last exit on the New York side of I-95 before the George Washington Bridge. The bricks, obviously beige at some point, are now mostly black from years of continuous car and truck exhaust.

As the weather warms up, I start getting nosebleeds, like when I was a kid. They quickly increase in frequency and severity.

One night, when I come home from work with yet another blood-stained shirt and tie, Andrea says I should look for a therapist and another job and find a creative outlet. She hires a contractor to convert our backyard shed into a deluxe writing cabin. Electricity, insulation, a space heater, two big windows. It's maddening—to have so much and see it so clearly and feel so unworthy.

Later, when Andrea and Ruby are on the couch watching Dora the Explorer, I'm on the floor to the side, researching shotguns on my laptop. In the kitchen, I measure the distance from my shoulder to my index finger—I want to make sure I won't have trouble pulling the trigger.

The sick irony isn't lost on me—suicide would be less of a stigma than using heroin to avoid killing myself.

An ear, nose, and throat doctor says a deviated septum is causing my nose to bleed. Surgery will resolve the problem. I schedule it in August, days before we depart for our first family vacation—a week in a rented house in Camden.

Rows of flowers line the cobblestone path to the front steps, and a rope hammock and small round table with wiry cafe chairs sit on the wraparound porch. Archetypal Downeast oceanfront style: wide-pine flooring, turquoise paint on the wainscoted underside of the vaulted ceiling. The view is stunning—from the harbor and the islands in Penobscot Bay to the outline of Castine in the distance. We schlep our luggage inside and go for a walk.

On Sea Street, Andrea points to number twenty-eight, a green Federalist-style home with black shutters. "Ruby, that's where Daddy and I lived when we first got together. A taxi driver named Ali told Daddy to move here."

I turn away and close my watery eyes as Andrea tells the story. I see her in Kevin's office at the Workshops eight and a half years ago—when she entered and I thought, *Someday I'll tell her the Ali story, and someday, she'll tell our kids.*

"Bees, Mama. *BEES!*"

Ruby angles her body at the tall wooden masts rising from schooners in the harbor. We did promise her a boat ride. We board the *Mary Day,* and I hoist Ruby onto my lap and wrap my arms around her. A low, thin rope is the only thing keeping us from falling overboard.

The salty air is especially pungent as we sail past the lighthouse on Curtis Island. The water gets choppy. For two hours, my brain bakes in the sun. When we disembark, Andrea wants to hike up Mount Megunticook. I want to lie down in a dark, quiet room. I push myself, not uttering a word about my headache.

"This," Andrea says, freeing Ruby from her car seat at the mountain's base. "This is what I've been looking forward to most."

We take turns piggybacking Ruby to the summit, where there are blueberries—if you know where to look and you're not too distracted by the view: 360 degrees of ocean, islands, mountains, and lakes. Andrea picks berries sparingly in consideration of other hikers.

"I so miss it here," she says, laying an arm around my shoulder.

"Me too."

I put Ruby on my shoulders and spin around. I tell her this is one of those mental-snapshot moments.

My headache gets worse over the next few days. I drink a lot of water and take a lot of Advil as we show Ruby the area's greatest hits: walking around Beauchamp point, the Belted Galloway cows, Owl's Head's rocky beach. We drive down the St. George peninsula to Port Clyde, picnic on Rockport Harbor behind the Maine Photographic Workshops, and walk up Main Street in Rockport.

On Thursday, I wake to the feeling of ice picks stabbing my eyes from the inside. I finally say something to Andrea. We think it's the surgery. I call Dr. Grossman.

"I've performed this procedure thousands of times," he says, dismissively. "Never had an issue before." He tells me to avoid the sun and to switch to Motrin.

Twenty-four hours later, my brain is skewered. Intense pain shoots down my back and arms to my fingertips. I spend the day—our last—inside, feeling guilty beyond words. In the morning, we say goodbye to Camden.

The sun is a strobe light, blasting through leaves on the trees on the side of the road. I feel it, even with my eyes closed, in the passenger seat while Andrea drives. When we get home, she helps me into bed and looks up my symptoms in Louise Hay's *You Can Heal Your Life*.

"Headaches: 'Invalidating the self. Self-criticism. Fear.' Back problems: 'Guilt.'"

Sunday morning. Everything is blurry. Ice picks continue to stab my eyes. I roll out of bed and blood gushes out of both nostrils. I open my mouth to speak. No words come. We get in the car.

My mom is waiting at the hospital when we arrive. She takes Ruby's hand and whisks her away as a nurse hustles me into a small triage area. She asks if I'm allergic to any medications. Andrea says no, barely restrained terror in her voice. The nurse gives me a shot of morphine. No effect on the pain, no euphoria.

A neurologist appears. Dr. Baudelaire. He peels back my eyelids and shines a flashlight in my eyes as Andrea lays out the sequence of events. "This has to be related to the surgery, right?"

"Eh, no," Dr. Baudelaire says, with confidence and a heavy French accent. "Seems like a transient ischemic attack." He orders a CAT scan, MRI, blood work, and a spinal tap.

Please, don't let this be something terminal. Don't make Andrea a widow. Don't make Ruby grow up without a father. I don't know who I'm addressing.

The nurse pushes me into the hall in a wheelchair. Andrea walks alongside, holding my hand, sobbing. In a dark room, the nurse draws what feels like every drop of blood in my body, then hits me with another useless shot of morphine.

"Hang in there," she says. I picture the cheesy poster of a kitten clinging to a tree branch. We go from one scan to the next. Then I'm on a gurney. A soft male voice says to lie on my back. I open my eyes. The guy in the lab coat doesn't look old enough to drive. He futzes with a machine that resembles the X-ray camera in a dentist's office: a long telescoping arm that narrows at the end.

"We're going to do a spinal tap, or 'lumbar puncture,'" he says. "I'm going to insert a needle into your spinal canal and collect some cerebrospinal fluid. You shouldn't feel anything because of all the morphine in your system."

Wrong. And spinal tap is a misnomer. Lumbar puncture is generous. I howl in pain as the cold, fat needle jackhammers my spine. In and out.

In and out. In and out. Laughing nervously, Doogie Howser apologizes for "missing."

The nurse wheels me down a long corridor. We pass through a wide door and into a double-occupancy room split in half by a maroon shower curtain. My roommate is watching *Judge Judy* on TV and talking about a "gabagool sangwich."

Lying facedown on the bed by the window, I wince as the nurse swabs the inside of my elbow with rubbing alcohol and pushes in the IV. It connects to two tubes. One goes to three bags of fluids and the other to a padlocked red box. A long gray cable runs from the box to a remote, which the nurse places in my hand.

"Press this when you're in pain," she says. "It controls the morphine."

I press. One dose comes out. I hold the button. Nothing happens.

Andrea counts fifty-five holes in a wide swath of bruised skin on my lower back. She takes pictures and says we should sue the hospital. I fantasize about quitting my job and moving back to Camden to write books for the rest of my (hopefully) very long life. Then I think to stop thinking about lawsuits to avoid jinxing myself.

Dr. Baudelaire enters the room. Andrea heaves a sigh when he says I have a complicated migraine. He asks if I have a history of migraines. I shake my head. Until now, I thought "migraine" was a word wimpy people used interchangeably with "headache."

"There are many types of migraines. They all present differently and have different causes, but it's extremely uncommon to have so much pressure in your head that it damages your vertebrae."

Andrea clenches up.

"The MRI also showed a cyst on your pineal gland," Dr. Baudelaire says far too casually. "It's benign. Low probability of becoming malignant, but we'll keep an eye on it."

Andrea lies next to me, stroking my hand with her fingertips. "I asked Dr. Miller to recommend a therapist for you," she says.

"Why?"

thirty-nine

After two days in the hospital, Dr. Baudelaire clears me to go home. He writes a prescription for a drug to prevent migraines, another drug to fight them, and forty Percocet, 2.5 mg/325 mg acetaminophen—the lowest dose of the active ingredient, oxycodone.

I tell myself it's okay. The pain is legit, and Dr. Baudelaire is a doctor. Andrea isn't concerned.

At home, I take the prophylactic medicine as directed, have no need for the combatant, and I'm justifiably liberal with the Percs. When the bottle is almost empty, I call Dr. Baudelaire's office and ask the receptionist for a refill, slipping, without thinking, into the voice I used in high school, when I called in pretending to be sick.

"No problem," the receptionist says.

Andrea goes to our local pharmacy, the aptly named Drug World, to pick up the script: sixty pills, 10 mg/325 mg. In a few days, the pain is gone, but I keep taking the Percocet. When I'm down to the last three pills, I call Dr. Baudelaire for another refill.

"No problem," the receptionist says.

I swallow the last Percs and go downstairs. From the bottom step, I see Andrea and Ruby making another batch of "get well soon" cards.

Andrea says I look much better. She holds up a drawing of a bull running through a green traffic light. "Unstop-a-bull. Get it?"

Blinking back tears, I nod and turn away. Everywhere I see reminders of the life we're building, the love we have. Ruby's first painting on the dining room wall: pink and red blobs on a white canvas; the picture from Ida Applebroog; the collage I made for Andrea's birthday; the drawing she made of a speaker powered by pedaling a bicycle—inspired by one of the books I've talked about writing. Out the window, I see the writing cabin. In the hall by the door, a pile of red low-top Chuck Taylors in three different sizes, our books mixed together on shelves. Nothing is singular. Each of us in everything. We are one.

It's unfathomable to think I could piss this away.

It's impossible to think of not picking up the prescription.

"Ladies, I need to go to Drug World."

Ruby bolts out of her seat, asking to come with. "Bees, Dada." She and I set out on foot. Andrea leaves for the gym.

Coming down the hill behind the bank, I remember a dream I had when Ruby was a baby. She was floating in the ocean, in an inflatable yellow tube with a duck's head. From the shore, I begged her to come back. She just waved and smiled and drifted farther away.

We pick up the prescription and walk home, holding hands, my stomach in knots, pills in an opaque brown plastic bottle, shaking like a maraca. I carry Ruby upstairs and set her down in the bathroom. I take a long look at my daughter—this miraculous creature with short brown pigtails, happy and healthy.

"Ruby, take a mental snapshot and remember this moment forever."

I pour the pills into the toilet and flush.

Ruby runs out of the bathroom and yells at the top of the stairs. "Bees, Dada, *bees!*"

She's almost three years old, and her life's ambition is to conquer our steep staircase solo. We strike a deal—she'll hold the rail the whole time, and I'll go down backward in front of her, one step lower, every step of the way.

In the living room, I turn on the stereo and crank the volume on "Idioteque" by Radiohead. Ruby and I shake our cabooses without inhibition to the chirping, agitated beats.

I should come clean and enlist Andrea's help but I don't. I can't. I call the shrink her shrink recommended and take his first available appointment.

Dr. Aftergood appears to be in his fifties and has kind eyes behind roundish wiry glasses. His small square office is on the ground floor of a residential building in White Plains—a desk in the corner, two leather Eames chairs facing each other and an ottoman in the middle, a low leather sofa under a wide window framed by tall bookshelves. On the wall behind me hangs a print of the Buddha and the seven chakras in colored circles, each explained in small text.

I offer the most honest version of my life that I can muster, feeling self-conscious but removed—like I'm auditioning for the role of myself in a play. I talk about my parents and Daniel, Jane, Andrea, and Ruby. I tell him about heroin and the history of addiction on both sides of the family. I describe my fears and insecurities, and I name every therapist I've ever seen and every antidepressant I've been prescribed. Dr. Aftergood takes copious notes. When I finish, he lays his pad and pencil on the edge of his desk.

"Did any of the medication give you any relief?"

"No, but heroin did."

"Well, heroin is more of a blunt instrument than an antidepressant, no?"

"When you want to destroy something, a blunt instrument does the trick."

"Ah. And what are you trying to destroy?"

"My depression."

"Try looking at it differently. Our work is about building, not destroying."

I feel like I'm lying on an operating room table, watching a surgeon prepare to dig into my soul with a rusty scalpel. Too early to know if the surgery will be a success, but I know it's going to hurt like hell and the healing process will be lengthy.

Dr. Aftergood asks what I want to accomplish from our time together. It takes a minute for me to think of an answer. "I want to be content."

"What does contentment mean to you?"

Silence swallows me whole—I don't know how to respond.

"Have you *ever* experienced contentment?"

"The beginning of my relationship with Andrea. Ruby's birth. I've had other moments before and since—hours, or maybe a day or two, but other than that, I've been miserable for as long as I can remember. Unless I've been on dope. And even then . . ."

"Even then?"

"I'd see somebody worse off or read an article in the *New York Times* Neediest Cases series—kids without enough to eat, parents taking turns going hungry every other night. I know how good I have it, how lucky I am. I'd think, *What right do I have to be so miserable?* I couldn't stand that a speck of powder could make my brain work in ways I couldn't on my own. I must not deserve to feel this way."

"You're kind of glossing over it. By telling yourself that you don't have the right to be an addict, you're giving yourself an excuse not to deal with it."

A month after the complicated migraine, I haven't had another, but I'm averaging at least two standard migraines a week. The pain concentrates behind my eyes and I have to lie down in a dark, quiet room. Sometimes when I feel one coming on, I take Zomig, the combatant Dr. Baudelaire prescribed, but then I feel defeated. That's why I haven't been taking the prophylactic medicine. My "faulty logic," as Dr. Aftergood calls it, comes up a lot.

"If I can't vanquish a problem without a foreign substance, it means I'm weak. If I need a foreign substance, it might as well be heroin."

"You realize there's a difference between heroin and legally prescribed non-narcotic medication, right?"

"Obviously."

"And you know migraine is a medical condition, and so is depression and anxiety."

"Okay . . ."

"I can't see properly without glasses, so I wear them. Does that make me weak?"

"No."

"Taking medication is no different. It doesn't make you weak."

"Maybe it doesn't make you weak. But you're not me."

With Dr. Aftergood's help, patterns become clear in every aspect of my life: impossibly high, self-imposed expectations and unrelenting, unforgiving punishment. I keep raising the bar, setting myself up for failure.

"How are you feeling right now?"

"Like a failure."

"Because you're not living up to your own—"

"Because I know it's fucking insane and I can't stop it."

I reach for a box of tissues on the bookshelf. Dr. Aftergood says to breathe. He says, "You have to forgive yourself." At the end of the session, he writes a prescription for the antidepressant Wellbutrin. I fill it.

If my brain were a football field, each end zone represents the two states of being I've known throughout my life. One end is *even*, achievable almost exclusively with heroin. The other is my default setting: *not even*. Going from one end to the other is a catapult, not a pendulum. I've seen the enormous space in the middle only when flying past. Wellbutrin acts as a gate, keeping me from the most extreme reaches of my natural state. It's an improvement, but not much. To stick with the football analogy, the gate is under the goal post, a few inches from the out-of-bounds line.

I worry about the future. I want to believe I could resist if dope finds me again, but depression is excruciating. At some point, my threshold will reach its limit. Pain can't be willed away.

Wisps of steam rise from a mug of chamomile tea centered on the table between Rob and me.

"Buprenorphine," he says, no judgment in his voice, only compassion as he urges me to find a licensed doctor.

"I already kicked. There's no dope in my system."

Rob takes a long sip and waves his index finger—no. "It's not just for kicking," he says. "I told you. When you decided to kick at your mom's and made me leave you there with no money and no car."

I go home and google "buprenorphine." The first article says induction occurs when an addict is in the acute stages of withdrawal, and buprenorphine can be discontinued after five to seven days or used for prolonged periods for maintenance. The author describes it as a "highly effective, anti-craving medication, a godsend for addicts who are worried about relapse."

Unlike methadone, a full opioid agonist that can be dispensed only at clinics, prescriptions for buprenorphine, a partial agonist, can be filled at pharmacies. But the Drug Treatment Act of 2000 mandated a special X waiver that physicians must obtain to prescribe all substances containing buprenorphine and limited the number of patients to a hundred each.

Six licensed doctors are within two hundred miles of my house. One after another, they say I need to be in withdrawal to be induced. When I explain the obvious conflict, they refuse to bend the rules. I beg Dr. Wallace, the last name on the list, and he agrees to see me. He has an opening in an hour. I can make it.

Dodging crater-sized potholes, I pull into a spot in the parking lot across from a row of identical brick buildings. Some are connected via steel-enclosed second-story breezeways. The doors have no numbers or signs of any kind.

Through trial and error, I find the right building. An old, dusty smell hits me when I walk through the door. It must have been an elegant place at one time, but now threadbare carpet covers the floor and stairs, and thick coats of paint on the bannister obscure most of the intricate carvings. At the top of the stairs on the second floor, I follow a maze until I see a door with a paper sign taped to it. "Dr. Wallace."

The waiting area is tiny, the ceiling low and slanted. I sit on the edge of the stained brown couch and start thumbing through the old magazines scattered on the Formica coffee table. *Time. People. Psychology Today. Harvard Business Review.* The bottom right corner is torn off the cover of every issue.

Dr. Wallace opens the inner door. Short, middle-aged, in a crisp white short-sleeved dress shirt and a pastel-striped tie. He waves me into his office, a slightly larger version of the waiting area, with a less pronounced slope in the ceiling.

Before any discussion of buprenorphine takes place, he explains his fee structure: $500 for this session, $200 for each monthly session. He doesn't accept insurance or Medicare or Medicaid. He cautions me that most insurance companies don't cover the cost of the $400 monthly prescription.

I give a painfully honest, exhaustive account of my history with opioids. Dr. Wallace doesn't ask questions or take notes. When he swivels his chair toward a filing cabinet, I notice an orange sticker on the back of the seat: "PAID" in big block letters.

"Normally, you'd be in peak withdrawal and we'd start with one pill." He opens a drawer and takes out a white plastic bottle. The label reads, "Suboxone, 2 mg." He shakes two small orange hexagonal pills onto a blotter calendar and uses white plastic tweezers to ferry them to my hand.

Under my tongue, the pills taste like artificial orange flavoring and something I can't quite identify. They dissolve quickly into a chunky powder, which disintegrates.

Dr. Wallace says the active ingredient won't work if I chew or swallow the pills, and I'll immediately go into the most agonizing withdrawal of my life if I crush them up and snort them or inject them or combine them with any opioid. And buprenorphine has a seven-day half-life, he says.

For a moment, I worry about a situation where opioids might be necessary. Surgery. A car accident. What if I'm unconscious when the paramedics show up and hit me with a shot of morphine? I don't voice these concerns. I don't want to risk making him suspicious that I'm already planning to relapse.

"We'll start with four milligrams a day and ramp up to eight over a week. You can go as high as twenty-four milligrams a day if the cravings don't go away."

I happily write a check for $500, Dr. Wallace writes the prescription, and we schedule my next appointment. Then I make a harried exit and have to backtrack twice before I finally hear the stairs creaking rhythmically with my thumping footfalls. Once I reach the exit and push through the heavy door, I see my behavior for what it is: a force of habit. You don't stand around after a drug deal. You get the fuck out of there.

Outside, the tension melts away, and a familiar feeling takes hold—almost like a speck of heroin when I'm on the verge of withdrawal. My brain stops thrashing. I check for the prescription in my shirt pocket as tears roll down my cheeks. Brushing them away, I get in the car and twist the key in the ignition.

John Frusciante's "The Past Recedes" plays on the stereo. A simple three-chord progression on an acoustic guitar—an inverted funnel, narrow and focused. A deep blue sky goes on forever without a cloud. I pull out of the parking lot and coast down the hill, a straight road that leads everywhere.

epilogue

It would be a gross understatement to say buprenorphine saved my life. Buprenorphine *gave* me my life. For the first time, my focus shifted from surviving to healing. My emotional pain threshold was now above basement level, and I no longer had the constant distraction of trying to find and hide heroin or avoid thinking about it.

In weekly sessions with Dr. Aftergood, a lifetime of behavioral and relationship patterns crystallized once I began to see depression as a distorted filter of negative self-bias. Under a fresh lens, I understood that family and friends really did love me—but I knew I'd never feel worthy as long as I continued to deceive them.

Three months after my first appointment with Dr. Wallace, at a drugstore minutes from his office, a pharmacist refused to fill my prescription on a Friday night at six o'clock.

"Controlled substances are thirty days," she said, her unblinking gaze on me. "I can fill it tomorrow."

"I can't come back tomorrow."

"Sorry." She waved the next customer forward.

An older man approached the register, and I stepped to the right and pretended to be interested in the brightly colored hand-shaped back scratchers while staring at my reflection in a fish-eye security mirror. Suit and tie. Short, neat hair. Clean-shaven. Not a junkie.

When the older man paid and shuffled off, I slid back into position.

"I can't come back on a weekend. My wife doesn't know about the buprenorphine, and even if she did, I don't get to see my daughter much on weekdays."

"Then maybe you ought to stop doing drugs around her."

"I take buprenorphine so I *won't* use drugs. It shouldn't be a controlled substance."

"And yet . . ."

I left without the prescription but with confirmation of every shitty feeling I'd had about myself. Choking back tears, I practiced spilling my guts to Andrea in rush-hour traffic. It felt like an unforgivable betrayal—like I'd cheated on the only girl I never cheated on. When I got home, I grabbed last month's prescription bottle, dumped an orange, hexagonal tablet in my hand, and proceeded to tell Andrea about buprenorphine—except I said it was a new medication for migraines.

Overwhelmed with guilt and shame and in a world of hurt from my self-inflicted wounds, I understood buprenorphine's limitations for relieving pain—physical and emotional. Opiate receptors regulate pain and emotional well-being. Opioids kill pain by saturating your receptors. Heroin is to Vicodin is to buprenorphine as vodka is to beer is to the hard seltzer you might give curious toddlers when they won't leave you alone about taking a sip.

By 2018, after many gut-spilling practices and chickening outs, I'd been on buprenorphine for a decade without a single slip, and only three people knew: Dr. Aftergood, Rob, and Dr. Wallace. Everyone else believed I had been sober for twenty-three years.

Opioid addiction had become a national health emergency, and our response was driven by stereotypes, misinformation, and a pervasive disregard of science and evidence—in policy, treatment, and prevention. I was profoundly aware of the ways my silence was working against my relationships and every change I wanted to see in the world. How could I expect anyone else to talk about their struggles with depression or addiction if I denied the existence of mine?

I started writing this book. When the first draft was finished, I began to open up. Slowly. Andrea and Daniel. A few friends here and there. I didn't tell Mom until August 2019—the day before my first confessional op-ed was published in the *Los Angeles Times*. With few exceptions, everyone received my news with compassion. No judgment. They wanted to understand. And I launched a new career as a writer, activist, and advocate.

. . .

Addiction isn't an automatic result of exposure to opioids. Compulsive use is driven by the relief they provide. That's the draw—painkillers *kill* pain. Opioids don't know or care if you have a prescription or whether your pain is physical or emotional. They flood your brain with dopamine and serotonin and bind to your opiate receptors.

No other type of substance has its own natural target or takes hold with such ferocity. Within weeks of active use, the normal hierarchy of needs shifts and neurotransmitters are rewired to seek out their next dose. Latent neural vulnerabilities include reduced connectivity between areas involving emotional regulation, stress response, and reward processing. These changes occur at a cellular level and don't necessarily reverse when you stop using.

Even after long periods of abstinence, significant dysfunctional activity has been observed in opioid addicts' brains. If sobriety doesn't get easier for an opioid addict over time, it might not be physiologically possible without medication.

Sobriety focuses on abstinence, whereas recovery heals the wounds that led to drugs in the first place. It's a process. And it doesn't automatically start when you get sober. Why would it? Pain doesn't end when you stop using painkillers. It gets worse.

Chronic pain is defined as a distress that persists for up to three to six months or more. In this era of mental health awareness, beliefs persist that physical pain can't be willed away, but psychological distress is optional. Upwards of 70 percent of depressed adults do not receive care. Shame prevents many from seeking help. Others lack resources or access.

We know how opioids affect our neural pathways, yet conventional treatments emphasize *addiction* as the primary problem and insist that remission can be achieved only by replacing science and medicine with God and a support group.

When addiction is equated with moral failure and opioids are lumped in with recreational drugs, we invalidate the real cause of our national health emergency. If it were simply about getting high, we'd cut risk, cost, and time and drink instead. Alcohol isn't legal because it's safer. Alcohol is safer because it's legal. Legal is the difference between buying beer and knowing you're not drinking grain alcohol and fermented wood, as was the case during Prohibition, when alcohol overdose fatalities surged.

Drug laws are self-defeating and antithetical to public health and safety. Most overdose fatalities involve illegal drugs because potency is unknown and inconsistent. Another life is cut tragically short every nineteen minutes. In the hardest hit areas, as many as one in four kids has lost one or both parents. How can a national health emergency end when every harm-reducing, life-saving resource is stigmatized, criminalized, and restricted?

The American Society of Addiction Medicine considers medication-assisted treatment and counseling the standard of care for opioid addiction. Though abstinence-based care (forced or voluntary) is now associated with increased risk of relapse and overdose death, buprenorphine is offered in only a third of rehabs, owing to the predominance of abstinence-based models. They maintain that any kind of medication (including antidepressants) invalidates your sobriety.

It doesn't matter to me that buprenorphine invalidates my sobriety. I never kept track of "clean time" because abstinence wasn't my objective. I just wanted to feel okay in my own skin. I was too ashamed to let anyone know I was on it for more than a decade. Since I started opening up, many people have asked me when I'll stop using it. In November 2020, I appeared on the CBS *Doctors TV Show*, and the host asked me that question. I responded with a question: If it were insulin, would anyone ask when I'd get off the life-saving medication because my diabetes was in check?

Once a month, I drive to another state—an hour and a half each way—for a stigma-free experience filling my buprenorphine prescription. I pay out of pocket for the medication and doctor visit because my insurance provider doesn't consider addiction a medical necessity. They (reluctantly) offer partial reimbursement for Dr. Aftergood's fees.

Today, writing is my full-time job. Andrea is an art therapist. We've been together for twenty-one years. Ruby is fifteen. Her brother, Samuel Herbert Hoppipolla Poses, is eleven.

My family knows everything there is to know about me—including how I tracked down the framed print above my desk: a signed Kurt Vonnegut original, *Peculiar Travel Suggestions Are Dancing Lessons from God*, handwritten in purple ink.

acknowledgments

If writing is a solitary act, this book is more like Lollapalooza (circa 1992): a multi-city, multi-stage festival, where, in any given moment, you're profoundly grateful to be surrounded and supported by such capable talent and profoundly aware that, comparatively, you're barely qualified to sell crappy homemade burritos in some off-site parking lot.

From the first revision to the last, Ruby and Sam spoke only in the simple future tense ("when the book is published"). But if Andrea had reacted differently to the first draft, I would have deleted the file before anyone else knew it existed. I'm grateful beyond words for her acceptance of me and my story—and so profoundly sorry for the pain I caused.

Tesla will never make enough Teslas for me to repay Carol Giacomo for turning on the light at the end of this tunnel.

I never promised Amy Dresner a Tesla, but I owe her a hundred car washes for everything she's done for me.

To my friends and fellow writers, activists, and advocates—Michele Cannarella, Brandon del Pozo, Rob French, David Hollander, Jennifer Hornak, Josh Kaye, Aric Kupper, Ben Levenson, Jenn Lewis, Jeff McDaniel, Danielle Pak-McCarthy, Stephanie Papes-Strong, Jay Pearsall, David Richardson, Petra Schulz, Maia Szalavitz, and Carlyn Zwarenstein—thank you for your insight and support and for screaming louder than my insecurities.

Thank you to Rob, Chessa, Jane, Greg, and everyone else who corroborated my memories and made them memorable in the first place—especially Mom and Daniel, who is a much better older brother to me than I ever was to him.

To Sandra Jonas: thank you for believing in my story and message and in me as a writer. I couldn't have hoped to find a better partner for this book.

Thank you to my publicists, Jennifer Buonantony and Demetria Johnson and Press Pass LA, my occasional literary agent, Heather Schroder, and my outstanding editors, Maia Danzinger, Emma Dries, and John Kenny, who taught me what I should have learned in the writing classes I never took.

Endless thanks to Dr. David Aftergood for (among other things) helping me face and process the truth, and to Dr. Zevi Labins for optimizing my neural pathways with the right medication regimen.

Change doesn't happen until those who aren't affected are as outraged as those who are. To anyone who struggles with mental health or addiction issues, or who cares about someone struggling or has lost someone, and to all the people and organizations working tirelessly to bring about positive change in policy, prevention, and treatment, thank you for your strength and courage. Every day, I'm humbled, heartened, and honored to fight alongside you.

playlist

Long before I knew how to talk about my feelings, I used music to communicate, so it isn't surprising that music plays an important role in my story. Below are some of the songs that appear in *The Weight of Air*, along with a few others I added to round out the list. You can find the soundtrack on Apple Music: music.apple.com/us/playlist/the-weight-of-air/pl.u-91kWCxD2yD1.

"Bodies": Sex Pistols
"I Am a Child": Neil Young
"So What": Miles Davis
"I Touch Myself": Divinyls
"Lightning Crashes": Live
"Rosanna": Toto
"Adagio for Strings": Samuel Barber
"Reason to Believe": Bruce Springsteen
"Hey": Pixies
"Negative Creep": Nirvana
"Exit Music (for a Film)": Radiohead
"Karma Police": Radiohead
"Bonus Track 1": John Frusciante
"Bonus Track 2": John Frusciante
"Ab's Song": Marshall Tucker Band
"Love Is a Stranger": Eurythmics
"Natural Mystic": Bob Marley

"I Don't Like the Drugs (but the Drugs Like Me)": Marilyn Manson

"Paranoid Android": Radiohead

"Forever Young": Rod Stewart

"Small Dark Movie": Greg Brown

"Rated X": Miles Davis

"Five-O": James

"Horses": Be Good Tanyas

"I Can't Give You Anything but Love": Django Reinhardt

"Everloving": Moby

"Untitled #4 (Njósnavélin)": Sigur Rós

"The Wedding Toccata Theme": Modeselektor

"Idioteque": Radiohead

"The Past Recedes": John Frusciante

about the author

DAVID POSES is a writer, speaker, and activist. After hiding his struggle with depression and opioids for twenty years, he started opening up and challenging conventional drug treatment prevention and policy. With candor, humor, and a unique perspective formed by science and lived experience, he advocates for a shift from punitive, self-defeating prohibition laws and logic to an approach based on evidence, compassion, and the harm reduction philosophy.

David has been published by the *Washington Post, Los Angeles Times,* and *New York Daily News* and has appeared on national television programs, including *The Doctors TV Show,* and numerous radio shows and podcasts. He lives in Hudson Valley, New York, with his wife, Andrea, and two children, Ruby and Sam, and entirely too many guitars for such a mediocre player.

Website: davidposes.com
Facebook: @davidposes.author
Twitter: @davidthekick
Instagram: @david_thekick

CPSIA information can be obtained
at www.ICGtesting.com
Printed in the USA
LVHW111538090921
697455LV00009B/304/J